NAMES OF PORTRAITS.

ADMIRAL BARRINGTON.

6 The Rt. Hon. Gen. Lord Heath-field, K. B. Governor

4 Lieut. Gen. Sir Robert Boyd, K. B. Lieut. Governor

5 Major General De la Motte, commanding the Hanoverian Brigade

7 Major General Sir William Green, Bart. Chief Engineer

9 Major General Picton

8 Col. Dachenhausen, Reden's Hanoverian Regiment

11 Col. Hugo, Sydow's, late Hardenberg's

10 Col. Schleppegrell, De la Motte's

21 Colonel Lewis, Commandant of Artillery

12 Col. Trigge, 12th Regiment

20 Lieut Col. Vaughan, 39th Regt.

19 Col. Craig, 56th Regiment

16 Major Brown, 58th Regiment

17 Hon. Lieut. Col. Lindsay, late 2d Battalion, 73d Regiment

18 Lieut. Col. Hardy, Quarter Master General

22 Major Vallotton, Governor's first Aid-de-Camp

14 Lieut. Holloway, Aid-de-Camp to Chief Engineer

13 Major Perryn, 12th Regt.

15 Capt. Drinkwater, late 72d, Author of the History of the Siege of Gibraltar

D0311727

Key to picture reproduced on jacke
'The Defeat of the Floating Batteries at Gibralta
by J. S. Copley (*Guildhall Art Galler*

GIBRALTAR BESIEGED

Jack Russell

GIBRALTAR
BESIEGED

1779 – 1783

———

HEINEMANN : LONDON

William Heinemann Ltd
LONDON MELBOURNE TORONTO
CAPE TOWN AUCKLAND

First published 1965

Printed in Great Britain by
Butler & Tanner Ltd, Frome and London

To my mother

Acknowledgements

I WISH to acknowledge my sense of gratitude to all those who have helped in the preparation of this book, both in Gibraltar and in London. I am particularly indebted to His Excellency General Sir Dudley Ward, G.C.B., K.B.E., D.S.O., Governor of Gibraltar, to Darrell Bates Esq., Chief Secretary, to E. F. E. Ryan Esq., Secretary of the Garrison Library, and to Brigadier H. E. Boulter, D.S.O., Major R. T. Brett, and Sergeant A. E. Trimming. My thanks are due to Mr and Mrs J. Serfaty for their kind hospitality. I could not have started without the help of Kenneth Ewing Esq. or finished without that of David Burnett Esq., and the advice of the Hon. David Erskine undoubtedly improved the middle. I am grateful for the kind assistance I have had from the Staffs of the Public Record Office and the Manuscript, Print and Reading Rooms of the British Museum.

Unpublished Crown-copyright material in the Public Record Office is reproduced by permission of the Controller of H.M. Stationery Office.
Unpublished manuscripts in the British Museum are reproduced by permission of the Trustees of the British Museum.
I am grateful to the following for the illustrations:
    The National Gallery.
    The National Portrait Gallery.
    The Guildhall Art Gallery.
    Controller of H.M. Stationery Office.
    The Trustees of the British Museum.
The plans have been admirably executed by Miss Joan Emerson.

For the rest, errors and omissions included, I must take the responsibility.

London 1965   JACK RUSSELL

Contents

Illustrations

xi

CHAPTER I
Britons, strike home!

THE Great Siege of Gibraltar began on 21 June 1779 and ended on 3 February 1783: during this time, the British garrison, including a Hanoverian brigade, their families, and the townspeople of Gibraltar, endured a continual blockade, the depredations of smallpox and scurvy, bombardment by day and night for more than a year, near starvation, and finally the Grand Attack, made by ten huge Floating Batteries invented for the occasion, with the Combined Fleet of forty-four line-of-battle ships and hundreds of smaller vessels assembled in the Bay, the Combined Army of nearly 40,000 Spanish and French troops on land, 200 heavy guns and mortars in the Spanish batteries, commanded by generals and admirals of the highest reputation, in the presence of two Royal Princes of France and 80,000 spectators of every rank, and from all Europe. The garrison were not content only to endure, and, under their eccentric Governor, General George Augustus Eliott, they maintained a constant fire on the enemy, and made the Great Sortie, which is celebrated annually in Gibraltar. Three famous British admirals led the three Reliefs of the Rock Fortress, and, after the siege, the garrison received the thanks of the King and the Houses of Parliament. In a war during which Great Britain lost her American Colonies, Florida, Dominica, St Vincent, Grenada, Tobago, St Kitts, Minorca, was threatened with invasion, lost control of the sea, and fought without a single ally for her possessions from Cape Canaveral to Calcutta, the Rock of Gibraltar came to represent, to her people and to her enemies, her pride and her power. After the siege it became synonymous in the English language with invincibility, grit, courage, and endurance. This is the citation. What happened?

The first shot from the batteries on the Rock against the Spanish Lines was fired at six-thirty on Sunday morning, 12 September 1779. It had been rumoured in the town on Friday that the garrison were going to open fire on the enemy, a compliment that everyone expected would be swiftly returned, and, at a Council of War on Saturday, the Governor had expressly denied that he had any such intention. As it was unusual for His Excellency to give any notice of his intentions, positive or other, the officers and soldiers had hurriedly tried to move their families to the south, the fishermen and gardeners left their boats in the Bay and their cabbages on the Neutral Ground, and the Jews went to synagogue to pray for deliverance from Spain, before prudently shutting their shops and removing their valuables out of range of the Spanish guns. In the grey, hazy dawn of this autumn day it was not difficult to realize that something was afoot. The small company of Royal Artillery had paraded at five o'clock, and marched off up the hill to the batteries, followed by the Governor and members of the Council on their horses, the senior officers of the garrison, those subalterns who were not on duty with their regiments, and a bunch of intrepid ladies, hanging on to the King's mules, which usually carried grimmer if not heavier burdens. The soldiers of the line regiments, who mounted the guards and pickets every day, marched through the narrow streets, into the bastions and lines, the scarlet coats flowing like blood into the runnels and channels of the Rock, the natural forts and galleries, up to the great white, peaked head, until the whole North Front was alive with bustle and buzz.

The batteries crowned the high ridge that shielded the town from Spain, and lay to the east of the squat yellow tower of the Moorish castle. The north peak hunched a thousand feet above them, and they looked down four hundred feet to the flat sandy isthmus stretching to the mainland. These were Willis's Batteries, which mounted 68 cannons, firing 24-, 26- and 32-pound shot the size of croquet balls, and 43 mortars, from 4- or 5-inch calibre to the fat 13-inch which looked like cooking pots and hurled shells like Christmas puddings. There were six positions along the ridge, loyally named Queen's, Princess Ann's, Princess Amelia's, Princess Caroline's and Queen Charlotte's, and, after the Spanish revolutionaries who had fought with the British in 1705, Catalan. The foremost of these, on top of a cliff that had been scarped and scraped until the white limestone shone like a bone under a scalpel, was the Queen's Battery, and it was crowded with red-coated officers, blue-jacketed gunners, with a fringe of lilac and lace where the ladies gathered at the back. It was no more than an uneven platform cut from the rock, fronted by a thick stone wall, and roofed with timbers packed with cement and stones. There were embrasures in the wall for the guns, half masked by leather curtains to protect the gunners from the flashes of the explosions. Iron rings were sunk into the wall beside each embrasure, through which ropes ran to the wooden gun-carriages so that after every recoil and reloading they could be hauled back into position. Each gun had its long sponge and rammer, its barrel of powder and pyramid of cannonballs, its gunners and matrosses, its bucket of water, and its share of the general opinion that it was almost as dangerous to be behind the guns as in front of them. The battery was dark, and damp, and chilly. It was fifty years since a gun had been fired at an enemy from the Rock.

There was not room for everyone inside the battery, and many were gathered on the rising ground behind it. A little breeze from the east, heralding the sun, stirred the few scraggly bushes spared by the engineers' mattocks; a cicada woke up and began to scrape a tuneless song; an ape shrieked from far up the hill, and gulls drifted from the cliffs complaining. In the east the Mediterranean sea trembled like the curtain of a theatre just before it rises; the tops of the brown Andalusian hills falling from the Queen of Spain's Chair before them, down to Estapona, Marbella and beyond, began to glow; suddenly shadows started out like alarmed sentinels; the sun was up. The batteries were in the shadow of the Rock, and cold, and the flooding of the mainland with light and warmth increased the feeling of isolation of those who stood in them. Spain began at the Spanish Lines, a mile along the isthmus from the base of the Rock, it circled the Bay with brown hills, matted with a grey-green crop of cork trees, and then lay like a lost continent, a thousand miles between them and Great Britain. On their small dark Rock, for how long could they defy this huge burning country?

The junior officers shifted uneasily. This was their first war. It was a moment before the most nervous could appear the most casual. The older lieutenants and captains were gathered on higher ground, from where they could seriously study the enemy's positions, and point out targets to each other, and generally behave as officers do when ladies, or their superior officers, are watching.

The Spanish Camp was nearly three miles away, two lines of tents running from Point Mala on the Bay towards the Queen of Spain's Chair. There were two large tents: one, they guessed, was a hospital, and the other a laboratory for the filling and priming of shells. There was another small encampment in a quarry at the foot of the Chair for the Catalonians, who, being of an independent and quarrelsome disposition, were usually quartered apart from the rest of the Spanish Army. On a rise above the Camp there was a large house, used as a barracks by the cavalry and called Buena Vista. The Headquarters of the General, Don Martin de Alvarez de Sotomayor, were in San Roque, a sad dirty little town which called itself the City of Gibraltar in Exile, on a hill almost out of sight a mile further away. Every move in the Spanish Camp could be observed from the Rock, every crate of supplies landed at Point Mala or the Orange Grove could be counted, and every regiment that joined the Camp could be identified. There were eight battalions of infantry, 400 artillerymen, and two regiments of cavalry: in all, 8,000 men. There was also a large body of workmen, sometimes 500 at a time were working in the Lines, and many wagons and carts drawn by mules, which trundled from the Camp to the Lines day and night. The Spanish Lines stretched across the isthmus like a garrotte across the neck of some unlucky victim of Spanish justice. On either side, there was a strong fort of stone, St Philip on the Bay, and St Barbara on the Mediterranean. Between them there were several bastions and guard-houses linked by epaulements of sand, which were reinforced by timbers, casks and fascines. The whole constituted a wall, some eighteen feet high and as thick again at the base, with the forts and strong-points animated with cannons and mortars. The enemy had been opening new embrasures in the Lines and establishing dumps of shot and magazines of powder, which argued their intention of firing on the Rock as soon as their preparations were completed. The Lines were the target for the garrison gunners. Already, Spanish sentries had come out and were yawning in the sun, some officers were taking a morning ride before returning to Mass in the squat church at San Roque, and the first carts were creeping forward from the Camp. To the watchers in the battery they were no bigger than toys on a nursery floor, impersonal dots of colour to be struck at and smeared into the sand. The black embrasures showed that the enemy could, and were expected to, retaliate with the same stern impassivity.

The senior officers, majors and colonels, who knew what the effect of a shell or cannonball could be in a confined and rocky space, shifted about creating ripples of uncomfortable silence with their disapproving stares. There were five British regiments on the Rock, a Hanoverian brigade, nearly five hundred artillerymen, and about a hundred engineers and artificers. The exact total when the Spaniards had closed all communications with the garrison on 21 June, nearly three months before, had been 5,382 men, but since then six of them had deserted to the enemy. There were 209 officers, and a half of them were gathered about the Queen's Battery. To one crusted colonel they all appeared very young gentlemen. The majors and colonels who found themselves staring at each other, knowing they could neither advance nor retreat, neither move to a flank, nor anywhere but up and down the hill, inwardly hoped that the siege would end before they came to hate each other too much. The Rock was little more than three miles long, and nowhere more than three-quarters of a mile across, and only a small part of it was habitable; the town was a mile long, and three streets in width, and scarce a day passed when one did not see the same people five or six times. The 12th Regiment had already been stationed there for ten years. In this age of influence, when regiments and commands were the gift of the King and ministers, in this age of fierce political controversy, when the Government was for war, the Opposition for peace, and Parliament was packed with placemen, excisemen, Government contractors, sandwiched between sleepy squires of both complexions, the officers of the garrison were as divided as the members of the House of Commons. There was a ruling class, and most of them were from it, Tory or Whig from birth, their fortunes identified with those of their party. Lord North, who led a form of Tory government, had been in power since 1770.

His Excellency the Governor, General George Augustus Eliott, a phlegmatic Scotsman, a robust florid man who ate no meat and drank no alcohol, a powerful man of sixty-two, a veteran soldier who had risen by favour, a man of few friends and those young and handsome, a secretive, domineering, ambitious, conscientious man, yet a man who liked to chatter, to make puns, to unbend, stood squarely over his Rock and his garrison. He dominated them. He did not like them. Now he had taken up his position to the right of the guns, where he could see the enemy, and be seen by everyone else. The officers of the Council formed a polite semicircle behind him, not near enough to exchange a casual remark, but not far enough away to appear to have left him on his own. There were two sailors, Vice-Admiral Duff, the Commodore, by nature as by name, and Sir Thomas Rich, dashing and popular: Colonel Godwin of the Royal Artillery was talking to the Chief Engineer, Colonel Green, two experts in their own fields, anxious to witness the results of their plans and labours: there was Colonel Ross, leader of the Tory faction and of those who agreed that Colonel Ross was a better man than the Lieutenant-Governor, and, refusing to meet his eye, the Lieutenant-Governor himself, Lieutenant-General Boyd, sixty-nine years old, sick, and disappointed that his friends had been unable to procure the Governorship for him; he had been on Gibraltar longer than any of them, and was the automatic leader of the opposition, which comprised the major part of the officers: lastly there was Major-General De la Motte, commander of the Hanoverians, a pug-like man of unquestionable loyalty and dullness. They waited, in the growing morning, for the shot that would shatter the dome of silent hostility that imprisoned them.

General Eliott was aware at once of the strength of his fortress and the weakness of his garrison. His decision to open fire was based as much on this awareness as on any fear that the enemy would fire first. It had been apparent since July that the Spaniards were planning to starve the garrison into surrender by cutting the isthmus and blockading the Bay. His target was not so much the 'preparations making outside', but the distress and dissension growing inside, which he hoped to distract with the noise and business of the guns, as a nurse might shake a rattle at a crying child. When Spanish shot and shells came flying into the town, there would be other preoccupations than hunger and faction. Grimness suited him. He looked grim. He had the face of a grim Roman Emperor on the body of John Bull. His three-cornered hat was jammed grimly over his brows. Yet he kept cats, was reluctant to have his men flogged or hanged, and was determined to defend Gibraltar by whatever means he could.

The first carts were reaching the Spanish Lines, with the sentries sauntering towards them. The guns were loaded, the aims laid, the tapers lit. There was no reason now to wait, except the old tradition that still required some gesture before a battle. Men who, after the first shot was fired, might expect to die, deserved encouragement. But the General was no speech-maker. He turned to Colonel Green; there was an honour that his Corps had earned for their work in the batteries. The Colonel turned to Lieutenant Skinner, who had been married a month, and told him to fetch his wife to His Excellency. There was a stir as a startled and fluttering young lady was led through the crowd, and edged towards the nearest cannon. A taper was put into her hand as reverently as if she were in church, and a gnarled serjeant pointed at the touch-hole of the cannon. General Eliott raised his hat, shook it at Spain, and shouted: 'Britons, strike home!'

In the moment between the trembling move of the lady's fair hand towards the black touch-hole of the cannon and the arrival of the ball in the sand several hundred yards short of the Spanish Lines, it might be pertinent to discover what a British garrison was doing on the Rock of Gibraltar at all. (It is only fair to add that the honour of firing the first shot was allotted to a lady by one of the chroniclers of the siege: the others merely noticed that the firing had started, except for one who wrote that Major Loyd, R.A., fired the first shot. That ladies were present in the batteries is confirmed by Garrison Orders for 14 September two days later: 'No soldier except on duty, or soldiers' wives, to be allowed to go up the hill on account of their irregular behaviour.')

The Rock first emerges from the mists of time, which are considerably thicker than those that hang on a Levanter in the Straits, in the mythology of the Flood, with which it was associated. It was a Pillar of Hercules—Mount Abyla in Africa was the other—and was called Mons Calpe, possibly from the Phoenician 'cal-pen', or harbour-hill. Hercules is said to have founded the city of Carteia on the Bay, after having defeated Geryon, and established his temple at Gades (Cadiz) where there were two brass pillars, inscribed 'Non plus ultra'. So a Greek hero built a Phoenician city and wrote in Latin what was, in any event, untrue, as the Phoenicians well knew.

But military gentlemen have many wonders attributed to them, and Hercules was the first of a long line of soldiers associated with the Rock, as Colonel James noted in his History written shortly before the Great Siege:

> It must be remembered, that the dwellers of this part of Spain are to look to those of the honourable profession of arms as their founders and inhabitants, from Hercules downwards: or if you will, the three Geryons whom he slew. The Phoenician adventurers were soldiers, the Carthaginians the same, and the Roman colony planted in Carteia, were from Roman soldiers and Spanish mothers. The Goths were soldiers, and the Moors who built Algezira and Gibraltar from the materials of the demolished city of Carteia, were also military men, who had just conquered almost all Spain in an amazing short space of time. When Algezira was wrested out of their hands, Alonzo gave that town and the adjacent country to his soldiers, as a reward for their gallant behaviour, and persevering services, in the reduction of that strong city.
> ... After Gibraltar was taken by the English, the Spaniards built the town of St Roca, a military station, and the headquarters for the Spanish commanders of that district: and everyone knows, that the fortress of Gibraltar, principally consists of military men.

The Rock was certainly not occupied until the eighth century, except by the rabbits: Southern Spain was called by Catullus 'rabbitty Celtiberia' (the Phoenician word for a rabbit was 'span') until the Vandals devastated that as well, leaving their name in Andalusia. Greeks, Phoenicians, Carthaginians, Romans, Vandals and Goths crossed the Herculean Straits, and nothing was left but the ruins of Carteia. The narrow Straits were crossed again in A.D. 711 by a Moorish army led by a Persian freeman, Tarik-ibn-Zeyad, and the history of Gibraltar (Jebel-Tarik, the Rock of Tarik) began. Tarik's army was no small raiding force (that had come the year before under a commander confusingly called Tarif-ibn-Zarca), and having defeated the army of King Roderic the Goth, he overran almost the whole peninsula.

What the Moors gained in eight months they kept for nearly eight centuries, divided and overrun as they were by successive incursions from Africa. The Reconquista, vaunted as the crusade of enlightened Christianity against heathen obscurantism, was little more than a series of land-grabbing excursions by squabbling and illiterate overlords against a people who had made the land pleasant with their learning, industry and art. It is difficult not to feel regret that the Moorish masters of Granada and Seville, of Cordova and Valencia, should have been dispossessed by the brutal and bigoted braggadocios satirized by Cervantes in the early seventeenth century. The eyes of Spain were plucked out, the hands cut off, when the Moors and Jews were expelled. There were left rank and religion without substance and humanity, toil and indigence without reward and responsibility. The treasures of America came in time to bolster the first without alleviating the second.

In the year 1462, after seven sieges in which it had changed hands twice only, Gibraltar was surrendered by a weak Moorish garrison to Alonso de Arcos, Governor of Tarifa, and annexed to the Crown of Castile. After a short period when it was seized by the feudatory Dukes of Medina-Sidonia, the fortress, known for its strength and position as the Key of Spain, was reclaimed for the united Kingdoms of Castile and Aragon by Queen Isabella in 1501. For 200 years after this Gibraltar, which included in its jurisdiction the districts of Algeciras, Ronda and Marbella, grew prosperous as a free port, and achieved the distinction of becoming the seat of several holy orders, which, like many of their kind, desired to augment their mysteries by the awe-inspiring nature of their surroundings. In the reign of Charles V, after a raid by Barbarossa's pirates, the fortifications were extended from the Castle, built by the Moors in A.D. 725 (and still standing), and from the Moorish walls that faced the sea and ran up the hill south of the town, to include a second wall to the south: it was now considered impregnable. There was the Castle and the Key of Spain, the great Rock dominating the sea and the countryside, with a city of 1,200 houses which was the centre of trade and administration, a large church, three monasteries, a convent, two hospitals, and several shrines, chief amongst them the Shrine of the Virgin of Europa, situated in an old mosque on the rocky plateau facing Africa. The large silver lights of this shrine served as a warning to ships passing the Straits, and the small brass cannon answered their salutes. On 21 July 1704 it received an entirely unexpected form of salute.

The occasion was the War of Spanish Succession. The last Spanish Hapsburg, Charles the Mad, died childless, and nominated the French Prince Philip, grandson of Louis XIV, as heir to the Spanish

Empire. The union of France and Spain was intolerable to England, Holland and the Austrian Empire, and they in turn put forward the Austrian Archduke Charles as claimant to the throne. Queen Anne declared the war was 'for preserving the liberty and balance of Europe, and for reducing the exorbitant power of France . . . everywhere designing to invade the liberties of Europe, and obstruct the freedom of navigation and commerce'.

Whilst the Duke of Marlborough and Prince Eugene achieved brilliant victories in Flanders, Bavaria and Italy, there was little activity in Spain until in 1703 the Methuen Treaty was concluded with Portugal, which gave England the use of Lisbon harbour as a base for operations in the Mediterranean. Though England had abandoned Tangier in 1684 it had long been recognized, by Oliver Cromwell among others, that England needed a port in or near the Straits to divide France from France and Spain from Spain in war, and to support her Mediterranean trade in peace. In 1702 there had been an abortive expedition under Sir George Rooke to capture a port for this purpose. In 1704 an English and Dutch fleet commanded by Sir George, and carrying 2,000 marines under Prince George of Hesse-Darmstadt, sailed with diverse orders, to assist the revolution of the Cevennois in Languedoc, or that of the Catalans in Barcelona, or to seize a port in Spain for the claimant Charles. The two first ventures having foundered, this fleet was lying off Tetuan in July, six months at sea and nothing achieved. At a Council of War attended by both Georges, Sir Cloudesley Shovel, Admiral Byng (father of the one shot 'pour encourager les autres'), Sir John Leake, Sir Thomas Wishart and three Dutch admirals, it was decided to attack Gibraltar. Though Gibraltar was certainly not the first target of the expedition, it seems unlikely that the Council's decision was one of desperation, or that they considered Gibraltar an easy or unimportant prize. Out of desperation they would probably have attacked Cadiz, where many English admirals, including Rooke, had made or lost reputations. The natural strength of Gibraltar, and the enormous value of the Bay, were known to every sailor who had waited off an unfriendly coast for the east wind, without which there was no passage from the Mediterranean to the Atlantic. If Gibraltar had not been attacked before it was because it had always been considered unassailable. The Council's arguments are given by Colonel James:

First, because in the condition the place then was, there was some probability of taking it, which in case it had been properly provided, and had in it a numerous garrison, would have been impossible. Secondly, the possession of that place was of infinite importance during the present war. Thirdly, because the taking this place would give a lustre to the Queen's army, and possibly dispose the Spaniards to favour the cause of King Charles.

On 21 July the fleet of forty-five ships-of-the-line streamed into the Bay.

The strength of the Spanish garrison commanded by the Governor Don Diego de Salinas has been obscured by Spanish historians minimizing the difficulty of the capture: the extreme version has it that Rooke entered the Bay to take soundings whereupon the Governor surrendered. In a letter sent by the citizens to King Philip, they referred to 'the fatal chance of our not having any garrison for its defence, except a few poor and raw peasants, amounting to less than 300', and the historian Ayala allows 150 soldiers and, including the citizens, under 500 men. He does not mention the crew of a French privateer that was in the Bay, or how 1,200 houses could only supply 500 men; however, there is no doubt that the fortress was undermanned, the defences were crumbling, or that Don Diego was a bold man when he answered the summons to surrender, 'that being entrusted with the place by his natural lord and king Philip V, he should make a very ill return for the honour done him, if he gave up the place to his enemies without making any defence'.

Prince George and the marines were landed on the isthmus at Point Mala, whilst a party of 200 men went in small boats to Europa Point, where there was then a small beach, and a track up the cliffs used by fishermen. On the 22nd the letters were exchanged with the Governor, and on the 23rd the Fleet began to cannonade the town. This was a famous cannonade, and lasted five hours, during which 15,000 shots were fired. The effect was to drive the women and children from the town to take refuge in the Shrine of Europa, where they were seized by the party that had landed there. At the same time the Spaniards were driven from their guns at the New Mole, and Rooke made a signal for a party of sailors to go ashore under Captain Whitaker. Captains Jumper and Hicks who were lying near the Mole pushed their men ashore first, the Spaniards sprung a mine, and forty were killed and sixty wounded. Though Whitaker's men saw their companions blown up, they landed, rushed forward, and captured the defences of the Mole. The Europa party appeared with their prisoners, and the Governor yielded to the second summons to surrender. Bishop Burnet, who had a low opinion of Gibraltar, and a lower one of Rooke, wrote a more cynical account of the action:

> Rooke, that he might seem to attempt somewhat, fell upon Gibraltar, where he spent much powder in bombarding (or rather cannonading, though he might have flung in some shells) it to very little purpose, though there was no reason to hope he should succeed. Some bold men ventured to go ashore in a place where it was not thought possible to climb up the rocks, yet they succeeded in it. When they had got up, they saw all the women of the town were come out, according to their superstition, to a chapel, there to implore the virgin's protection; they seized on them, and that contributed not a little to engage those in the town to surrender.

There is an apocryphal story that Prince George ran up the flag of Austrian Charles, and that Rooke pulled it down and claimed the prize for England. The terms of surrender were signed by Prince George and allowed that the Spanish garrison should march out, but that anyone else could remain provided they swore fidelity to Charles, so it would appear that Gibraltar was still Spanish. However, except for one woman and a few men, the whole population quitted the Rock, even the elderly nuns, few of whom survived the journey inland. It was not so much that they preferred a French king to an Austrian one, but the brutal excesses committed by the marines and sailors in the town, particularly against the women, forced them to leave. Prince George's men completed the ruin of Gibraltar begun by the cannonade: they sacked the shrines and churches and performed such acts of bestiality and barbarism that nearly eighty years later in the Great Siege Spanish soldiers refused to be rescued by the British from burning ships because they feared they would be tortured to death.

Early in August, Rooke sailed to meet the French fleet at the bloody battle of Malaga which, though inconclusive (Rooke had expended half his powder battering Gibraltar), was the beginning of seventy-five years of British naval superiority in the Straits, and Prince George was left to defend the prize with the marines. He was unable to make any excursions from the Rock to the mainland, and many of the original inhabitants of Gibraltar took their archives and the pieces of their Saints to San Roque, from where they could see their homes, and hoped to return to them after the barbarians had been defeated. When these hopes had faded, this sad little town was dignified with the title City of Gibraltar in Exile, and still elects a Mayor of Gibraltar.

The twelfth siege in 1705 was conducted by the Marquis de Villadarias with 9,000 Spanish and 3,000 French troops, against Prince George's 2,000 marines, whose numbers were soon halved by disease. It might have succeeded had the Marquis not wasted his attack against the North Front, whilst the sea was left to Sir John Leake and his squadron stationed at Lisbon. When the French Marshal Tessé came to take over the command he found the besiegers in a miserable state, and abandoned the siege. His opinion of the Spaniards was to apply through the century:

> The general spirit of the Spaniards, even of the most zealous, is to fore-see nothing, to think that they are exculpated from the misfortunes they bring on themselves, by yielding to superior power. The king himself seems occasionally to desire that chance should furnish what can only be hoped for from the best combined precautions, and his specific orders have an air of obstinacy which must injure his service.

The war dragged to a standstill. Prince George went off to die in a second attempt on Barcelona. The Archduke Charles, who had been acclaimed at Gibraltar, succeeded his brother as Emperor, and could no longer be thought of as King of Spain. The Rock, which had been captured for him by his Dutch and English allies, was kept by England.

In 1713 the Treaty of Utrecht was signed, which established the pattern of power in Europe for the century. Philip V was recognized as King of Spain, with the proviso that the crowns of France and Spain would never be united: the Hanoverian succession was en-sured in England: France, acting for Spain, ceded to England, Minorca and Gibraltar, and the right to trade in slaves to the West Indies (the Asiento): France ceded Nova Scotia, Newfoundland, the Hudson Bay territories, and St Kitts: the Dutch retained the Spanish Netherlands, and Prussia and Savoy were rewarded with recognition and territories from the dismembered empire. There were conditions, which were customary, attached to the cession of Gibraltar; the town and fortress alone were ceded, the boundary was left undefined, but there was to be no open communication with the mainland; there was to be freedom of worship for Catholics, but no Moors or Jews were to be allowed to reside there; and finally, should Great Britain ever give up the Rock it was first to be offered to Spain. An opinion prevalent in some circles was expressed in 1783 in a pamphlet by John Sinclair:

> The possession of these two places [Gibraltar and Minorca] was a bribe which England accepted for the desertion of her allies . . . it was privately understood among the parties that neither of those places, or at least Gibraltar, should long remain in the possession of this country.

The English forced the Dutch to withdraw any claim they entertained to a share in Gibraltar by threatening to make a separate peace, but both Gibraltar and Minorca were a *sine qua non* of the English terms from the start of the peace negotiations. When, after a few years, Gibraltar appeared to be more of a liability than an asset, King George I and his ministers began to consider returning it to Spain.

Gibraltar was a considerable liability. Though it had been declared a free port by its first British Governor (Colonel Roger Elliot, the uncle of General George Augustus), the Spaniards would allow no commerce with it across the isthmus, and its harbour, which was shallow and treacherous, could not bear comparison with that of Port Mahon or Lisbon. The Government was obliged to maintain a garrison of regular soldiers, which they and the country disliked, and which was estimated to cost £90,000 a year in peace-time. It was hot, dirty, ruined, disease-ridden, with a garrison famous for the amount of drink it consumed, and which attracted a colony of 'Jews and girls' from Morocco and Genoa, the only people who benefited from it apart from its rapacious Governors, who made private fortunes by imposing taxes on everything carried on, off, or about, the Rock. Its greatest liability was that, whilst it was held by Great Britain, no lasting peace was possible with Spain.

In 1718 Gibraltar was offered to Spain in return for her participation in the Quadruple Alliance to prevent a war in Italy. Spain prolonged the negotiations until the war ended them. The offer was renewed during the peace negotiations of 1720 with a new purpose. Lord Stanhope wrote: 'By means of this restitution we will be able to prevent for a long time to come the union of Spain with France in order jointly with her to make war on us.' Stanhope died in the next year but his successor, Lord Townshend, was equally hopeful that a Franco-Spanish compact could be averted by the retrocession of Gibraltar. In this year, George I wrote to Philip V of Spain: 'I do no longer balance to assure Your Majesty of my Readiness to satisfy you with regard to your Demand touching the Restitution of Gibraltar, promising you to make use of the first favourable opportunity to regulate this article with the Consent of my Parliament.' This letter only served to embitter relations between the two courts, as Philip claimed that it was a definite promise to restore Gibraltar, and signed a treaty advantageous to Great Britain in that belief, whereas the British pointed out that it was a promise to raise the matter in Parliament, where there was little chance of it being contemplated. The popular and nonsensical view was expressed repeatedly by pamphleteers like Thomas Gordon:

> Dares anyone to propose to a British King the delivering up to a baffled and subdued enemy the most important place in the world to the trade and naval Empire of England, the key of the Mediterranean, the terror of our enemies, and the best pledge of our new friendships?

Fortunately it prevailed.

In 1727 the Spaniards attempted to achieve by force what they had failed to do by negotiation. Reinforcements were hurriedly thrown into Gibraltar. The North Front was strengthened by the flooding of a triangular marsh, the Inundation, and by the erection of Willis's Batteries. A powerful squadron was kept cruising in the Bay. The Spanish General, the Conde de las Torres, ignoring the lesson of the previous siege, sat down with 20,000 men and 164 cannons on the mainland, and proceeded to burrow along the isthmus. Six months later, with less than 13,000 men and only 19 cannons, he turned his back on the Rock. During the peace negotiations there was a new proposition to exchange Gibraltar for a port or territory less offensive to Spanish pride. Lord Townshend replied:

> What you propose in relation to Gibraltar is certainly very reasonable, and is exactly conformable to the opinion which you know I have always

entertained concerning that place. But you cannot but be sensible of the violent and almost superstitious zeal which has of late prevailed among all parties in this kingdom against any scheme for the restitution of Gibraltar upon any condition whatsoever. And I am afraid that the bare mention of a proposal which carried the most distant appearance of laying England under an obligation of ever parting with that place would be sufficient to put the whole nation in a flame.

The Treaty of Seville in 1729 made no specific mention of Gibraltar, but renewed and confirmed the Treaty of Utrecht. The Spanish Court then set about making the most of those conditions. A line of permanent fortifications was erected across the isthmus, the Spanish Lines, and all communication was temporarily closed. The British were urged to expel the Jews and Moors from Gibraltar. With the mainland shut off, provisions for the garrison had to come from Morocco, and the Governors were obliged to maintain friendly relations with the Emperor, which they could not do by expelling his subjects. Moreover the Jews provided the taxes that were worth £20,000 a year.

After the thirteenth siege the Rock was better governed and the fortifications were greatly strengthened. It was during this period that the town was altered from a crumbling and unhealthy ruin into a stark but not unpleasant barrack fortress. Emigrants were encouraged to come from Genoa to fish and cultivate the garden in the Neutral Ground. Gibraltar was not attacked again before the Great Siege, though there were two wars, the war of the Austrian Succession and the Seven Years War. Since 1733, and the signing of the First Family Compact between the kings of France and Spain, Spain had followed, often reluctantly, in the wake of her dominating partner. The French and British were irreconcilable enemies, contestants for the world's trade which was slipping from the weak hands of the Dutch and Portuguese. Spain had little to gain in this struggle, and much to lose, but the little there was to gain was Gibraltar. This was the spur that made her run with France, and each time the Family Compact was renewed the French king promised secretly to assist his cousin to regain the Key of Spain. However, during the wars there were never French troops and ships available to besiege Gibraltar, and at the peace conferences French diplomats were found persuading the Spaniards not to insist on its return in case the negotiations broke down. Though Spain wanted Gibraltar, and Great Britain seemed several times to be on the verge of restoring it to her (William Pitt offered to exchange it in 1757 for Spanish help in recapturing Minorca, for the loss of which his outraged countrymen had just shot Admiral Byng), it was never in the interests of France for the retrocession to take place, because it would have removed the strongest incentive the Spanish had to join her in her wars against Great Britain.

The Treaty of Paris that ended the Seven Years War in 1763 was considered generous by the British, who had ended the war with a blaze of triumphs, and humiliating by the Bourbon kings, Louis XV and Charles III. British power was at its zenith in the century, from America to India her enemies were floundering, her allies flattering. Yet within ten years her power had so far declined that she had no friend, the American Colonies and Ireland were on the brink of rebellion, the country was divided as it had not been since the Civil War, her Navy was rotting in harbour, her Army was inadequate, her policies were illiberal and short-sighted. This was the difference between George II and George III, the king who led the army at Dettingen and a regiment of mistresses at home, but who left government to his ministers, and the king who led a blameless life, who wanted to govern in the light of honesty and fairness, and for the good of his subjects.

When the smouldering resentment of the colonists in America burst into flame, both France and Spain added fuel to the fire by sending money and arms to the insurgents. However, they were reluctant to appear openly hostile, Spain because she feared the epidemic of freedom might spread to her own American colonies, and France because there seemed little hope that the American backwoodsmen could defeat a trained army, and she had no wish to find herself facing Great Britain alone. An unknown American was of the same opinion when he wrote in 1777 after three years of war:

Our Affairs are as dark as they can be and I really think the Game is up . . . the whole Continent is starving, I could scarce get anything on the Road. The Continental money is not worth a Curse, nobody will take it without being forced, and everybody jumps to give 14 paper Dollars for a Silver One; in short everybody is tired, and those red hot Virginians who were so violent are all crying out for Peace.

In the same year, Benjamin Franklin wrote to King Louis XVI and his minister the Comte de Vergennes, in terms both desperate and wheedling:

It must be remembered that the first resistance of the Colonies was not to obtain independency but a redress of their grievances, and that there are many among them who might, even now, be satisfied with a limited subjection to the British Crown. A majority have indeed put in for the prize of independency, but they have done it partly on a confidence that France, attentive to her most important interests, would soon give them open and effectual support. But when they find themselves disappointed —it is very probable that despairing of foreign aid and severely pressed by their enemies and their own internal wants and distresses, they may be inclined to accept of such terms as it will be the interest and disposition of the British Government to grant them.

France was not impressed, until on 17 October 1777 an event of startling impact occurred which shook her out of her cautious neutrality. A British Army under General Burgoyne, the victim of the armchair strategy of Lord George Germaine and the baffling tactics of General Howe, surrendered to an overwhelming American force at Saratoga. In England the effect was to strengthen the Opposition in their clamour for peace, and to open the eyes of George III and his friends to the possibility of defeat. But before the Peace Commissioners hurriedly assembled by Lord North could sail, Vergennes had signed a treaty with the Americans. This treaty (February 1778) was to come into effect in the event of war being declared between France and Great Britain, its essential and direct end was the establishment of the liberty and independence of the United States, and neither side was to cease hostilities until this had been achieved. A month later a French squadron sailed to the west.

On 30 January 1778 Lord Weymouth, Secretary for the Southern Department, wrote to Lord Grantham, Ambassador at Madrid:

There is great reason to suspect that a Treaty is forming and perhaps even concluded between the French Court and the Americans in Rebellion, which makes the event of a War more probable. If this should be founded in Truth it is most likely that the designs of the Court of Madrid are not less hostile towards Great Britain.

The first reaction of the Spanish Court to the treaty was anger that Vergennes should have acted without consulting Charles III or his minister Floridablanca. 'His Catholic Majesty is very piqued indeed,' wrote Lord Grantham. Spain had no desire to see the American colonists free themselves from Great Britain. Not only did they fear the result a successful revolution might have on their own colonies, on whose tribute the Spanish economy was somewhat perilously balanced, but the Americans were great smugglers who had only been restrained by the British from preying on the West Indian trade. However, Vergennes pulled the rein of the Family Compact, and pressed the spur of Gibraltar. Spain was not ready for war: the yearly Flota bringing gold from the west had not yet arrived: her fleets and armies were not assembled. In order to gain time, Floridablanca resorted to the old expedient of offering to mediate between the opposing camps. It was hinted to Great Britain that the price of the mediation would be the surrender of Gibraltar, thus ensuring that there would be little chance of it succeeding. Lord Grantham believed the Spanish government to be sincere when they offered the Mediation, but then he was no match for Floridablanca. When he expressed surprise that there were twenty warships arming at Cadiz he was told: 'If the sea was covered with British, French and American Fleets it was necessary that the Spanish trade should be protected', and when he asked why so many cannons were being collected in the south, he appeared satisfied with the answer that the iron artillery at Cadiz was being changed for brass. In January 1779, when the Mediation had been prolonged for nine months, he could still write: 'I really believe this Court sincere in wishing to bring about a Pacification.' It was not until June, when he was presented with his passports, that he finally accepted the failure of negotiations never intended to succeed. In his last long dispatch he wrote:

> With regard to the Plan of Operations which this ill-advised Court will pursue, it is impossible to penetrate it; but I presume to think that their object is to strengthen the French Fleet and according to events to employ the Cadiz Fleet against Gibraltar. There is no Point but that, and the weakening if possible our Navy, which can be a Temptation to Spain.

This penetrating presumption was enclosed in a packet marked 'Most Confidential—by a Spanish courier'.

There was no Pitt in the British Cabinet to control the war, as in 1761 when Spain was forced to commence fighting before she was ready. Lord Weymouth carried on the farce of the Mediation, presenting the British demands and refusing to accept the French, until it petered out at the beginning of 1779. Floridablanca was still not ready to disclose his true intentions, as the Spring Flota would then be at the mercy of hostile British ships. He proposed another time-wasting solution to settle the differences between Britain and the colonies, which he called the Ultimatum. The British government carefully studied the terms, which included a twenty-five-years truce in America, *de facto* recognition of American independence, each side to remain in possession of the territory it then occupied, and compensation to France for her interference, whilst the Flota sailed safely into port, the Spanish Fleet joined the French off Coruña, and more regiments arrived outside Gibraltar at San Roque. Weymouth earnestly replied to the Ultimatum:

> The Terms to be granted to Colonies in such a Predicament, cannot be submitted to other Powers, who cannot be judges of the line of Authority which the Mother Country should extend over her Provinces, and the Terms which might be thought reasonable in Europe might be rejected in America.

They undoubtedly would have been, as at that time the British were still in possession of New York, Long Island, Rhode Island, most of Georgia, and large areas in the north-west territories. On 12 April 1779 Floridablanca signed the secret Convention of Aranjuez, committing Spain to open hostilities against Great Britain, and to join her navy to the French navy for the invasion of England that summer; in return, France guaranteed that war would not cease until Gibraltar was recovered by Spain. The Convention was a success for Floridablanca, as there was no mention of American independence, and France was committed to assist in the reduction of the Key of Spain. The signing of the treaty put an end to the bogus negotiations between Spain and Great Britain, and was followed by the presentation of the Spanish Manifesto, in effect a declaration of war. The Spanish Court had considerable difficulty in finding an excuse to commence hostilities, and the Manifesto was a list of petty complaints fabricated for the occasion: twelve outrages to Spanish ships, eighty-six insults to the Spanish navy, eleven invasions of Spanish territory, a plot to raise the Chatca, Cheroquie and Chicacha Indians

against the innocent inhabitants of Louisiana (fortunately foiled by
the honest Chatcas) and finally a claim that the failure of the Mediation was an insult to the 'august Mediator' Charles III. Spain entered
the war on 21 June 1779.

The treaty between the United States and France engaged both to
carry on the war until the independence of America was recognized
by Great Britain. The Convention between France and Spain engaged both to carry on the war until Spain regained Gibraltar. As
one American said: 'Our Fate here depends absolutely on the turn of
affairs in Europe.'

In Europe a cannon thundered. The ladies jumped. General Eliott
noted, with less satisfaction, that most of his officers had jumped too.

CHAPTER II

The dead man

THE Spaniards called it 'El Plaça', and sometimes 'the dead man' from its outline when seen from Algeciras. The troops marching to join the Spanish Camp from Malaga could see its humped back all the way along the coast, past the old watch-towers, through Marbella and Estapona, until the road wound up into the hills behind the Queen's Chair to San Roque. Those coming by boat from Cadiz saw it from the Straits, reaching out towards Africa, and the spires of the Atlas mountains, not hunched, but seeming low and rambling. The nearer they approached from either direction, the more ominous it appeared.

From the isthmus the North Front rose perpendicularly nearly 1,400 feet to Rock Guard on top of the peak: a great white limestone wedge, rising steeply from the Mediterranean and shelving down towards the Bay. It was possible to approach the Rock on the east side, past the ruined Devil's Tower, but thereafter there was nothing but towering cliffs and a giant sandbank, piled up in some ancient flood: the ridge from north to south was once climbed by the enemy in 1705, at Middle Hill, but was now scarped and walled and inaccessible: from Mount Misery and Sugar Loaf Point, the highest part of Gibraltar (1,403 feet), the cliffs fell vertically to the sea. On the west of the isthmus were the cemetery and the Genoese gardens, dominated by the ridge, on top of which were Willis's Batteries and the tower of the Moorish Castle: running below the batteries, like steps cut out of the rock on two levels, were the Prince's, Queen's and King's Lines, each with a stone parapet, a covered way, and bomb-proof shelters for the guards: they ran from the foremost point of the Rock down towards the Bay, overlooking the triangular Inundation. At the point where the Lines, the Inundation and the Old Mole defences met, there was a ditch, crossed by a drawbridge, a ramp, covered by a *place d'armes* and a battery, and the only entrance to the fortress from the land, Landport tunnel, which twisted underneath the Grand Battery. At Waterport and on the Old Mole, which the enemy called the Devil's Tongue, there were guns covering the Causeway between the Bay and the Inundation. The whole front was palisaded, with two gates, Bayside barrier, and Forbes barrier. From the isthmus there was barely a shrub to be seen, only the white wall of the Rock and the grey batteries and bastions with their black embrasures. The Spaniards in 1727 called this, the one approach by land to Gibraltar, the 'bocca de fuego', and it had been considerably strengthened since then, the latest addition, under the supervision of Colonel Green, being a small battery 900 feet up on the face of the cliff which he called the Superior Battery, but which the Governor later named Green's Lodge.

The prospect from the sea was less dramatic but almost equally formidable. From the Old Mole and Orange's Bastion, the Bay was fronted by a massive Line Wall, running the length of the town to the South Bastion and Ragged Staff, a small wharf where boats brought the stores unloaded from shipping in the Bay. Jutting out from the wall opposite the Spanish Church was the King's Bastion, begun whilst General Boyd was Acting-Governor. The General made this prophetic speech after laying the foundation-stone: 'This is the first stone of a work which I name the King's Bastion: may it be as gallantly defended, as I know it will be ably executed; and may I live to see it resist the united efforts of France and Spain.' This bastion was a miniature fortress, mounting twenty-six cannons and mortars, and with room inside for 800 men, complete with kitchens and ovens and a niche where General Boyd desired to be buried. There were several gun emplacements along the rampart of the Line Wall, and the Bay beneath was six feet deep and strewn with sharp rocks. The South Bastion was considerably higher than the other works, and its guns covered both the Bay and the Red Sands to the south. From this bastion a wall ran up the hill to Southport Gate, built in the reign of Charles V and having the arms of the Empire and Spain over the arch: this wall ended against a high cliff, on which was a battery covering the approach to the wall and the ditch before it. From the cliff the old Moorish wall stretched up the Rock to the ridge at the top, and to the south of this there was Charles V's Wall: between the two walls, on the ridge, stood the Signal House from where the watch could see to the horizon of the Mediterranean and over the Spanish hills to the Atlantic. From the South Bastion the Line Wall continued to the New Mole, enclosing the Red Sands, the remains of another huge sandbank on the north part of which the town was built: there was an eight-gun bastion in the wall and, parallel behind it, the Princess of Wales Lines, covering the sands and the Bay at that part. The wharf at Ragged Staff contained a basin where a ship could come in to take on water. However, as the Bay from Ragged Staff to the north was within range of the guns in St Philip's Fort and the Black Battery, most of the shipping lay off the New Mole, where it was deep enough for a ship-of-the-line to heave down. The New Mole was protected by a battery at its head and a fort at its foot, where there were also two magazines each capable of storing 2,100 barrels of gunpowder.

The wall was continued south of the New Mole to Rosia Bay, where it was possible to make a landing, though the rocks on either side were inaccessible; and then on to Camp Bay, Little Bay and Europa, where the cliffs fell vertically to the sea, and the approaches were guarded by shoals of rocks. Wherever there appeared any weakness in the natural defences, cannons were placed, and guards mounted. At Europa Point the cliffs had been scarped so that there was no trace of the rocks up which the marines had climbed in 1704; however, the wall was continued round to the overhanging precipice beyond Europa Advance and Cave Guard, and the plateau of Europa was covered by the raised positions on Windmill Hill. In short, the whole Rock was a natural fortress, and for a thousand years its defenders had added walls and bastions to those parts that nature had left unprotected: the British, after the siege of 1727, had been particularly adept and industrious at this, and the majority of the works mentioned still stand as a monument to their efforts.

The town of Gibraltar, whilst it was nearly all destroyed in 1704 and again damaged by the Spanish bombardment in 1727, had been rebuilt on the same foundations as the earlier Spanish town. Main Street ran from Landport to Southport, and a curious mixture of Moorish and Spanish and British military architecture was piled on either side of it. Next to Landport there was the Picket Yard, and a concretion of a block and a guard-house, a bastion, a barrack and a bomb-proof shelter, all constructed with the ingenuity of Army engineers to be difficult to get in to and almost impossible to get out of, and to trap the yellow torrents that poured down from the hill in the winter. Then came the town proper, 'the rotten part of the town' as Governor Eliott called it, a quarter of a mile of dense wood and plaster buildings, arching over narrow alleys, with balconied windows shuttered against each other and strong doors, for it was a garrison town. These doors might reveal, for the briefest glance, a shaded courtyard with a pool, green vines and orange trees, or, more likely, a rickety staircase and a clutch of dirty squalling babies. There were some four hundred houses, and where they were dirtier, closer, and more tottering, between Main Street and Orange's Bastion, it was called Irish Town. Above the town there was a row of private storehouses, belonging to the merchants, and another hundred steps up, the Castle, though little was left but the square Torre del Hominage, and the upper wall, which enclosed a sloping oblong patch with Moorish remains and the more recent litter of the garrison. Behind the Castle ran a good road to the batteries, along which were two magazines of excellent construction so as to be dry and cool, and a shed containing spare gun-carriages. (The plaster on the magazines has fallen off on all but one side, and there may still be seen the initials of soldiers, perhaps scratched whilst they stood on guard, among them those of Mr Ince, of whom more later.)

The Grand Parade that ran from Main Street down to the Line Wall was like a clearing in the forest of houses: there were green benches around it and a whipping post and the whirligig (a wooden cage which could be spun round, used for the punishment of prostitutes), the prison and Black Hole in one corner, and coffee-rooms in the houses about it. At the foot of the Parade was the water fountain where the winter rains, collected in the huge tilted saucer of the Rock and filtered through the Red Sands, were carried on an ancient aqueduct, to flow out all the year round. A few yards from the Parade, opposite the King's Bastion, stood the Spanish Church, which had survived the early bombardments, and which had, in accordance with the terms of the Treaty of Utrecht, been open to the Roman Catholics for worship: when the siege commenced, this was considered too much of an indulgence, and it was converted, as the other chapels and shrines had been, into a store-house for flour. Up the hill from the Spanish Church there was a garden belonging to the Governor, one of the three large gardens on the Rock. Further south, the Lieutenant-Governor had his house, a short way from the Convent, which was the Governor's residence. This was the building from which the nuns had made their unhappy way, whilst the walls echoed with the screams of the victims of the assault of the marines in 1704. It was a pleasant, regular, red-brick building, with a paved courtyard and a fine view across the Bay, and it had the second garden, which was convenient for the vegetarian General. The Chapel adjoining the Convent, the King's Chapel, served the garrison and the town; as the bells had disturbed the Sunday morning sleep of Governor Cornwallis when he was in residence, the congregation were summoned to church by the beat of a drum. The Victualling Office and King's Stores, large stone buildings of which the Army was very fond, were on the hill above the Convent. The town ended at Southport and Charles V's wall. There was one other building of little architectural merit but some antiquity near the sea in Irish Town, and that was the Moorish galley-house, which had been converted into the Admiralty store-house. Every building in Gibraltar town was flattened or suffered great damage during the Great Siege; in 1779 it was a small, squalid heap of houses, not to be compared with the Spanish city that had once stood there, but not dissimilar to the more crowded parts today.

South of the town there were a few officers' houses, little more than cottages, though Colonel Green had laid out the third large garden around his. On the hill above the New Mole stood the South Barracks, a plain building, with a parade in front of it, and room for a regiment to encamp behind it. Above Rosia Bay there was the Naval Hospital, with wards for 1,000 men, a pleasant airy building with a gallery on the upper floor for the sick to sit in the sunshine. Behind the Hospital another regiment could encamp on the sloping ground below the hill, and among the rocks at the foot of the hill was a place set apart for the townspeople to build huts, which the garrison was not slow in calling New Jerusalem. On Europa there was the ruin of the once famous shrine, now a guard-house, with a small tessellated pavement before it, and a large sunken bath, cut out of the rock, eight feet deep, seventy feet long, and forty-two feet wide, which was full of leeches.

The Rock itself was always impressive, with a strange mixture of ugliness and beauty. Francis Carter the antiquarian, who stayed in Gibraltar in 1773, wrote of it:

> The shape and face of Gibraltar rock is neither promising nor pleasing and it is as barren as uncouth, not a tree or shrub hardly to be seen on it above the Town, and this not owing to its natural sterility, but to the modern policy of our military gentry.

and also:

> After Christmas you will see the hill everywhere beautifully enameled with them [flowers]; they spring immediately out of the dry ground, without rising an inch, or having any green leaves about them, and often form little groups of six or eight, resembling an embroidery of tapestry.

It was a naturalist's treasure-store, and Colonel James listed over three hundred varieties of wild flowers from 'Acacia, June, back of hill' to 'Wormwood, Roman, April, front'. He also listed dozens of shell-fish and fish to be found in the waters around the Rock, and the insects, birds and animals which lived on it, of which there was a surprising variety. The larger animals inhabited the parts of the Rock which were practically inaccessible to the garrison and therefore still covered with trees and bushes. There were rabbits and foxes, snakes and lizards, centipedes and large hairy spiders (which lived in the South Bastion), partridges, pigeons and bats, eagles and vultures journeying from Africa, and 'the true lords of the hill', the apes, which were no friendlier then than they are now, and threw stones at the Signal House guard. The place was full of holes, caves and wells, the most famous being St Michael's Cave (the British patriotically called it St George's Cave, but the old name stuck). This was (and is) 1,100 feet up in the hill above the South Barracks, with a small entrance, opening up into a great cavern apparently supported by stone columns, stalactites and stalagmites joined together, giving it the appearance of 'a gloomy Gothic cathedral'. In many of the caves the fossilized bones of men, elephants, leopards and other animals dating from the Stone Age, were discovered, and on top of the Rock, 1,400 feet above the sea, fossilized molluscs clung where they had been when the mountains were thrust up from the ocean bed.

The climate of Gibraltar, one of the few things the garrison could not change, is pleasant for most of the year, with the heat of June, July and August, tempered by the sea breeze, which used to be called 'the Doctor'. In winter it grows cold, but seldom enough for there to be a frost, and it is barely high enough to reach the snow that lies on the mountains of Granada and Africa. There are storms in December and January, sometimes tremendous, with gales, thunder and lightning, and torrents of rain which carry rocks and rubble down into the town, blocking the drains, and flooding cellars and streets. These are more welcome than otherwise, as they supply the water for the next year. The bane of Gibraltar are the levanter winds, then as now, as Francis Carter wrote:

> Eight months in the year are disfigured with the levanters that blow in whirlwinds round the hill, obscure the sky with mists and clouds, and render the atmosphere heavy and unsupportable: they cause such a dampness that all the furniture mildews and rots, steel and iron utensils rust, be they covered ever so close, and no provisions will keep a day.

The inhabitants of Gibraltar, 'to the amount of about 3,600 of all countries, and all religions, amongst which many of suspicious characters', which was General Eliott's opinion, had come from Morocco and Genoa to fill the gap left when the Spanish population quitted the Rock in 1704. They were at best Jews who could trace their descent from those banished from Spain two centuries before, Genoese labourers, or Spanish and Portuguese exiles: and at worst, brothel-keepers, prostitutes and pedlars, attracted by the garrison. By 1777 there was a generation of Gibraltarians who regarded the Rock as their home, and the garrison as their livelihood. The Governor referred to them again in October 1777: 'The inhabitants amounting to 4,000 will need great help if we are shut up as they have no store of provisions', and in July 1779 he wrote to Lord Weymouth:

> My Lord, it is believed Spain intends to prevent our Supplies; therefore all sorts of Provisions should be sent at any Risk to make up a sufficient Stock for a Year at least, besides daily Consumption, and this for three or four Thousand Souls over and above the garrison, One Half of which will Labour or bear Arms, the Remainder cannot lay in Stock for subsistence any Considerable Time.

At a census in 1777, the civilian population was calculated at 3,201 people: there were 519 British, 1,819 Roman Catholics from Genoa, Portugal and Spain, and 863 Jews. The British were for the most part retired soldiers who had served in the garrison, civilians employed by the Government, some merchants, and the troop entertainers of the day—the proprietors of wine-cellars and the prostitutes. The Spanish historian Ayala wrote about the townspeople of Gibraltar:

> The richest mercantile houses are the English, and besides the Military and civil officers of the Government, there are other Englishmen who keep inns and pursue various occupations. The Jews for the most part are shopkeepers and brokers, as much given to cheating and to lending money at exorbitant interest there as their brethren are elsewhere. . . . The Genoese are traders, but the greater part of them are fishermen, sailors and gardeners. . . . It is a barren rock, and the Governor and garrison are the principal customers.

Ayala expresses the traditional Spanish hatred of the Jews, and it is not surprising either to find Colonel James giving this opinion as his own:

> What the Jews call other men, are the Christians, Moors, Turks, and Pagans, whom they may cheat or rob with a safe conscience, when they have an opportunity, provided they give some part of the gain to raise the fortune of such of their own as are fallen to decay, and to keep their poor from Begging: in this particular their charity is wonderful; for when a man has lost all he had, they will set him up again three times, that he may live of himself; and if fortune still frowns on him, he is maintained amongst the poor; but the wicked ways they find to support them, will convince any man how cautious he ought to be in his dealings with them.

The Jews were isolated by their religion and by the caste system that placed a soldier above a shopkeeper, but without them there would have been no private stores in Gibraltar to feed the townspeople, little contact with, and therefore few shipments of food from, Morocco, and no core of civilian resistance to Spain. They were brokers because prejudice allowed them to be little else, and if they charged a high rate of interest for their money it was because the borrowers were dishonest, not the lenders. The Genoese who came to settle on the Rock were mostly sailors attracted by the opportunity of smuggling, or finding a ready market for their fish. They stayed to become the gardeners, on the Neutral Ground, and, the garrison suspected, to cultivate the Spaniards as well as their cabbages; there was always the danger that the Genoese would sell information to the enemy, and this accounts for some of the Governor's attempts at secrecy—the garrison however usually knew what was happening. Apart from the 519 British civilians on Gibraltar, one of whom was to be honoured with a mention in Garrison Orders for 20 July 1778: 'Mary Sayse alias Minorca Moll, being ordered to quit the Garrison if any Soldier or Soldier's wife presumes to Harbour or secrete her they will be severely punished', there were the families of the soldiers and officers of the British regiments. The number of these can only be estimated during the siege, as one soldier wrote, 'we Marry and breed faster than ever known in peacable times'. There were five regiments, and a reasonable estimate would be about five hundred wives, and perhaps a thousand children. Twenty years before, Colonel James estimated there were 1,426 'women, military, and children' and 414 other British civilians, and there appears little to suggest that these figures had altered drastically. So apart from his garrison of 5,382 men, Governor Eliott ruled over a population of some 4,700, living in the town. This figure was almost immediately reduced, as, once the siege had started, no boat left Gibraltar without being crowded with inhabitants escaping from it, with the full encouragement of the Governor.

Whereas the townspeople were a drab agglomeration, living in each other's pockets in the heap of buildings about Main Street, the garrison were bright, neat lines and squares, every man numbered and accounted for. (See page 31.)

Though the regiments were, in the main, recruited from the counties with which they were later identified, and were as diverse in their drills as in their accents, on the Rock they became a corporate unit, and men from Suffolk (12th), Dorset (39th), Essex (56th) and Northampton (58th), together with the newly raised Royal Manchester Volunteers (72nd), formed a body of unified activity and opinion. The Hanoverians drafted from the Elector's dominions to provide him with a revenue, which as King of England he paid to himself, tended to live a separate, more ordered existence, but were on the best of terms with the British troops. They were a garrison, and Gibraltar was their fortress. As in any muster of 5,000 men, there were thieves, homosexuals, adulterers, lunatics and potential deserters

THE GARRISON OF GIBRALTAR

General G. A. Eliott, Governor
Lieutenant-General R. Boyd, Lieutenant-Governor
Major-General De la Motte, Commander of the Hanoverian Brigade

	Off.	Staff	Sjts	Drums	Rank & File	
Artillery	25	0	17	15	428	Col. Godwin
12 Regt.	26	3	29	22	519	Lt.-Col. Trigge
39th	25	4	29	22	506	Lt-Gen. Boyd Col. Ross
56th	23	4	30	22	508	Maj. Fancourt
58th	25	3	29	22	526	Lt-Col. Cochrane
72nd Royal Manchester Vol.	29	4	47	22	944	Lt-Col. Gledstanes
Hardenberg's	16	13	42	14	367	Lt-Col. Hugo
Reden's	15	12	42	14	361	Lt-Col. Dachenhausen
De la Motte's	17	16	42	14	367	Maj-Gen. De la Motte Lt-Col. Sclippergill
Engineers & Artificers	8	0	6	2	106	Col. Green
	209	59	313	169	4632	

THE NAVY AT GIBRALTAR

Vice-Admiral Duff, Commodore
Sir Thomas Rich, Bart.

	Guns	Officers & Men
The Panther	60	400
The Enterprise	28	200
The Childers	14	90
The Gibraltar	12	40
The Fortune	10	30
	124	760

among them: they were ignorant but not stupid, loyal but not servile, rough but not cruel; they liked to keep pets, birds, dogs, lizards and snakes, they liked to eat meat, and they liked to get drunk. They were remarkably good-natured and good-humoured, and submitted to barely tolerable privations and disciplines. On occasions they were to defy their officers, but during the siege when a large part of the garrison was in a state of semi-mutiny, the guards and pickets paraded and the Governor wrote: 'I have no reason to suspect that any care is wanting at the Post next the Enemy.' Each soldier had his best uniform for parades and fighting: tricorn hat, scarlet coat with facings of his regimental colours, white waistcoat and breeches, black gaiters and boots, a cross-belt, cartouche box, short sword, bayonet, and Brown Bess musket; he was clean-shaven, and his hair was worn long, drawn back and 'clubbed' and, at the beginning of the siege, powdered with flour; for work, he wore a loose tunic and breeches usually patched, and washed to a uniform pink. He had his bedding and some camp equipment, and a weekly ration of dry and salt provisions, which on Gibraltar was:

Bread	7	lb.
Salt beef	$2\frac{1}{2}$	lb.
Salt pork	1	lb.
Butter	10	oz.
Pease	$\frac{1}{2}$	gall.
Groats	3	pts.

He was paid $4\frac{1}{2}$d. a day, in Spanish currency, with which he had to buy every other requirement: a drummer and a corporal were paid 6d. a day, and a serjeant 9d. The Royal Artillery, who wore dark blue coats, were paid slightly more. The duties of the garrison consisted of mounting pickets and guards, day and night, and providing working parties, under the supervision of the artillery or the engineers, who did everything from dragging guns and powder up the hill to digging defences and collecting wood for fascines, most of which, however, was pilfered and burnt for warmth. Every year the Articles of War were read to the men, which gave the officers power to have them tried by courts-martial, and if convicted, flogged or hanged. Some had already been on Gibraltar for ten years, others for a year; at the beginning of the siege most hated it, at the end, most agreed with Private Gordon of the 73rd Regiment (which joined the garrison in 1780) when he wrote:

> A common soldier, though he has an equal share of danger with the commander-in-chief, is far from having an equal share of the glory, nor has he any title to expect it. Yet I know not how it is, I have a desire, and I believe everyone has the same, that it should be known I was at Gibraltar, and fought and conquered.

The officers of the garrison, apart from those in the Royal Artillery and Engineers who had graduated through Woolwich, had purchased their commissions. The junior officers had had the minimum of training and few studied their profession seriously. For them, Gibraltar was the worst garrison in the world, as there was little opportunity there for either pleasure or promotion. They were constantly under the Governor's eye. The senior officers were unavoidably involved in the niggling war of the two factions, which apparently agreed on one essential only, that of keeping the Spaniards out of Gibraltar. They received the same weekly provisions as the men, but in greater proportions: a Warrant-Officer, Ensign and Lieutenant was allowed two rations, a Captain three, a Major and Lieutenant-Colonel four, and a Colonel six. The Lieutenant-Governor and the Governor received twenty-four rations each. When there were private supplies of fresh food in the garrison the officers used to sell their rations to the shopkeepers, but shortly after the start of the blockade this practice ended. Their pay (the total pay for the year 1780 was £7,500 and there were 225 officers in Gibraltar at that time: a little under £34 per annum each in proportion from Ensign, 3s. 8d. a day with reductions, to Colonel, £1 4s. od. a day) had to be drawn in Spanish currency at the prevailing rate of exchange; at the height of the siege, Captain Drinkwater noted, they lost 6d. in every 3/– because of the unfavourable rate. They, like the men, received virtually nothing for their families. Once the communication with the mainland was closed, and the hunting trips and picnics ended, there was little to do on Gibraltar but drink and argue in the few hours free from the burden of command and administration. Several officers kept journals of the siege, but few allowed themselves to comment on the routine events they recorded. They were, however, the garrison's voice, and it is in the pages of their journals and diaries that the siege still lives. (After the diarists and after the siege came the painters, who paid more attention to the faces in their pictures than to the credibility of the background, and in them several of the garrison's heroes can be seen.)

The most admirable of the contemporary writers was Captain Drinkwater of the 72nd Regiment. This is his account of the story of Lieutenant-General Boyd, who was born in 1710.

> He was originally in the Civil Service of the Ordnance—a storekeeper at Minorca, and was dispatched, at considerable hazard from the Garrison then besieged, to communicate with the British Admiral Byng —who was sent to the relief of the fortress but by not attacking the Enemy's fleet eventually lost his life. Mr Boyd afterwards proceeded to Germany as a Commissary to the British Army and so ingratiated himself with Prince Ferdinand that the Prince, it is said, wrote to England that they had sent him Storekeepers or Commissaries fit to be Generals and Generals not fit to be Commissaries. On some brilliant success—the victory of Minden I believe, Mr Boyd was made the bearer of intelligence to England—written as reports gave out with a pencil on his back in the field of battle—being the harbinger of such good news and patronized by so popular a General as Prince F. Mr Boyd obtained immediate notice and Promotion in the Army. He soon rose to high military rank, and at the time Col. D. [Drinkwater] first knew him he was Colonel of the 39th Regiment of Foot and Major-General in the Army and Lieutenant-Governor of Gibraltar. During the blockade and siege of Gibraltar Col. D was too young and of too humble rank himself to belong to any Party. He was therefore received civilly by both chiefs.

The General's reputation did not depend entirely on the use to which his back was put at Minden. The great Merchant-General Lord Clive, recommending Boyd to the Directors of the East India Company for the post of Commander-in-Chief Bengal, wrote: 'He is esteemed as one of the best, if not the best officer in the King's Service.' General Boyd was not without influence, and before the siege commenced Lord Chatham, eldest son of the great Earl, was his A.D.C., but his party was not in power.

The chief of Gibraltar, Cock of the Rock, His Excellency the Governor, was General George Augustus Eliott. He was the seventh son of Sir Gilbert Eliott (usually spelt Elliot) of Stobs in Roxburghshire, born on Christmas Day 1717, a gentleman of a border family

of some significance, Hanoverian affinities, and estates in England.
Young Eliott studied languages at Edinburgh and Leyden, and his
chosen career at the French Military Academy of La Fère. When he
was eighteen he served as a volunteer in the Prussian Army, the
model army of the day, and later entered the engineer establishment
on which the Military Academy was founded at Woolwich, where he
was commissioned as a field engineer. In 1739 he was gazetted to
the 2nd Horse Grenadier Guards, then commanded by his uncle,
Colonel James Eliott, and was promoted Lieutenant and then Adjutant to the regiment. He served during the War of Austrian Succession, and was wounded at Dettingen, where he was brought to the
notice of George II. After the war, he purchased his commission as
Major, and married a Miss Anne Pollexfen; the marriage produced a
son and a daughter before Mrs Eliott died. A Lieutenant-Colonel in
1754, he was appointed A.D.C. to King George, who liked him, and
who, four years later, commissioned him to raise a regiment of light
horse, similar to those employed by Frederick the Great. The 1st
Light Horse (later the 15th Hussars), Colonel Eliott's, saw service
during the Seven Years War, and Colonel Eliott received the thanks
of the same Prince F. who scribbled on Mr Boyd's back. As a
Brigadier he took part in one of the raids on the French coast in 1761,
and in the next year he was appointed Major-General, and made
second-in-command to the Earl of Albemarle in the expedition to
Cuba, undertaken when Spain entered that war. Though he was
barely mentioned in the accounts of the siege and capture of Havana,
he was very much in evidence when the prize money was distributed,
and his share amounted to the fortune of £24,539 10s. 1d. He returned to England a Lieutenant-General and bought an estate at
Heathfield in Sussex. He was with his regiment when they were
reviewed by George III in Hyde Park after this war and, when the
King offered him a favour, asked that they should become a Royal
regiment. This was accorded, and with it a continuance of royal
patronage. At the outbreak of the American war Lieutenant-
General Eliott was appointed Commander-in-Chief of the separate
and important military establishment in Ireland. Here, however, he
had the first setback in his career. Before he had time to unpack his
bags, he found himself in conflict with the civil government of that
country, which was on the verge of revolution itself. He returned to

England almost immediately, and was passed over, fortunately for him, for the commands of the armies in America. In 1777, at the age of sixty, he was sent to govern Gibraltar.

There are two ways of judging a man: by what others say about him, and by what he says about others. Little was said about Governor Eliott before the siege, and most of what was said afterwards was coloured by his victory. This description was given of him in 1787, four years after the siege, by his nephew Sir Gilbert Elliot:

> Elliot of Wells carried me yesterday to Lord Heathfield [General Eliott] who received me with great politeness and appearance of friendship. He is a fine old man, and preserves a sort of beauty which is his character and consists in tolerable freshness and features of a marked and commanding style. But his age appears by the total decay of his teeth. He seems wrapt up in his profession, and more particularly in his own province of Gibraltar, where he is to return at the end of next summer, in the intention of leaving his bones under that Rock which will indeed be a noble and proper monument. I expected to have found something more dignified, more silent, and more saturnine in his manner, from what we know of his severity in discipline, his extreme simplicity and abstinence in living, and his unpopularity in the garrison. But he has a brisk, lively manner, full of attention and civility, a great deal of conversation, approaching even to rattle, and no starch of any kind that I could perceive, although no want of dignity appears either. I should have thought that he must have been the most popular general in the service, and I still suspect that all the obloquy he fell under was the consequence of his adherence to his duty and the dislike of the garrison to do theirs.

Much of what General Eliott said will appear in the course of the story of the siege, but he was on Gibraltar for two years before the siege started, and he spent that time in arming and equipping the fortress that had been too long neglected. He arrived in the *Worcester* on 26 May 1777, and was warned shortly afterwards by Lord Weymouth of the preparations the Spaniards were making at Cadiz. He answered: 'No vigilance on my part shall be wanting, in case of service the garrison must be increased considerably more than double the present numbers, especially artillerymen.' (At that time the garrison was complete apart from the 72nd, and some companies of artillery.) General Eliott (he was promoted in April 1778), insisted

that the minimum number of men required for the garrison was
8,000, and when told he could expect one new regiment and no more
wrote: 'The reinforcements propos'd for us will I fear not exceed
One thousand seven hundred effective men, after their arrival our
whole will then consist of five thousand men everything included: the
raw men will feel the difference of climate and all duties bear much
harder on them than Old Soldiers.' But he was pleased with the 72nd,
as he was with the others: 'The several Regiments in this Garrison
are good and are in the most perfect order—their vigour may be
depended upon', and with the Hanoverians: 'A most perfect har-
mony subsists between these Corps.' But he wanted things for them,
and everything had to come from England, as he said himself,
'Gibraltar however tremendous is immoveable.' Nothing was too
small or too large for him to demand from Lord Weymouth. He
wanted camp kettles, 'no utensil of that kind being sold here', and a
general hospital: 'a private soldier who discharges his duty with
courage, fidelity and patience, has a just claim to every assistance the
State can afford him'. Above all he wanted provisions: 'Our present
stock of Beef Pork Pease and Butter is scarce the complement for five
months; Flour including Biscuit three months; Oatmeal the same.
The usual regulation is always to have six months provision in store—
in the present circumstances it ought to be no less than eight months
for five thousand men.' He also required a quantity of rum. The
other concern of the Governor was the state of the fortifications, and
he sent Colonel Green to London in 1777 to have the Colonel's plans
for improving the defences approved, adding: 'This will be a tedious,
expensive, but necessary work for maintaining the fortress, and
added to it must be many internal accommodations in barracks,
bomb-proofs, store-houses, hospitals, magazines.' The garrison was
put to work, the Lords of the Treasury were awoken, and the
General was sent most of what he asked for. On 22 June 1779, he
could write, 'I have taken every necessary precaution', and his justifi-
cation was that nearly four years later the Rock still belonged to
Great Britain.

This was Gibraltar, the garrison, and the Governor before the
Great Siege. For a description of Southern Spain and the Spaniards
at this time there is no better authority than Colonel James:

Spain is very pleasant in spring, but excessive warm in summer; was it not for this heat, the climate in this province would be as fine as any in Europe: however, it has not the violent heat of Africa, the damp of Holland, the frosts of Germany and France, nor the stormy winds of England: the rains are seldom in those refreshing showers, but descend in cataracts, and accompanied with severe lightnings and thunders, particularly in the dog days, and the months of October and November.

The climate, however, in general, is temperate, and the soil fruitful; vast quantities of fruit the earth produces of various kinds, and on which the poor peasant feeds almost the year round. I hope it may not be prejudice, but I do not think their fruits so delicious as those of England: the reason is, because they have not the art or industry of our husband-men and gardeners: the vine is exuberant, their produce generous, and variety almost infinite; for there is hardly a village, but whose vintage varies: here is plenty of corn, wine, oil, and honey: Andalusia boasts the preference to all these.

Here is plenty of cattle, sugar, silks, wooll, vermillion, and vast woods: the sea, which surrounds almost all Spain, produces plenty of fish; however, they are supplied in great measure from the English, with salt cod from Newfoundland, particularly the Portuguese, who were very uneasy when the French took that island in the last war: there are very few rivers, and fewer lakes; the salt fish is therefore very acceptable to the inhabitants, whose religion is of the Roman Catholic faith. The inhabitants from the most early ages, have always been a brave people, but have, like other nations, had various vicissitudes: however, they foiled the Roman glory more than any other people. They are even now a brave nation, and if men of honour may be credited, their soldiers will never quit the field, unless the way is shewn to them: if a Spanish gentleman gives his word you may rely on him.

They are of a sallow complexion, and in some towns near high moun-tains (where the sun in summer is violent, and the frost in winter severe) of a cadaverous aspect: the peasant is sturdy, and well limbed, their diet plain and simple; they drink much water and devour fruit. I do not recollect to have seen three Spaniards drunk in the streets, or in the fields, during the nine weeks of two summers I was in that country.

The Spaniards still retain many of the Moorish customs, and are al-most as extravagant in their amours: in short, many idle customs and ceremonies prevail among them: the women, are by the generality of husbands, preserved with a very watchful eye, and very seldom feel the sun beams but when they go to mass: they are very fair and delicate;

but in general prone to venery: they are rude to strangers, and think all
nations greatly their inferiours, and the men are ridiculously fond of
boasting of an imaginary pedigree. To such a degree does this folly
prevail, as to affect strangers, who may enjoy some post in that government, as, without noble or ancient lineage, they cut but a very indifferent figure among that people who are a century and a half behind
all Europe. I have heard a branch from an English stem, to keep in
high opinion with the don, trace his pedigree back to king John! but,
that which is more ridiculous, in their boasting of having no Moorish
blood in their veins. Whoever deals with a Spaniard, must have great
patience; for they are slow in their actions, and very deliberate in their
speech, drawing their words from their mouths, as they do their legs
from the earth: they sleep in summer from twelve at noon till four in the
afternoon, dining a little before twelve; so that their siesto is in the heat
of the day: they have a saying, that none but a dog and an Englishman
will be seen out in those four hours; which is literally true, for I have
been barked at, from one end of a village and town to the other: however this be, I know as an Englishman, that there are too many hours
idly spent; for what with religion, siestos, idleness, and pride, industry,
husbandry, manufactures, and literature, doze, for want of being put
into motion: when they awake at four in the afternoon, and the village
again becomes peopled, it is admirable to see their walk, which may be
rather termed marching in slow time, and seldom casting their eye upon
the earth, as if they despised it. Mr Howell tells us a merry tale of a
Spaniard, who having broke his nose by a fall, rose up in a passion, and
in a disdainful manner said, 'This is the consequence of walking upon
the earth.'

There are old sayings for a complete woman: 'Let her be English to
the neck, French to the waist, and Dutch below; and for hands and feet,
let them be Spanish.'

Again: 'Let the French women grace the dance, the Dutch woman
the kitchen, the Italian the window, the English the board, and the
Spanish lady the bed.'

This may be: but no nation can boast of having their women so complete in general as the English.

The Spaniard marries his daughter very young; and the women are
generally past child-bearing at thirty: they go veiled, and appear so
much alike each other in that dress, or disguise, that it is difficult to
know a don's lady from a taylor's daughter: they are much freer than is
generally conceived; and as for the country wenches, though they have
rustic romantic notions of gallantry, yet are easily to be won: in

general they are buxom lasses, and too many maritornes are amongst them. In short there is no travelling but Cervantes is hourly verified.

It was the Spain painted by the young Goya for the tapestries of Madrid. And it might have been separated from Gibraltar by the Channel as by the mile of sand for all there was in common between them.

CHAPTER III

Mamma, some bread!

Two days before the Court of Spain found the insults of Great
Britain as enumerated in the Spanish Manifesto too much to bear and
declared war, General Eliott and his Staff took a ride to San Roque
to congratulate the Spanish commander at that time, Lieutenant-
General Mendoza, on his recent promotion. Relations between the
camps had been cordial for many years, several British families were
staying at San Roque, and there was a party of officers on a hunting
expedition further inland, but on this Saturday (19 June 1779) the
Spanish General's reception was stiffer and more formal than was
merited by his new gold braid, and the Governor and his party were
not offered the usual cup of chocolate. Had they known Mendoza
had dispatches from Madrid in his pocket advising him that war was
imminent, and that a messenger was on the road with orders to shut
all communications with the Rock, they would not have stayed the
short time they did. The next day, the families and officers in San
Roque were given a few hours to move, so short a time that Lieutenant Witham left his watch behind and Mr Booth a little article of
private property, and it was not until April 1780 that these were returned to them at the request of the Governor. The shooting party,
which included Colonel Ross, who was to lead a desperate sort of life
on and off Gibraltar for the next few years, were obliged to make
their way to Portugal in disguise, and arrived back a month later in
a rowing boat from Faro. On Monday, the last of the refugees arrived,
and the mail did not, and at 3 a.m. the next morning, the ports in the
Spanish Lines were closed. As M. Almodovar, the Spanish Ambassador, was angrily demanding his passports in London, and Lord
Grantham was sadly packing in Madrid, the pickets at Forbes and

Bayside were lying on their arms, and the French and Spanish captains of the fleets that had joined off Coruña were discovering that they could not understand each others' signals. The plan of the Court of Spain was to venture a fleet with the French fleet in an invasion of England, and to starve Gibraltar into submission. Floridablanca hoped for an advantageous peace in six months. The invasion fleets lay off Coruña until August, and must be left for another chapter, eyeing each other with contempt and suspicion, whilst the aged Admiral Cordova and the tragic d'Orvilliers engaged in long, polite and futile councils. The threat to Gibraltar, whilst less obvious, was considerably more effective.

During the seventy-five years of British occupation, the Rock had often been cut off from the mainland, but the needs of the garrison had always been met by supplies of salt provisions and flour from Britain, augmented by fresh provisions, livestock, vegetables and fruit, from Morocco and Minorca. During these years, there had been no significant challenge to British naval superiority in the Straits, and the ancient enmity of Morocco and Spain, kept alive by the presence of a Spanish garrison in Ceuta, had ensured a British ally in the Emperor of Morocco. Now, however, the combined fleets of France and Spain lay between the Channel and the Mediterranean, and Floridablanca was offering friendship to the Emperor, which to this avaricious monarch was always associated with presents, with the intention of barring the ports of Tangier, Tetuan and Larache to British ships, and forbidding the dispatch of supplies to Gibraltar. By the persistence of General Eliott, and the efforts of the Consul in Tangier, Mr Logie, the British Government had been persuaded to counter the Spanish offer to farm these ports, with a better one of fitting out four Moroccan frigates from the Naval Stores at Gibraltar. The last of these frigates was still in the Bay, with Vice-Admiral Duff refusing to part with any more of his ropes and spars, when the second line of the Spanish blockade was drawn round the Rock early in July. The Governor wrote to Lord Weymouth on the 7th: 'Two or three Spanish ships are cruising East of our rock.' As yet the blockade was hardly effective, and Sir Thomas Rich increased his popularity by taking the *Enterprise* over to Tangier and returning with a fleet of small boats that allowed two weeks fresh provisions for every soldier. When this was gone, another boat came in carrying cattle, which provided 760 lb. of beef. Mrs Green, the Colonel's wife, got 2 lb. 6 oz. but there was not enough to share amongst the men. The system that General Eliott imposed and maintained throughout the siege was extraordinary for the day, as no one was allowed to import provisions privately. The Governor had first option to purchase any cargo from a neutral vessel or prize, the price to be fixed by a Court of Arbitration. Any other goods were sold by auction. Naturally, once the goods had been bought they were re-sold at twice or three times the price piecemeal, but the auction ensured that every article went to the highest bidder. The customary perquisites of priority were replaced by the prerogative of riches—as the soldiers knew neither, the system served only to offend the officers, and enrich the merchants.

July saw considerable activity in the town and the Neutral Ground. The garrison mounted pickets at Forbes and Bayside, and sent a guard every day to the Devil's Tower; the Genoese still cultivated their garden, and with a large party of Jews, 300 in all, they were put on levelling the banks of sand that had collected around it, and which might have served as cover for a Spanish advance. Any horse in the garrison the owner of which could not supply 1,000 lb. of forage was ordered to be shot, and the Governor gave up one of his mounts. All stray dogs were supposed to be killed, but as this order kept appearing, they presumably acquired temporary owners when the executioners were about. Chimneys were swept. The guards were ordered to mount unpowdered, an economy of flour which the garrison wits claimed was inspired by their vegetarian Governor's liking for puddings. An Ensign was court-martialled for dicing, and a Hanoverian deserted. He was followed by a serjeant of the 39th. During this month Consul Logie was brought across from Tangier to persuade Vice-Admiral Duff that unless the fourth Moroccan frigate was equipped there would be no more supplies from that quarter, and General Eliott issued Letters of Marque to legalize any privateering against the enemy undertaken from the Rock, whereupon the Jews took out a longboat and captured a neutral Dutch dogger full of wheat. On Sunday the 11th the Navy lost the opportunity of capturing a convoy of sixty sail indifferently guarded, because Vice-Admiral Duff was on Windmill Hill observing it, instead of on the *Panther* attacking it. On the 16th the Admiral was relieved from even considering any offensive action by the appearance of a Spanish squadron in the Bay, comprised of two 74-gun ships-of-the-line, two frigates, five xebecks, and a large number of galleys and longboats. This squadron was commanded by Admiral Barcello, and it was said his officers were wearing keys on ribbons round their necks as an earnest of the recapture of the Key of Spain. They nearly caught Mr Logie on his way back to Tangier in a Moorish row-galley, but he hid in a small scuttle, with General Eliott's dispatches in a loaf of bread.

As the summer passed, the Governor appointed his Staff from the more handsome or better connected of his officers, and the Spanish Camp increased with the arrival of boatloads of men and materials almost daily. Some neutral ships came into the Bay, and one or two small boats sent by Mr Logie slipped in at night past the galleys lying off Cabrita Point. Though the ships arrived with poor cargoes, they left rich, and crowded with townspeople, who preferred to leave their homes rather than risk the discomforts or worse of a siege. They were encouraged to leave. On 25 August, General Eliott wrote: 'Our duty is hard but the garrison is in very good health: we have done much work, repairing old defences, constructing new, still have much to do.'

There had been no convoy from Britain since April, fresh provisions were scarce, and prices were up 50 per cent. On Saturday, 4 September, Colonel Green was given 'soup meagre' for dinner: Captain Spilsbury of the 12th Regiment was more fortunate, but he had to pay 7/– for his duck and a small plum pudding. It started to rain. Rain was usually welcomed on Gibraltar, as without it there was no water, but as it streamed down the mountain into the town, across the streets and into the basements and casemates, it aggravated the feelings of dissatisfaction, discomfort, the unpleasant sensation of being ignored or forgotten. There was no news from England. The nights were cold. There was little fuel. The enemy were working openly in the Lines, and men joined the Spanish Camp from every direction. Another Hanoverian deserted. There were rumours that Colonel Ross and Lieutenant-General Boyd had quarrelled again. Lieutenant Burleigh, who had been given command of a squad of sharpshooters, made a slighting remark about Lieutenant Witham's retreat from St Roque. The Governor decided to open fire.

After the first barrage on 12 September he noted: 'The enemy slacken'd in his work and desisted entirely from transporting stores during daytime. This fire has continued ever since at intervals, but they are now so buried that scarce a head is to be seen.' Immediately the garrison was in good spirits. The dull thunder of the guns seemed to comfort them, and there was work to do. In order to decrease the effect of the expected retaliation, the Governor ordered Main Street to be ploughed up from Irish Town to the Grand Parade; the cupola of the White Convent and the upper part of the King's Chapel were taken down, and later, the steeple clock and bells of the Spanish Church followed, all possible targets for the enemy gunners; the Rock was stripped of shrubs and what stunted trees within reach that remained, for fascines; and casks of earth were piled behind the defences to fill any breaches that might be made. However, after a few days, and the enemy not having fired a single shot, the garrison relaxed again, and the townspeople returned from their huts in the south, and opened up their houses and shops, though there was little enough to sell. Though the Spaniards had given up working by day and their carts and shovels could be heard at night, the artillery blazed away as if they were at the gates. The cannonballs ineffectually buried themselves at the first impact, and the shells had a tendency to burst either high in the air or under the sand. This did not deter the artillery, who fired some two thousand times in the early barrages in September. Eventually Captain Mercier had the idea of firing small shells from cannons, which gave them less elevation and greater accuracy. After much practice, another 1,500 shots in October, they were able to burst shells over the Spanish Lines, but by now there was little to fire at, and the rate dropped to eight or nine shots a day. The Spanish Camp spread like a cluster of mushrooms along the foot of the Queen of Spain's Chair. In October it was reported to consist of 14,000 men, and Lieutenant-General Mendoza had been replaced by Lieutenant-General Don Martin de Alvarez de Sotomayor. In the meantime, the garrison were employed on guard, on picket duty, and in working parties; when off duty the single men lounged about the town, in the wine-shops or the smaller rooms above, or leaned on the sea-wall gazing hopefully to the west. The married men, driven by the cold and hungry looks of their children, climbed up the hill for wood, or even roots for them to eat. The Artillery, who had their numbers increased by 180 men drafted from

the line regiments, dragged a 24-pounder from Middle Hill to a platform below Rock Guard, and fired a few shots. It was called the Rock
Gun.

During October enemy working parties increased their activities
at night, raising the parapets of the Lines, and throwing up new
epaulements near the Bay. Lieutenant Witham invented a light ball,
a form of flare, and on the night of the 19th several of these were fired
without any working parties being revealed, perhaps because the
balls gave out as much smoke as light. In the morning, the officers of
the guard saw that thirty-five embrasures had been opened in the
Lines, in three batteries, two, of fourteen guns each, facing Willis's
and one of seven guns aimed at the town. Lieutenant Burleigh made
a disparaging comment about Lieutenant Witham's light balls, and
the garrison prepared to receive a bombardment. But the Spaniards
still did not open fire. If they knew of the circumstances in the town,
and it seems likely that they did from the gardeners who still ventured out into the Neutral Ground, they had good reason to expect
the blockade to succeed, and the Rock to fall without their firing a
shot. Whilst the Governor could remark that the troops were 'uncommonly healthy', the families and townspeople, particularly the
Jews who could not eat the salt meat and there was little fresh left,
were in increasing distress. On 23 October a prize taken by a privateer was sent in, the first for six weeks, and its small cargo of rice sold
for 8d. a lb. or five times its normal price. (In England at this period
bread cost 2d. a lb. and meat 4d. a lb.) Mrs Green noted in her diary:
'The Chief distress is the want of Flour and Firing—two very great
wants indeed.' Smallpox broke out amongst a Jewish family living
in Irish Town. They were immediately confined, and all soldiers
who had not had the disease were sent to the South Barracks, and
their places taken by those who had. Captain Spilsbury reported
an incident which showed how General Eliott was reacting at this
time:

> It seems one 58th was overheard saying that if the Spaniards came,
> damn him that would not join them: the Governor said he must be mad
> and ordered his head to be shaved, to be blistered, bled, and sent to the
> Provost on bread and water, wear a tight waistcoat, and to be prayed
> for in Church.

The old soldier was obviously not prepared to tolerate any nonsense.

November started dismally, with driving rain and nothing to do. No ships had come in since the rice ship, and the little excitement caused by the appearance east of the Rock of the privateer *Peace and Plenty* was put out when it ran aground on the isthmus and was set on fire by the Spanish gunners. The garrison were bored. Two Garrison Orders showed the results:

> October 31st. The service of the batteries is much interrupted by Officers not on duty crowding upon them. Spectators are therefore desired not to go upon any part of a Battery from which there is firing.

> November 2nd. No wine or strong liquor to be carried to non-commissioned officers or soldiers on duty.

In the town the bakers opened for an hour or two every morning to sell the day's ration of bread, and the fishermen and gardeners brought their few goods to market. The soldier's 4½d. a day could buy little, when six small fish like sprats cost 2/-, a small bunch of cabbage leaves 5d., and a pint of milk and water 1s. 3d. The very rich could still buy a duck for a guinea, or two fowls for 18/-, prices which in England would have bought them a flock of either. The very poor, and that meant the greater part of the population, gathered round the wickets that had been set up in the doorways of the bake-houses and were guarded by sentries, to buy a slice or two of sour bread with their pennies. Quartermaster Ancell of the 58th Regiment left this description:

> It is really grievous to see the fighting of the people for a morsel of bread, at a price not to be credited by those who never knew hardship or their country's service. Men wrestling, women intreating, and children crying, a jargon of all languages piteously pouring forth their complaints.

The cold wind blew in high places. Captain Spilsbury wrote in his journal on 7 November: 'Nineteen shillings given for a pig's head. The Governor does not care how dear things are, but he has left off treating with hock and claret.' But General Eliott did not need either hock or claret, and may have considered that a little abstemiousness would not come amiss in his officers. He was called cold, unfeeling, lacking in sympathy, but he did not ask his men to do one thing he was not prepared to do himself. He went further. Captain Drinkwater of the Royal Manchester Volunteers, whose name amused the

General so much that he was honoured 'with a Hob-nob in wine with His Excellency whenever he dined at Headquarters', recorded:

> It was about this period that the Governor made trial what quantity of rice would suffice a single person for twenty-four hours, and actually lived himself eight days on four ounces of rice per day. Sir George is remarkable for an abstemious mode of living, seldom tasting anything but vegetables, simple puddings, and water; and yet is very hale, and uses constant exercise.

It presents an extraordinary picture of the stout, elderly, red-faced General, sitting in the Convent over his rice pudding, and refusing to accept the possibility of surrender. Since very few ships had arrived at Gibraltar since the start of the blockade he had no sure way of communicating with the Government in London, or of hearing when, or even if, the relief convoy would sail. He sent his dispatches, three or four copies at a time, by whatever ships there were, even if they were destined for ports as far apart as Antwerp or Leghorn, and on occasions risked sending a row-boat across to Morocco and Mr Logie. The last message he had received from Lord Weymouth was dated 11 August, and read: 'The Ordnance Stores designed for your Garrison are ready to sail. Provisions are upon the sea to endeavour to make their way to Gibraltar,' but that was nearly three months ago.

Suddenly on 14 November everybody thought that the convoy was approaching. At 8 a.m. the look-outs reported a cutter standing for the Bay from the west, with all her sail crowded. The wind was a brisk north-westerly. The Spaniards saw her, and ran up red signal flags on the watch-towers along the coast. As she entered the Straits the sails of the Spanish squadron at Algeciras were shaken out, and two xebecks, two frigates, and the *St Jean Baptiste*, Admiral Barcello's flagship of 74-guns, moved out to intercept her, followed by a host of galleys and smaller ships. As the cutter came abreast of Cabrita Point, the galleys stationed there opened fire, which she returned; when her captain saw the Spanish squadron bearing down on him, he tacked and stood for the Barbary coast. The Spaniards came sweeping out of the Bay, only to be blown to the leeward of the cutter, which appeared to hang in the swift westerly current like a gull, as the larger ships were forced clumsily to the east. Still holding the windward gauge, the cutter tacked, and stood once more for the

Rock. Barcello, who had dropped behind his squadron, managed to fire one ill-judged broadside, before being blown ignominiously off into the Mediterranean. The cutter saluted the Spanish Admiral with its stern-chasers, and came into the harbour. By this time, the walls were crowded with excited soldiers and townspeople, who cheered the captain ashore, and kept on cheering until they learned that, as opposed to being the fore-runner of the Fleet, the cutter was the *Buck*, a privateer, and Captain Fagg had come in for provisions himself. However, his manœuvre had confirmed the garrison's opinion that Admiral Barcello was, among other things, no seaman, and had broken the blockade, for, as long as the wind blew from the west, the Admiral could not return. Captain Fagg was toasted, and the Governor allowed him to buy provisions from the Stores, and rewarded his crew with 5/- each.

Now that Britain once more ruled the waves, Vice-Admiral Duff held a Council to decide whether to take out his ships to attack the enemy's small craft in the Bay. No one was really surprised when nothing was done. Mr Logie, whose eyes were always turned to the Rock, sent over a boatload of bullocks a few days later, which, though many died from the journey on the water's edge, gave some, but only the sick in hospital and the officers, their first taste of fresh meat for months. On 26 November the wind changed, and Barcello's squadron sailed back into the Bay.

One of the odd circumstances during this winter of 1779 was the small number of deserters from the garrison compared to the number of the enemy who deserted to the garrison. There must have been a great temptation to leave the Rock, where there seemed every prospect of starving to death; though it was exceedingly difficult to do so, and some men fell to their deaths trying to climb down the precipices on the east side. There can have been little temptation to come to it, and the men who did were mostly Walloons; but they had to risk running the mile between the Spanish Lines and the barriers, and as there were usually some cavalry there, several were cut down, or dragged back to be hanged the next day. Early in December a formal deputation came from the enemy to return Colonel Green's mule that had deserted the day before.

December was a cold, quiet month. Captain Drinkwater summed up the scenes and feelings in the garrison:

The bakers had long been limited to the quantity of bread daily to be issued to the inhabitants, and sentries were placed at the wickets where it was delivered to prevent confusion and riot. The strongest nevertheless had the advantage; so that numbers of women, children, and infirm persons, returned to their miserable habitations, frequently without tasting, for some days, that chief and perhaps necessary support of life. The inhabitants were not the only sufferers in this scene of distress; many officers and soldiers had families to support out of the pittance received from the victualling-office. A soldier, with his wife and three children, would inevitably have been starved to death, had not the generous contribution of his corps relieved his family: one woman actually died through want; and many were so enfeebled that it was not without great attention they recovered: thistles, dandelion, wild leeks &c. were for sometime the daily nourishment of numbers. Few supplies arriving from Barbary, and there appearing little prospect of relief from England, famine began to present itself with its attendant horrors: had there been a glimmering hope of assistance from home, it would have enabled many to support themselves under this accumulation of distress; but alas! we seemed entirely abandoned to our fortune.

On 20 December the *Buck* sailed, only to be sunk shortly after by a French frigate. Mrs Green wrote in her diary: 'Christmas—this holiday time (as it used to be called) . . . Everybody tried to appear Easy and Contented! Only think of the poor!' On Boxing Day there was a great storm, thunder, lightning and driving rain. Everything seemed against the garrison. But the next morning they found the shore below the Line Wall strewn with wood and cork, which had been washed across from the Spanish depot at the Orange Grove, enough fuel for six weeks. The diary exploded into capitals: 'It was Truly a God Send and Highly Worth to be Remembered—and it was Likewise a Loss to the Enemy!' On the 28th the *Fly* packet-boat arrived from Tangier. The bad weather kept the Spanish Admiral in harbour. On board were forty goats, some fowls and eggs, but no mail. A Walloon deserter reported that the whole Spanish Camp was under water. Things were looking up.

On New Year's Day 1780 General Eliott paraded at dawn, as usual, and there was a cold east wind whipping round his legs. The guards and working parties drawn from the regiments in the town marched off, and small groups of townspeople began to gather round the bakers' doors. If he walked down to the King's Bastion he would have seen the masts of Barcello's ships outlined against the yellow houses of Algeciras, and across at the Spanish Camp huts were being erected to replace the sodden tents; he might have seen the Lieutenant-Governor, who came down to the Bastion whenever he could, and he might have avoided him, as they seldom talked together. After six months of blockade there was little social life amongst the officers, and each family was reluctant to share its precious stock of food and fuel. The men, with the extraordinary powers of endurance and resilience that soldiers have, made the most of their cold casemates and meagre rations, patched up their worn uniforms, stuffed their boots with paper, and found time to sympathize with the sufferings of the poor inhabitants.

> How children cry'd 'Mamma some bread',
> And mother wept when this they said,
> What crowds at bakers' doors were found
> And every tongue with piteous sound,
> And numbers went without each day,
> And money scarce would pass for pay.

This was written by a soldier, and preserved in the back of General Boyd's Log Book.

On 8 January the Governor was just finishing a dispatch to Lord Weymouth in which he wrote: 'No vessel has got in here, the Spanish cruizers are so vigilant, consequently no supplies—our Provisions daily consuming—many Inhabitants near starving', when a cargo ship from Naples was driven in under the guns on the New Mole. On board there were 6,000 bushels of barley, another 'God Send' for the garrison. Two days later, the garrison witnessed the first execution since General Eliott had become Governor. The victim was a soldier of the 58th Regiment, and had been condemned to death for stealing. Mrs Green noted that he would not go to church or even allow the Clergyman to visit him. She added, 'Monday 10th. The Man went out at Southport!!' The gallows were at Southport. The next day, the Clergyman must have felt even less appreciated when, whilst officiating at the burial of a soldier in the graveyard in the Neutral Ground, he was shot at four times from Fort St Barbara. The corpse was dropped and the funeral party hurried back. After that, a part of the Red Sands outside the town was allocated as a burial ground. At

8.30 the next morning two shots were fired at the town from Fort St Philip, and at 10.30 three more, one of which occasioned the first casualty of the siege. It was a woman. Finding herself a heroine, she undoubtedly repeated her story of the incident until it assumed heroic proportions, and Mrs Green became exasperated:

> The woman who keeps a Milliner's Shop happened to be going by at the same time; had her leg struck by some part of the Splinters of the Roof or by some of the Shell Work out of the front of the house. She was thrown down, and insisted upon it, both at that time and since, that it was the Ball that hit her Leg. However that was impossible as it must have broke her Leg. She was more alarmed than any real hurt.

These few shots started a general rush of the inhabitants to the south again, though they returned that night, when there was no further firing.

How the garrison got wind that the relief convoy was near, nobody knew. Suddenly the town was abuzz with rumours. One said that the Spanish gunners had been ranging on the town preparatory to a bombardment when the convoy arrived, and another that a Walloon deserter had reported an action off Finisterre in which the Spanish had defeated the British Fleet. The official reaction was hardly encouraging. On the evening of 13 January Colonel Ross called the commanding officers of the various regiments to his quarters and told them that the Governor had ordered the weekly rations to be cut by $\frac{1}{2}$ lb. of beef, $\frac{1}{4}$ lb. of pork and 1 pint of pease. When this was announced to the men the next day, it was accepted without a murmur. Captain Drinkwater suspected that the Governor knew that a relief was at hand and was testing the morale of the garrison. Perhaps the garrison suspected the same. Their hopes were increased when the Navy, in the person of Vice-Admiral Duff, was seen down at the New Mole, looking out to sea. There were two more days of anxious waiting. On Saturday the 15th the look-outs saw some vessels sailing to the east, when one unexpectedly altered course and stood for the Bay. As she approached they could see she was a brig flying the British flag. A xebeck and several galleys started out from Cabrita Point to intercept her, but she was too fast for them and their shots fell short. The scene at the New Mole as she came in was riotous. The whole garrison seemed to be there. The townspeople were laughing and cheering, and the Jews, who had suffered most of all, gave the loudest huzzas. The brig was the *Sophia*, carrying ordnance stores, and her captain reported that he had been separated from the main convoy five days before in the Bay of Biscay. The enthusiasm of his reception was dampened when he added that he had seen nine enemy line-of-battle ships lying in Cadiz, but the mere fact that the British flag was once more flying in the Straits was enough to justify Mrs Green's comment for the day, 'Three cheers!'

In spite of the uncertainty about the fate of the convoy, the price of flour dropped the next day from 2/– per lb. to 6d. and the shops displayed goods for sale that everyone believed had been consumed long before. But there was little time for shopping. Hundreds lined the sea-wall, hundreds more scrambled over the rocks to the south, and a few of the younger men climbed up to the Signal House, from where, on a fine day, the masts of ships passing Cape Trafalgar could be seen. Unfortunately the day was cloudy, and there was nothing to see except the Spanish ships being warped in behind the boom at Algeciras. It is not recorded what Admiral Barcello's officers did with their keys. In the evening a second brig came in, carrying flour, and the news that the convoy was approaching, escorted by a British Fleet of twenty-one sail-of-the-line, commanded by Admiral Sir George Brydges Rodney, and that off the coast of Portugal they had fallen in with and captured six Spanish warships and sixteen merchantmen belonging to the Caracca Company, a tremendous prize. The garrison had to wait another day, but the name of Rodney and the size of his fleet banished all doubts that the enemy might have attempted to intercept the convoy off Cadiz. On the morning of the 18th one of the prizes was brought in by a midshipman, who said that the enemy had attempted just that, and there had been an engagement off Cape St Mary. The doubts returned. The arrival of a second prize that evening did nothing to dispel them. As it grew dark, the eyes of Gibraltar were strained to the west. Then, off Europa, coming from the Barbary coast, the convoy and the Fleet appeared, illuminated by flashes of lightning, as they were taken by the current past the Rock. One or two merchantmen managed to get in, and the *Apollo* frigate, Captain Pownall. It was from the Captain that the Governor and then the garrison learned of Rodney's victory over the Spanish Admiral off Cape St Mary: four Spanish ships-of-the-line had been

c

captured, including the Admiral, one had been wrecked, and another blown up. The news spread through the town, and there was continual cheering as Captain Pownall made his way across to the *Panther* to pay his respects to Vice-Admiral Duff. He was surprised not to find the Admiral aboard his flagship, but only the opinion of him 'that he was a quiet man!'

The garrison did not care. Relief was only round the corner.

CHAPTER IV

A joyful confusion

THE first action of the French ministry after signing the treaty with
the Americans in 1778 had been to send a squadron of twelve ships-
of-the-line and five frigates, commanded by the Comte d'Estaing, to
assist Washington's army, which was camped outside New York, the
headquarters of the British army. This squadron was of little effect,
partly because of the caution of d'Estaing, who was unwilling to risk
his ships in any action where there could be no territorial gains for
France, and partly because of the superior seamanship of Lord Howe.
In October 1778 Washington wrote: 'If the Spaniards would but
join their fleets to France and commence hostilities my doubts would
all subside. Without it I fear the British Navy has it too much in its
power to counteract the schemes of France.' The reputation of the
British Navy was justified (Howe with 6 64s, 3 50s, and 6 frigates,
outmanœuvred d'Estaing with 2 80s, 6 74s, 3 64s, 1 54, and 6 frigates),
but its strength was far below the figures Lord Sandwich, the First
Lord of the Admiralty, optimistically presented to Parliament, and
which made Spanish participation in the war so important to Vergennes and Washington. They appear in the Navy Lists of 1778.

SHIPS-OF-THE-LINE OF 50 GUNS AND ABOVE

	1st Rates	2nd Rates	3rd Rates	4th Rates	Total
British	3	15	94	25	137
French	8	30	30		68
Spanish	9	42	11		62

The enemy were as misguided as His Lordship, as the figures for the
British Navy included every nameplate, whether it was on a rotting
hulk, or a pile of new timbers in Portsmouth dockyard. In March

1778 when Admiral Keppel was appointed to command a fleet of forty-two ships, he found only six ready for sea. Moreover those ships the British had were scattered from the Chesapeake to Calcutta. It was impossible for them to carry out the traditional strategy of keeping the French fleet blocked up in Brest, and dividing the enemy. So it was that after the signing of the Convention of Aranjuez the Brest fleet sailed south under the Comte d'Orvilliers to join the Spanish fleet off Coruña. Fortunately for Great Britain the advantage of combining the fleets, which must have seemed so obvious in Paris, was more than compensated by the disadvantage of the distrust and disunity of a divided command, and of sailing good French ships with bad Spanish ones. Nevertheless it was a formidable armada that finally sailed up the Channel in August 1779. There were sixty-six ships-of-the-line under d'Orvilliers and the old Spanish Admiral, Don Luis de Cordova. A French army of 50,000 was waiting at Le Havre and St Malo for the defeat of the British Grand Fleet and the signal to embark. The Grand Fleet, thirty-five ships-of-the-line, was commanded, not by Howe (who had returned from America to share the Government's prosecution of his brother the general), or by Keppel, who was being persecuted for failing to win the Battle of the Ushant, but by the elderly Sir Charles Hardy, about whom Kempenfeldt said: 'There is a fund of good nature in the man but not one grain of the Commander-in-Chief', but who was of the right political complexion. Hardy backed up the Channel and disappeared behind a boom at Plymouth. All England was gripped with the fear of invasion, and Horace Walpole quoted the Duke of Bolton as saying, 'Everything at sea but our fleet.'

But Vergennes' plan had the seeds of failure sown in it; prepared for June, it had been delayed by the unreadiness of Spain until August, when the provisions on board the ships were nearly exhausted and the diseases of sailors pressed from prisons had spread throughout the fleet; at the last moment the proposed attack was diverted from Plymouth to Falmouth, where, even if it had been taken, there was no shelter for a huge fleet from the Channel gales. For days the Combined Fleet rode in the Channel, its only action being to commit its dead to the sea, until decision was taken out of the hands of its commanders by an easterly gale, which drove it from the shores of England back to its silent ports.

This was the largest force to threaten the invasion of England since the Spanish Armada, and its humiliating retreat caused a rift between the Spaniards and the French, which led to the events described in the next chapter. It had another effect of importance to Gibraltar: so great was the fear of invasion in England that only once in the next three years of war was the Grand Fleet allowed to leave the Channel, and without the Fleet there could be no convoy, and no convoy meant no food, no fuel, and no reinforcements.

On 14 September 1779 Lord Sandwich wrote in his 'Thoughts upon Naval Measures to be Taken': 'As to the first [Gibraltar], something Must without delay be attempted—at least to throw in a Supply of Stores and Provisions', and he went on to recommend that a convoy should be prepared to sail in one month. In order to collect the men, provisions, stores and ships for a convoy, it was necessary to go through every department of government and administration from the Minuting Clerk at the Civil Branch of the Office of Ordnance to the King. The latter had to agree with the recommendation of the Commander-in-Chief, Lord Amherst, to send a regiment: the former, and his Board, supplied ammunition and artillery, the Artillerymen to fire it, but not the carts to carry it to the ships or the horses to pull them, which had to be hired privately: victuals came, not from the Victualling Board, but from army contractors engaged by the Board on the instructions of the Commissioners of the Treasury, and were collected at Cork, which was then the army's store-house; medical stores were purchased from a private monopolist through the Apothecary-General: and the transports and store-ships to carry it all were hired by the Navy Board. When this great concourse of ships, soldiers and stores had finally been assembled, an admiral prepared to serve under Lord Sandwich had to be found, and a fleet manned and provisioned for him—so the whole process had to be repeated. When convoy and fleet were ready, then they had to wait for any merchantmen who wanted to take advantage of an escort through the Channel. Finally, with a fair wind, and providing there was no sudden change of policy, they could weigh anchor and sail away—in Rodney's case, three and a half months after the project was planned, which was fairly expeditious.

He sailed on 29 December 1779 with the *Royal George* (100), the *Prince George* (98), the *Sandwich* (90), 16 74s, and 2 64s, and 9 frigates;

as well as the relief convoy for Gibraltar and Minorca, there was a fleet of merchantmen destined for the West Indies. Rodney and part of the fleet were sailing for the west, but after he had seen the convoy safe to Gibraltar. On 7 January the West Indian traders took their own course, escorted by four frigates. The next day, off the coast of Portugal, the fleet ran in with a Spanish convoy of sixteen ships of the Caracca Company escorted by one ship-of-the-line and six frigates, and captured them all. This was a great prize (in Gibraltar they estimated it as worth £400,000), but the Spanish prisoners told Rodney that the Spanish Fleet was preparing to meet him in the Straits. His almost legendary good luck held when, a week later, approaching the Straits, his look-outs saw, not the fleet, but only eleven Spanish ships-of-the-line advancing to meet him.

After the fiasco of the invasion attempt, the idea of further combined operations had little appeal for either France or Spain. However, when it was learned that a convoy was preparing to sail to the relief of Gibraltar, it was agreed to collect forty ships in Brest to oppose it. Cordova was on his way to Brest with fifteen ships when it was discovered that Rodney had already sailed, and he returned south to join Admiral Langara, who was coming from the Mediterranean with eleven ships. Whether the confusion was in Madrid, where Floridablanca believed the British convoy to be escorted by no more than twelve ships-of-the-line, or between the two admirals, is not apparent, but Cordova, hearing of the size of Rodney's fleet, took refuge in Cadiz, whilst Langara sailed confidently out, expecting to meet equal odds, and to be reinforced at any moment. He was soon disillusioned.

The Spaniards had two advantages as they turned to run for Cadiz: they were not far from safety, and it was late afternoon, with a storm blowing up. They had two disadvantages: the British ships were copper-bottomed, and therefore faster, and they were commanded by a daring admiral, who, though he might have been confined to his cabin with gout, transmitted his orders through an equally daring flag-captain, Captain Young. Langara's ships were caught at about 4 p.m., and the British, leaving the windward position and ignoring the danger of being blown onto the rocks that fringed the Spanish coast, cut in between them and their port. The action continued until 2 a.m. when six of the enemy ships, including

Langara's flagship the *Phoenix*, had been taken and one blown up. The weather stayed stormy, and one of the prizes was wrecked and another stranded, and several of the British ships were in danger until two days later, when in calm weather they rejoined the convoy off Cape Spartel to count their victory. Then they sailed on to Gibraltar.

The town was awake before dawn on Wednesday 19 January. Small hoarded stocks of luxuries, tea, coffee and rum, were recklessly shared, and the ladies put on their best bonnets and joined the throng jostling along the Line Wall waiting for the ships to come in. The parole that day was 'Victory', and General Eliott ordered a 21-gun salute to be fired from Willis's. The Artillery officer in charge ordered the guns to be aimed at Fort St Barbara for the salute, with commendable caution, as the enemy had unmasked one of the 14-gun batteries in the Lines, and the guns of Fort St Philip were menacingly raised. As the last shot echoed across the Bay, fortunately not answered by the Spanish guns, the crowds from Orange's to the New Mole cheered, and the *Edgar* came round Europa escorting the captured flagship, the *Phoenix*. There were more cheers when Admiral Langara was carried ashore in a sedan chair, and his escort were obliged to push back the more inquisitive ladies who were trying to catch a glimpse of the Spaniard, who, it was reported, had been wounded in the groin.

That night the *Prince George*, under the flag of Admiral Digby, and aboard which Prince William Henry, George III's second son and later William IV, served as a midshipman, came in with twelve more ships, and the Prince stepped ashore for a spell at noon. It was universally agreed that he made a fine figure in his sailor's suit. The 20th was the King of Spain's birthday and, across the Bay at Algeciras, Admiral Barcello hung out his flags, under the protection of a land battery that had been hastily constructed. Some more ships arrived on the 21st, but Admiral Rodney was delayed because he would not leave his prizes, some of which were dismasted and could not make the Bay without an east wind; so the Governor invited the Prince to dinner without him, and heard the story of how Admiral Langara had remarked, on seeing William Henry going about his humble duties: 'Well does Great Britain merit the empire of the sea, when the humblest stations in her Navy are supported by Princes of the

Blood.' He could not know how William was entirely suited to be a midshipman, and not at all so to be a king.

The Bay was now filling with vessels of all kinds, and unloading had begun; a growing heap of boxes, barrels, sheep, casks and bales spread in confusion along the New Mole. Confusion, joyful confusion, as Mrs Green called it, was the order of the day: confusion when four warships drifted towards the enemy camp and had to be towed back; confusion when the officers of the Navy accepted too many invitations; and the worst confusion when three ships, sent across to Tetuan to fetch cattle and wood collected by Mr Logie, were discovered to be transports fitted out to carry troops, and so full of provisions that there was no room to carry a fascine or a cow, when the wind changed and they were obliged to return to the Rock. Mrs Green, who had been sent seven sheep from England and given two more by Admiral Digby, wrote: 'No sort of fresh supply from Barbary, by which means the Garrison was as badly off as before.' A Newfoundland ship arrived laden with 500,000 lb. of salt cod, which the Governor bought for the garrison, and together with the Government stores and the cargoes of Rodney's prizes which were also purchased, this seemed so much food that there was no attempt to send other ships to Tetuan until the fleet had gone, and then, being unprotected, they were taken by the enemy.

The Spaniards could do little whilst the Fleet was in the Bay, and their own Camp and the garrison at Ceuta were blockaded, as Gibraltar had been blockaded. There were daily parleys as conditions were agreed for the return of Rodney's prisoners, and, on 25 January, an unpleasant incident on the isthmus when;

> About eight this morning, a corporal and five Walloon deserters, who made a push for the Garrison, were pursued by a party of horse and foot, the corporal was taken, and two they knocked down and run them through with their bayonets, afterwards beat them with the butts of their firelocks, and slashed them with their swords; one of them they carried off in triumph: We shot one of their horses in the hind leg, in their retreat, who remained on the isthmus or neck of land during the day; three escaped the massacre, owing to the activity of their heels, and the one whom they left on the sands, a party of our people brought in, so miserably hacked, that he was shocking to behold.

Mr Ancell also mentioned that they hanged the corporal the next day.

Admiral Rodney arrived in the Bay on the 25th, and General Eliott, Lieutenant-General Draper, who was bound for Minorca where he was second-in-command to General Murray, Lieutenant-General Boyd and Vice-Admiral Duff, went on board his flagship, the *Sandwich*, for a Council of War. The subject under discussion was the 73rd Regiment, the 2nd Battalion of Lord McLeod's Highlanders, which was originally destined for Minorca, but which General Eliott wanted to keep in Gibraltar. Lord Weymouth, before he resigned and was succeeded by Lord Hillsborough, had indicated that, should circumstances require it, the regiment could be retained in Gibraltar, and the Governor persuaded the Council to this effect. He later wrote to Lord Hillsborough that there were 4,330 effective men in the garrison, and the daily duty required 2,250. So the 73rd, consisting of 36 officers, 72 N.C.O.s and 944 rank and file, commanded by Colonel George McKenzie, were landed, to the delight of the spectators, wearing their kilts; they could not have had much else to wear, as in the same dispatch, the Governor asked his Lordship for clothing for them. The relief had brought no wine or rum, and he added:

> The want of strong liquor will perhaps be more severely felt by the Soldier than the curtailing a small part of his provisions, and possibly might affect his health, from the alteration of a habit he is accustomed to.

There is another instance of his concern in this dispatch:

> I shall send home with the transports all useless mouths amongst which many women and children, who upon their arrival in England will need some assistance till they are in a way of getting their bread.

The rule he made, though there is no indication that it was rigorously enforced, was that those wives and children who were not provided with a year's provisions of 250 lb. of flour or 360 lb. of biscuit per person, must prepare to leave Gibraltar with the Fleet. Before the end of the month the sick and wounded Spanish prisoners were carried across the Bay in the *Fortune*; the Governor entertained Admiral Rodney and his prisoner, Admiral Langara, Admiral Digby and Prince William Henry, and Langara declared that the French had deceived him; the *Childers* was sent to England with dispatches;

the convoy bound for Minorca sailed; and three more Walloons deserted to the garrison, bringing the total since the opening of hostilities to twenty-two.

February began with a storm. As the store-ships were unloaded, others took their places. The Governor bought the cannons and the powder from the captured Spanish battleships, and asked the Admiral to leave what wine, coal and provisions he could spare from his ships. The Navy felt a particular comradeship with the garrison of Gibraltar: General Eliott once referred to himself as a 'half-sea officer' and Rodney, like Darby and Howe who followed, sent a boat round his ships to collect what they could spare for the Rock. The Walloon deserters joined the Navy, and on the 10th Admiral Duff went on board the *Royal George* on his way back to England. There was no ceremony, and he appeared 'a good deal discomposed and disconcerted' according to Mrs Green. The following day the invalids and families who were to leave embarked, whilst the town was crowded for the departure of Admiral Langara into Spain. He had agreed with Rodney that the Spanish prisoners returned before him should be exchanged for the same number of Englishmen from Spain, who would eventually man the vessels Rodney was obliged to leave. On Sunday, 13 February, the Fleet raised sail, watched in silence from the walls that had echoed with the cheers of the garrison a month before. Some officers climbed the hill to take a last look as dusk closed down on the distant sails.

Rodney had left behind the *Edgar* (Commodore Eliott succeeded Admiral Duff), which, with the *Panther*, the *Enterprise* and *Porcupine* frigates, and the *Fortune* and *Gibraltar* sloops, guarded the ships left to be manned by prisoners. The Spaniards delayed returning these men, until in March the Commodore made a formal demand and asked, if the prisoners were not to be sent over, that Admiral Langara and his officers should honour their parole and return instead. The provisions were gradually sorted out and the estimate of how long they would last was given to the Governor:

Bread and flour	607 days
Beef	291
Pork	407
Pease	164
Oatmeal	104

Butter.	.	.	.	.	.	183 days
Oil	.	.	.	.	.	25
Salt fish	.	.	.	.	.	160
Wine and spirits	.	.	.	.	.	50

The figures, however, did not take into account the rottenness of the provisions, for the contractor who had supplied the garrison on this occasion had been treasonably dishonest, and after a few weeks the flour was rotten, the pease maggoty, and the meat stinking.

But at the time the garrison thought they were well off and laughed at the Spanish prisoner, who, as he was leaving the fortress looked up at the Rock and said, 'Give up that to us and all will be well.'

CHAPTER V

His own comedy

SPAIN entered the war with limited objectives, and even more limited resources. She was not at all concerned with American independence, and her king, Charles III, when asked to recognize the claims of the revolutionaries, might well have answered in the words of the Emperor Joseph, 'I am a royalist by profession.' The possession of Gibraltar, Minorca and Jamaica would have realized the highest hopes of Minister Floridablanca, and he would have given up the attempts on Minorca and Jamaica for Gibraltar, and thrown in the Family Compact in the bargain. After six months of war with Great Britain, after the fiasco of the invasion, and the defeat of Langara, and after the relief of Gibraltar, the Court of Madrid had nothing but humiliation and the feeling of being cheated and despised by France.

Great Britain had been at war for four years, and, since the entrance of France on the side of the colonists, had lost Dominica, St Vincent and Grenada, whilst capturing St Lucia in the West Indies. She had been forced to maintain troops and ships in the defence of England which King George would have dearly loved to employ in the subjugation of the rebels. The campaign in America had recovered from the setback of Saratoga, and there was a new plan to attack the Southern States from the sea and to prise them away from the Union, but this, as did every other British strategy, relied on her naval superiority. The importance of French ships to the American cause was underlined by General Washington: 'In any operation and under all circumstances, a decisive naval superiority is to be considered as a fundamental principle, and the basis upon which every hope of success must ultimately depend.' The atmosphere up and down the back-stairs of the Courts of Madrid and London was conducive to the resumption of the negotiations started by the Mediation for a separate peace. How far each Court was sincere in desiring, or even capable of concluding, such a peace can be judged from the instruments chosen for the negotiation by Floridablanca and Lord George Germaine. This latter nobleman, court-martialled for cowardice after the Battle of Minden and sentenced to be barred from holding military office under the Crown, had progressed with the favour of George III to become Secretary of State for the American Colonies and director of the war in America. He was a single-minded man who led a blameless domestic life and was harshly criticized by men the King considered his own enemies, which served to recommend him to George III, and to make him the prime mover in the Government where the placid and pliable Lord North was the Prime Minister. After Minden, Germaine's sole preoccupation was the vindication of his honour and talents; in the American war this became part of a greater crusade for the King's honour against his recalcitrant subjects and every other policy was subordinated to it.

The tools chosen for the secret negotiation were an English playwright and an Irish priest.

Richard Cumberland claimed to have written more plays than anyone else (he wrote thirty-five plays, four operas and a farce, which says something for his industry if not for his talents). He was the original of Sir Fretful Plagiary, in Sheridan's *The Critic*, an earnest, pompous, figure, who might well have said, with Sir Fretful: 'A dextrous plagiarist may do anything. Why sir, for aught I know, he might take out some of the best things in my tragedy, and put them into his own comedy.' In the winter of 1779 he was forty-seven and, through the patronage of Lord George Germaine, Secretary of the Board of Trade. In November he was approached by the Abbé Thomas Hussey, who said he wanted to buy some mathematical instruments. Father Hussey was a known Spanish spy. He had been chaplain to the Spanish Embassy in London and had bribed a certain William Wardlaw to provide him with documents relating to the strength of the Navy and the defences of Gibraltar—how distantly relating may be guessed, as Wardlaw was a British agent. In August Hussey took a trip to Paris, returning in September, and two months later, with Gibraltar blockaded but still holding out, he was sitting in

Richard Cumberland's office, adroitly turning the conversation from compasses to peace with Spain. It seems likely at this stage that Father Hussey was acting on his own initiative, as was one of Germaine's henchmen, Commodore Johnstone, who commanded the British squadron at Lisbon and who had been announcing to all and sundry that Great Britain was ready to buy a peace with Spain by ceding the Rock of Gibraltar. Cumberland, with visions of acting the hero for a change, hurried Father Hussey off to Lord George, who gave him a vague letter of commendation, and sent him to Madrid on 3 January 1780. On 16 January Rodney defeated Langara and relieved Gibraltar. On the 31st Hussey was back in London with Floridablanca's proposals.

The first Spanish offer was that if England would surrender Gibraltar—pretending, in order to save face, that it was starved out—Spain would grant an honourable capitulation, pay for any stores left there, and allow the garrison to return home; she would withdraw from her alliance with France, and would put pressure on France to break with the American Colonies. As Gibraltar had just been supplied with provisions for almost a year, even Germaine balked at such scanty terms. In due course, and after private conversations with the Cabinet, he produced his own terms—in return for Gibraltar, Spain should cede to Great Britain Puerto Rico, the fortress and territory of Omoa, a harbour and territory near Oran, should purchase all stores and artillery left on the Rock and pay £2,000,000 towards the improvements to it made by Britain, should renounce all her engagements to France, and should assist Great Britain to reduce the rebellion in the Colonies, or at least refuse to recognize the colonists in any way. It seemed to Father Hussey that the British were not taking the negotiations seriously, particularly as the proposal was not even made officially. However, he persisted, and in March 1780 he received a letter from Floridablanca promising the good offices of Spain, and suggesting that if he could conclude the principal heads of a treaty, it could be formalized and extended by discussions to be held in Lisbon to cover the cessation of hostilities and the exchange of territories. Floridablanca suggested ingeniously that, as the treaty between France and the United States depended on a declaration of war between France and Great Britain, and there had been no such declaration in spite of the outbreak of hostilities, it might be possible for France to withdraw from it, with honour, and without fear of complaint from the Americans. Armed with this letter, Father Hussey went to see Lord George, but found himself instead with Lord Stormont and Lord Hillsborough, Secretaries for the North and South Departments respectively. They were sympathetic but unhelpful, disowned outright the brash utterances of Commodore Johnstone, and eventually Lord Stormont said that if the map of the Spanish Empire was spread before him, he could not lay his finger on that portion of it, which he, as Minister, would treat for upon exchange for Gibraltar. It seemed to be the end of the affair.

Hussey went to see Richard Cumberland in a rage, swearing that he had been taken for a fool. Eventually the playwright pacified the priest, and together they composed a letter to Floridablanca in which Hussey wrote:

> The tender of Gibraltar as a previous and indispensible article of the treaty, is what the Cabinet could not be brought to grant. They offer to treat upon the basis of the Treaty of Paris; and then Spain may start the subject under the title of Change of Territory . . . and if Your Excellency will allow me a conjecture on it as it stands, I really believe that they will cede Gibraltar upon terms; but for this I have no authority from the British Cabinet either written or verbal.

On the basis of this letter Hussey was invited to Madrid, and, according to Cumberland, both Floridablanca and Hussey insisted that he should attend himself. They set out for Lisbon together with Cumberland's family, under the pretence that they were going there for the health of his daughter, and with strict instructions from Lord Hillsborough that Cumberland should not admit in the preliminaries any article for the cession or exchange of Gibraltar, and that he should not proceed from Lisbon without receiving the assurance of the Spanish Court on this point. Hussey went on to Madrid, whilst Cumberland stayed in Lisbon, where Commodore Johnstone continued to broadcast that the British were prepared to give up the Rock. Hussey was sent back from Madrid with instructions to fetch Cumberland there, without committing the Court one way or another. This he did in an ambiguous letter, appealing to Cumberland's friendship, which, when they were travelling through Spain, he abused by copying out his secret instructions and his letters to London, and sending the copies on to Floridablanca. This helped little, as

Bernardo del Campo, Floridablanca's secretary, wrote: 'It appears to
me that the negotiation has gone infinitely backward from the first
word, as you will see from the secret copy of the instructions which
Cumberland carries.' Hussey, Cumberland and his family arrived in
Aranjuez, the summer residence of the Spanish king, in June 1780.
Cumberland wrote: 'I have grounds to think that Spain upon my
first coming would have given Magnificent conditions' which he
thought might have included Puerto Rico, and added, 'The invincible prejudices of the Catholic King for the recovery of Gibraltar
must be taken into account before any man's opinion ought to decide
against what I assert.' Cumberland was encouraged in his hopes by
a flattering reception at the Court, and by the conference he was
granted almost immediately with Floridablanca. They agreed that the
basis of the negotiations should be the Treaty of Paris, and arranged
to meet again, with Father Hussey and del Campo, when Cumberland had written down the preliminaries specified by Britain. Believing that he would shortly be the peacemaker between two great
powers, he wrote to Lord Hillsborough, giving his account of the
conference and asking for further instructions, and then, in the intervals of riding out and attending the Court, he copied out all the
clauses in the Treaty of Paris in which Spain and Great Britain were
mentioned together. His dream was short-lived. In July, reports were
received in Aranjuez of the Gordon Riots, and were exaggerated so
that Floridablanca believed that there was a national uprising, and
said to Cumberland, 'of the extermination of the Ministry no question could be made', whereas the greatest indignity ministers had
suffered was to be turned upside down, and un-wigged. When it was
later learned that order had been restored in London, the negotiations were renewed, but Floridablanca was no longer prepared to
talk about the Treaty of Paris. Cumberland's presence in Aranjuez
had been noticed by the French emissaries there, who were beginning
to show a willingness to pledge France to co-operate more actively
with Spain. Moreover, Cumberland had received no new instructions
from London, only a letter from Lord Hillsborough rebuking him for
putting anything in writing. Floridablanca, who must by now have
taken the measure of the English playwright, suggested that they
should come to an immediate accommodation, saying at one moment,
'Gibraltar is an object for which the King my master will break the

Family Compact and every other engagement with France', and, at the next, suggesting that it was impossible for Spain to desert her allies without a pretext, and that Britain must offer equitable terms to the Colonies, which, even if they were rejected, Spain could use as a reason for withdrawing from her engagements. Cumberland was under a considerable disadvantage at this meeting, not only because he was unused to diplomatic phraseology, but because it was conducted in 'the Spanish language which tho' I understood sufficiently well I was not master enough to reply in'. Eventually he wrote to Lord Hillsborough: 'If His Majesty shall be advised to cause some declaration to be made of his gracious disposition towards a reconcilement with his deluded subjects in rebellion . . .' which was the one thing His Majesty refused to be advised to do, as everyone knew except Richard Cumberland. In August 1780 whatever small chance of peace there was vanished. The Combined Fleet under Admiral Cordova ran into, and captured, the British East and West Indian merchant fleet of fifty-five ships and carried them into Cadiz, where the inhabitants were wild with joy as the British ships they usually saw fired at them. The French and the Spanish were acting in partnership again. 'Stupid Cumberland with his fantastic genius', as Bernardo del Campo called him, was ignored at Court, and threatened by Floridablanca, who invited the American plenipotentiary John Jay to Madrid and claimed that he was about to ask the Empress of Russia to mediate between Spain and Great Britain. Poor Cumberland fell off his horse and broke his arm.

The mediation of Russia and Austria, proposed by Count Kaunitz, was never seriously entertained by either Spain or Great Britain, as Spain demanded the cession of Gibraltar which she knew would not be granted. It was another part of Floridablanca's scheme to force France into a more active participation in Spanish designs, and to isolate Great Britain from the Continental powers, by making the one demand which he knew she would reject, and so letting the onus for the failure of any mediation fall on her.

Father Hussey, who now wrote Cumberland's dispatches for him, was sent to London in October 1780 with an ultimatum from the Spanish Court, offering, at the price of the Rock, to arrange a peace, in an unspecified way, that would allow some form of American independence. It was unacceptable. The country was on the brink of an election, Lord North told Hussey, 'Gibraltar is a forbidden word which must never pass my lips', and Lord Hillsborough added that as far as he was concerned it would please him if it were ceded to Spain, but that he dared not advise it to the King, for if the nation revolted it might cost him his head. Hussey, who had once boasted that he had Gibraltar in his pocket, reported failure, and was not permitted to enter Spain. Floridablanca sent him back from Lisbon with a message which ended:

> The negative therefore put, in such absolute terms, by the Court of London on this matter is to us an undeceiving proof that Great Britain does not desire to be the friend of Spain, nor indeed never can whilst this apple of discord subsists between both Nations.

This ended the negotiations which, but for the playwright and the priest, would never have been more than the echo of Commodore Johnstone's braying in Lisbon. Father Hussey became a travelling tutor and a marriage broker; he returned to Ireland, was made Bishop of Waterford, and died in the sea at Tramore in 1803. On 9 December 1780 Lord Hillsborough wrote to Richard Cumberland saying that he saw little utility in his remaining at Madrid. He stayed on until 24 March 1781, before starting home with his family across France. He suffered all sorts of trials on the journey, mainly because no one would accept his bills of exchange. When he at last arrived in London, he wrote, 'I am compleatly and effectually ruin'd by the Expedition.' He claimed that he had not received a farthing from the Government and that he had expended £4,500 of his own money on his mission and by defraying Father Hussey's expenses. Eventually, and like many others of Lord North's petitioners, he was paid on His Lordship's last day in office in 1782, at the rate of £5 a day for the time he spent in Spain, and on this he lived until 1811. He could not have lived on his plays, the best of which had twelve performances.

It is difficult to believe that either Great Britain or Spain took Father Hussey and Richard Cumberland as serious negotiators whose efforts might lead to peace. Rather they were expendable pawns, hazarded in the hope of drawing some larger piece out of position. That this was possible appears in a letter from Vergennes to the French Ambassador at Madrid, written on 21 April 1780:

I do not deceive myself any more than you do Monsieur, that if Spain treats separately it is all up with American Independence: but it would be equally necessary to sacrifice that if we were ourselves to undertake any separate negotiation.

If Floridablanca appears as an astute diplomatist in his manipulation of Richard Cumberland, this opinion is confirmed by his juggling of the neutral powers in Europe into a maritime alliance that came to be called the Armed Neutrality.

In the eighteenth century British sea-power had so prevailed that the ships of the other European nations were obliged to submit to being searched in peace-time, and to being detained and their cargoes commandeered for an indemnification during a war. At Gibraltar, blockaded by the Spanish navy, the sailors captured Danish and Dutch ships, and the Governor bought their cargoes, though both countries were neutral. All belligerents shipped naval stores, provisions and armaments in neutral ships, but only Great Britain claimed the right, and had the power, to stop these ships and to seize enemy cargoes. Whilst the first moves were being made in the negotiations instigated by Father Hussey, Floridablanca was engaged in another intrigue which he described himself:

To deprive our enemies of every maritime alliance . . . I cultivated a good correspondence with the Court of Russia . . . France entered into similar ideas, and we not only prevented Russia from uniting with England during the war, but even prevailed on her to send us purposely two of her frigates charged with naval stores, at the time when the war prevented the transport of them, for the equipment of our fleet. We also succeeded in inducing the Empress of Russia to place herself at the head of almost all the neutral nations to support the honour of her flag.

He claimed too much, as there is no indication that Russia had any intention of uniting with Britain, whose power she believed, with Prussia and Austria, to be on the wane. However, he continued, that in order to anger the neutral powers the Spanish Cabinet passed a law entitling her navy to stop all neutral shipping passing the Straits of Gibraltar, and to seize all goods being carried to or from Great Britain.

I was attacked by the ministers of Sweden, Denmark, Holland, Russia, Prussia, Venice, Genoa and others, to put a stop to the injuries which their commerce suffered by the detention of so many vessels. To these clamours we constantly answered that if the neutral powers would defend their flags against the English, when conveying Spanish effects, then we would respect that flag, even if conveying English. The matter being thus prepared to throw the odium as was just, upon the English, and to incite the neutral powers to the defence of their flag, Russia brought forward an idea, of which we dexterously profited.

On 26 February 1780 Catherine the Great issued a declaration to which all the neutral maritime powers except Portugal subscribed. They agreed to defend their right to transport all goods except arms and munitions freely from any one port to another, providing that the port was not actively blockaded. Floridablanca exaggerated the importance of the Armed Neutrality, which Great Britain ignored, and the Empress herself referred to as the 'Armed Nullity'. Neutral ships were still stopped, and cargoes were still seized, and neither Denmark nor Sweden nor Russia were prepared to put their trade at the mercy of the Royal Navy by provoking a war with Great Britain. Only Holland fell a victim to Floridablanca's scheme, forsook her old friend for her old enemy, and had war declared on her by Britain in December 1780. Though Holland gained nothing in the war, and lost St Eustatius, Trincomalee and Nagapatam, Floridablanca succeeded in uniting all Europe, even if it was only a nominal union, against Great Britain.

CHAPTER VI

Contradiction only!

AFTER the triumph of the relief, Rodney's victory, the sight of the captured Admiral Langara, the visit of Prince William Henry, even the departure of Admiral Duff, the Gibraltar garrison might have been expected to be in the best possible spirits. They had survived six months' blockade, and had provisions for about a year in store; their strength was increased by the thousand men of the 73rd Regiment; the Navy was reinforced by the *Edgar*, which Rodney had left to guard his prizes until sufficient prisoners were exchanged to sail them home; and they had the satisfaction of learning that, whilst the British Fleet was in the Bay, the Spanish garrison at Ceuta had suffered from privations as great as their own had been. Most of all, they had been remembered by the Government and people at home. Yet no sooner had Rodney's sails dipped below the headland to the west than old quarrels were renewed, and dissatisfaction and unease, as bad as a Levanter, embittered the air, lengthened the days, and troubled the nights. The Fleet had brought no news of the war, either in America or at home, which gave any hope of its conclusion. By incompetence the cattle that Mr Logie had collected for shipment to the Rock had not been brought over. The first victims of scurvy were lying in the hospital wards, and smallpox had broken out again. When, on 16 February, Barcello's ships were warped out from behind the boom at Algeciras, it became apparent that the blockade was to be renewed, and those families who had not taken the opportunity to leave with the Fleet began to regret their decisions. On the 27th four ships of the line, two frigates and a xebeck came from the west to join the Spanish squadron. It was too late for regrets.

Everyone blamed the outbreak of smallpox on the Spanish prisoners of war. Perhaps they were infected, but so were the British sailors, and the captain who took the *Phoenix* allowed Admiral Langara to stay on board his own ship as the British ship was carrying the disease. However, Mrs Green had noted that Captain Evelegh's boy had smallpox on 14 January, the day the *Sophia* arrived at Gibraltar. On the 25 February she wrote: 'The smallpox is beginning to be very fatal to the children. The Governor does not give leave for inoculation.' The question of inoculation was to trouble anxious mothers in the town for many months, but the Governor was adamant. At first he said that he would allow it if the infection spread to the troops, but even after about fifty men of the 73rd Regiment had died, he persisted in his refusal to permit it.

> *Dr Baynes:* Smallpox—if it happened in a family where there were more than one child would it not be a better way to Innoculate the Rest of the Family?

> *The Governor:* No! by no means! I could not answer it to my conscience.

Mrs Green recorded this, and more, as her daughter Charlotte fell ill and her maid died of the disease.

> 11th April. Smallpox raging very bad—children dying every day.

> 7th May. On each side of our house and directly opposite three very fine children have died since yesterday after being 9 days bad.

> 22nd May. Every day five or six buryings. Everyone alarmed and unhappy. It is to be wished the Innoculation had been allowed.

Charlotte, who was five years old, recovered, but five hundred others, mostly children, were less fortunate. Mrs Green's bitterness, and the bitterness of many women, can be felt in this entry for 6 June:

> More and more bad accounts of the fatal effects of the Small Pox, and Many Severe things said in consequence. It cannot be wondered that the Lower Degrees of People should be much hurt at all these bad times, their Provisions so bad, nothing to be got to assist them or their poor families, and the losing so many fine children, has been a heavy Stroke upon them, but we hear that a Great Person in the Garrison says he thinks it a fortunate Circumstance to those Soldiers who have Large families to Lose three or four Children.

The epidemic was over by August, though then the garrison had other troubles to contend with. Whether General Eliott was ruled by his conscience, or whether he felt that the crude form of inoculation then practised would only spread the disease amongst the men who had not taken it, his decision isolated him, and brought him into disfavour with the wives of the garrison. The children were gone, buried in hundreds of unmarked graves in the Red Sands. The siege went on.

Mrs Green mentioned that by June the provisions were bad, and yet only four months before the troops and townspeople had been wild with joy at the sight of the stores landed from Rodney's victuallers. At the beginning of March the Governor instituted a new scale of rations, to include the salt cod he had purchased from the Newfoundland ship. A pound of bread a day was issued weekly for every man, the remainder monthly.

	Soldiers		Officers
	1st & 3rd weeks	2nd & 4th weeks	Per month
Salt beef		1½ lb.	3 lb.
Salt pork	1 lb.		2 lb.
Fish	2½ lb.	2 lb.	9 lb.
Pease	2 pts		8 pts
Wheat	½ lb.	1½ lb.	5 lb.
Rice	1 lb.	1 lb.	4 lb.
Oatmeal	1½ pts	1½ pts	6 pts
Butter	5 oz.	5 oz.	40 oz.
Raisins	¼ lb.	¼ lb.	

The Genoese still brought their fish and vegetables to market, and occasionally a small boat slipped the blockade to come in with a few chickens or sheep, a little oil, honey and wine, but as many were taken by the galleys cruising at the entrance of the Bay. But few soldiers could afford the prices paid for these luxuries, and most were obliged to live, with their families, on their meagre rations. To make things worse for them, the Governor's fish began to stink very soon. Those officers fortunate enough to have bought or been given some sheep or a cow when the fleet was in the Bay, or rich enough to have obtained one of those brought in from Morocco afterwards, found themselves the unwilling objects of their friends' kind attentions, and when the animal was slaughtered were obliged to reciprocate them. Mrs Green left this history of a small cow worth £30, and killed on 21 March: A sirloin to General Boyd: part of the ribs to Colonel

Godwin: a piece of the loin to roast and a small piece to boil to
Captain Phipps: a part of the forequarter and a little piece for soup
to Colonel Gledstanes: a part of the sirloin to Dr Baynes: a part of the
ribs to the Engineer's Mess: a piece for boiling for Mrs Skinner: a
piece for roasting for Mrs Booth: a piece for roasting for Captain
Evelegh: a round for Mrs Power: a shin or two for some sick families:
the head and liver between Serjeant Grant and a married servant:
and presumably, the little piece that was left for the Colonel, Mrs
Green and Charlotte. Two months later, when the cow was a memory, she remarked: 'The Governor says he has not any objection to
have the Fresh Meat as dear as possible. It is not very easy to know
his Reason for it—Contradiction only!' She might have said Vegetarian only! because, while the General took little interest in the
meat market, he was concerned to make the Rock produce as many
vegetables as possible. All officers with gardens were instructed in the
Garrison Orders of 16 April to send their surplus produce to be
auctioned, and several, including Captain Witham, promoted
A.D.C. to the Governor, were given ground to cultivate. Lieutenant
Burleigh took to fishing.

In the meantime the enemy did remarkably little. The extent of
their activity on the land can be measured by the number of times
the garrison guns fired at them: eleven shots in February, twenty-
seven in March, six in April and fourteen in May. During March
Rodney's prisoners were exchanged for British sailors captured by
the Spaniards, who were put on board the prizes in the Bay. Four
men deserted in this month, the troops were instructed not to stamp
with the right foot when ordered to March Quick but step off at once
with the left, and Colonel Ross, to everyone's surprise, appeared on
parade with the 39th. He had not done any duty since he had arrived
from Faro, and had made a point of ignoring his Commanding
Officer, General Boyd, even when they dined together at the Governor's, so the garrison wondered what had prompted his sudden decision to take the General's usual place at the head of the regiment.
Boyd wrote a letter to Lord Hillsborough, congratulating him on his
appointment, which started, 'In my present state of insignificancy',
and went on to request a permission to return home, as General Eliott
persisted in slighting him. The Governor's attitude at this time
offended more than the Lieutenant-Governor. Mrs Green noted on

8 April: 'The Colonel not exceedingly well pleased at the Mode of carrying on Business. N.B. Nor is any of the Commanding Officers satisfied—so little attention showed to Them.' Others in the garrison would have been pleased with this inattention. Garrison Orders, 13 April: ' Whenever any boys are observed throwing squibs or firing powder they are immediately to be taken to the next Officer's Guard and whipped by the Drummers to the discretion of the Officer.' Life in the little town huddled under the Castle and in the shadow of the great hill was dull, and if the boys played with fireworks it was because the men appeared to be doing the same. However, it was no game to the Governor, whether parading at dawn with the working parties, or sitting with his secretary, Mr Rawleigh, in his room at the Convent, coding dispatches to Lord Hillsborough, or walking alone in his garden, or riding his white horse, shod with several layers of wool, round the sentry posts at night. He was the first up and the last to bed. His garrison now comprised over 6,000 men, and though many families and townspeople had left in the empty victuallers, there were still some 2,500 remaining, and nearly 2,000 sailors on the warships and prizes in the Bay. They all had to be fed. And, in the face of General Alvarez's army, and Admiral Barcello's fleet, the Rock had to be defended. Now the Government had ordered the *Edgar* to join the Grand Fleet, and the *Panther* to follow with the ships left behind by Rodney. In spite of the Governor's protests, the frigate *Hyena* arrived on 15 April to escort the *Edgar*, and on the 20th they sailed before Barcello could pull up anchor in pursuit. The defence of Great Britain, which was not going to be attacked, was deemed more important than that of Gibraltar, which was.

On 3 May Mrs Green took time off from tending Charlotte's sickness and the Colonel's dinner to note:

> The Officer at Forbes saw two dogs digging near the Mill Tower. The Officer at the Lines saw two men. The Officer at Forbes insisted that they were dogs. The Officer at the Lines was annoyed, and said he could tell the difference between two dogs and two men, and sent in a report to the Governor that the Enemy was advancing.

The enemy, however, did not advance, except for some deserters who were caught and executed. On the 6th the guards in the Lines were surprised to see the whole Spanish army marching out of their Camp. Quartermaster Ancell described the scene:

This afternoon the Spanish army were arranged in two divisions, and
about four o'clock, began a sham fight, similar to an attack on the
garrison, as one division took post on the rising ground under the Queen's
Chair (supposed to be the English) while the other division in the valley
on the common, endeavoured to dislodge the troops above and take
possession of their intrenchments: The fire was warmly returned by
those from the height, and briskly supported on both sides for three
hours, when the English forces were entirely routed;—they had several
field pieces and some cannon with them. I assure you, that the sight
afforded great entertainment, and the army displayed some merit in
their performance.

There seems a slight uneasiness in the last comment, but Ancell was
not one to be down-hearted. A few pages later in his Journal he burst
into pentameters:

> But should great Mars, not deign to bless our cause,
> And proud Iberia gain a triumph'd conquest,
> If Britons in the battle are o'erpower'd,
> By numbers far superior, full of vigour,
> Nor worn out with the heavy toils of war,
> Yet first they'll fight with martial desperation,
> Nor yield to Spanish arms the envied fortress,
> Not while a man is spar'd to fire a gun!
> But this is only mere imagination,
> Such valiant officers as bear command,
> Boyde, De la Motte, Green, Pickton, Hugo, Curtis,
> M'Kenzie, Gledstanes, Horsfall, Lewis, Maxwell;
> With many more experienc'd hard vet'rans,
> (To mention all their names, 'twould tedious prove)
> Like tygers to their prey the men will lead,
> And cheer each valiant soldier doom'd to bleed.

He did not mention the Governor, but then he was determined not
to be tedious. (To be fair, Ancell was always more concerned with
drama than with accuracy: for example, Captain Curtis did not
arrive at Gibraltar until almost a year later.) There was no attack
from the land, and no more activity at the Mill Tower, by dogs or
men. Consul Logie continued to send boats from Tangier with oil
and leather (most of the garrison now wore canvas shoes with rope
soles), and some got through and some were taken by the enemy.

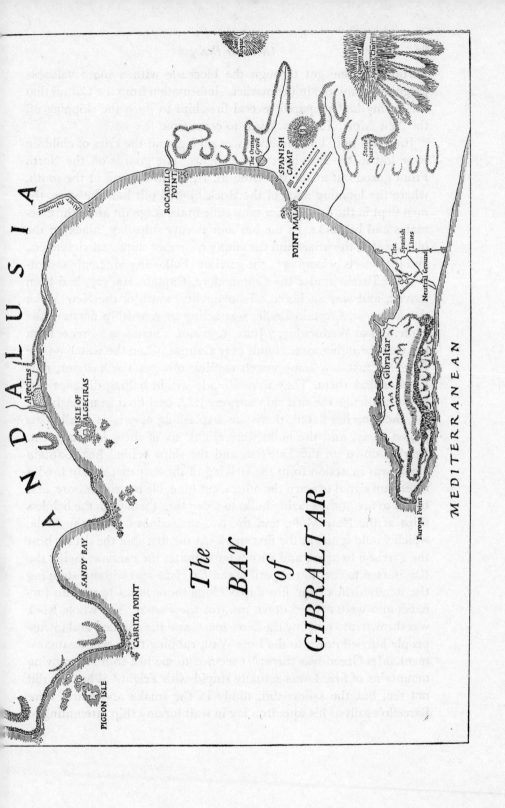

The
BAY
of
GIBRALTAR

ANDALUSIA

MEDITERRANEAN

Algeciras

River Palmones

ROCADILLO POINT

POINT MALA

The Orange Grove

SPANISH CAMP

Stone Quarry

Queen of Spain's Chair

San Roque

The Spanish Lines

Neutral Ground

Gibraltar

Europa Point

ISLE OF ALGECIRAS

SANDY BAY

CABRITA POINT

PIGEON ISLE

Fortunately one got through the blockade with a more valuable cargo than any sold in the market—information from the Consul that the enemy had prepared several fire-ships to burn the shipping off the New Mole. The attack was to come from the sea.

June was hot. The smallpox was raging, and the cries of children were lost in the heaviness of the nights. The guards on the North Front gazed out at the still isthmus. In the town, and at the south, where the looming mass of the Rock blotted out half the stars, the men slept in the open rather than stifle in the stagnant air of the case-mates and barracks. In the harbour twenty ships lay, black on the black water, the prizes and the empty ordnance ships and victuallers, and the vessels belonging to the garrison. Following Mr Logie's warn-ing, the *Panther* under the Commodore, Captain Harvey, had been moved, and was anchored off Buenavista, south of the New Mole; the *Enterprise*, Captain Leslie, was acting as guardship north of the Mole. It was Wednesday, 7 June, 1.30 a.m. There was a breeze from the west, bringing some clouds over Cabrita, when the watch on the *Enterprise* first saw some vessels drifting towards the harbour, out-lined against them. They were already within hailing distance and to his challenge the first ship answered: 'A beef boat from Barbary', but then torches flared, there was a splashing of oars as small boats pulled away, and the hulks were alight, six of them in a crescent, bearing down on the *Enterprise* and the ships behind her. Captain Leslie was in action from the striking of the first match. He fired a three-gun signal to warn the others, cut his cable to drift inshore, and began to fire at the blazing hulks to try to turn them from the helpless ships at the New Mole, and the two magazines behind the Mole, which would ignite at the first spark. At the first shot the drums beat the garrison to arms, and within ten minutes the cannons facing the Bay started to fire, to the peril of the *Enterprise* and without stopping the steady drift of the fire-ships. Three more hulks burst into fur-naces and were carried down towards the *Panther*. The whole Rock was thrown into relief by the fierce glare, and the garrison and towns-people hurried down to the Line Wall, rubbing their eyes in amaze-ment. Mrs Green was there: 'It seemed to me just so many moving mountains of fire. I was actually stupid with Fright.' What she did not see, but the sailors did, dimly in the smoke and glare, were Barcello's sails as his squadron lay in wait for any ship attempting to escape to the sea. At the moment when it seemed inevitable that the arc of fire must fall on the defenceless shipping, now brightly lit by the flames high above them, the wind dropped and the cracking, roaring ring appeared to pause before descending on them. In this respite the longboats were ordered out, sailors piled into them, seized the oars and began to row towards the hulks. When they were so near that faces scorched and paint blistered, grappling hooks were hurled into the flames and every man pulled desperately to drag the fire-ships clear before the rope burnt through or the ship, perhaps loaded with powder, blew up taking them with it. One by one the hulks were grappled and towed away to burn out their fury harmlessly against the shore. Three of them were linked with chains and cables, and these had to be hacked apart, with the small boats bobbing between two pillars of fire which threatened to close upon them. Five ships were dragged away and were burning out of danger when the sixth, drifting directly down on the Mole, was turned by a bar-shot from a 32-pounder on the Mole head and diverted into Rosia Bay. In the meantime, the *Panther* was fighting a desperate battle with one of the hulks sent against her. With the pitch on her sides melting, she fired broadside after broadside, forcing the fire-ship from her with the impact of the shot, until her own boats grappled it and hauled it out into the current where it was taken with the two others round Europa, to dwindle into the darkness of the sea. As dawn broke the flames flickered out in a hiss of steam and there were only the blackened spars and ribs on the Red Sands to tell the story. Barcello had returned to Algeciras. The sailors with blistered hands and grimy faces were off watch. The garrison was going about its duties. General Eliott was writing to Lord Hillsborough: 'We depend on guard boats . . . if the magazines blow up we all go with them.'

This spirited action gave the garrison some cause for alarm, because it revealed a significant weakness in their defences towards the Bay, and more cause for satisfaction, because they had witnessed the courageous conduct of their sailors and obtained a welcome supply of fuel from the hulls of the fire-ships. There were reports that Admiral Barcello had asked General Alvarez to support his attack with a barrage from the land, and the garrison were puzzled why, with 18,000 men and a great quantity of artillery, the Spanish General held his fire. Had they known that whilst they were literally sweating it out on Gibraltar, the British Government was flirting with Florida-blanca's peace proposals which were based on its cession to Spain, they might not have gone about their duties and suffered Eliott's stinking fish with such high resolve. One advantage was that whilst the negotiations were in process, the order to General Alvarez to open fire was withheld in Madrid.

Admiral Barcello did not need an order. When his ships of the line, which had left their station on 14 June, returned on the 24th, they exchanged several broadsides with the land batteries and shipping at the south. And three days later, at 2 a.m., everyone was woken up by firing and tumbled out of bed to see the *Panther* and the guns along the Line Wall shooting at some small craft out in the Bay. The enemy only fired four or five shots, which caused little damage, but had discovered a way of harassing the garrison which was to cause a lot of lost sleep and frayed tempers later. This was the first visit of the gunboats, and Captain Drinkwater left this description of them:

These boats were strongly built but ill finished: they had a small mast inclining forward from the centre of the boat, almost over the bow; upon which was hoisted a latine yard and sail, which, at anchor served as an awning to the men on board. They rowed astonishingly swift, and each carried a twenty-six pounder in the bow. We never had a good opportunity of making any satisfactory observations on them, but judged from their size, that they were about 70 feet long, and 20 broad.

On 3 July the *Panther* sailed, and was followed a week later by the prizes and transports. The gun-boats came again twice in this month, but otherwise the enemy's activities were confined to patrolling the Straits and unloading stores for the Camp. They began to establish piles of timber and brushwood behind the Lines, which gave the gunners more target practice, though their 246 shots took little effect. The extreme heat of this summer drained a man's strength, as the glaring light took the colour from his uniform. Few small boats came in, and those mostly from the East and carrying a few luxuries, wine, sugar, oil, or onions, whilst the Spanish squadron took a brig and a packet-ship coming through the Straits. The provisions in the storehouses began to deteriorate: flour became mouldy and bitter, butter melted and congealed into lumps of rancid grease, peas shrank to bullets, salt meat swelled up, bursting the barrels and oozing obscenely green where it met the heavy air, Eliott's salt cod lay in stinking piles, scarcely recognizable. The smell of a meal made from these ingredients, and there was nothing else for the soldiers, was enough to turn a stomach. But the poorest townspeople did not have even that. Odd things began to happen. The surgeon's mate of the 72nd poisoned himself. Major Horsfall sold his cow for fifty guineas and a pint of milk a day. Six sailors suddenly took a boat and rowed over to the enemy. When Colonel Mawhood of the 72nd died, the surgeons found, according to Mrs Green, 'A mortification in his Bowels had taken place and likewise a Stone as large as a pistol Ball was found in his Gall bladder.' The oddest thing occurred on the Grand Parade on 23 August, when the Articles of War were being read out to the various regiments. (This was a yearly procedure in the Army, required by Parliament, and the reading of the Articles placed the soldiers under Military Law for the following year.) The incident was omitted in all the published journals, but survives in Mrs Green's diary:

> Upon the parade of the 39th something very disagreeable passed. The Lieutenant-Colonel, Colonel Ross, went there under a visible agitation: after the Regiment were Drawn up He asked if General Boyd as Commanding Officer of the 39th was upon the Parade. He was told Not. He then ordered the Articles to be Read, after which to the surprise of everybody he addressed the officers and soldiers talking first of the True Meaning of those Articles, and afterwards attacking the Colonel of the 39th calling him Bob Boyd, and the Regiment the Storekeepers Regiment, and said a vast deal tending to hurt General Boyd in the Eyes of the Men; and He also ordered the Adjutant to tell the General all he had been saying! but as he declined it one of the General's a.d.c.'s did. It is supposed this will occasion much confusion.

The next day Lieutenant-General Boyd had Colonel Ross placed under arrest. The same day Apes Hill opposite the Rock in Africa caught fire, and black clouds of smoke drifted across the Straits and the heat was intense. Colonel Green presided at Colonel Ross's court-martial, and presumably told his wife about it in the evenings.

> Colonel Ross read a long paper and related some past circumstances respecting an old regimental coat which he had worn for the first two days of the Court Martial, and which was only to bring in what passed

between himself and General Boyd 5 years ago—he then desired the Court to indulge him for 2 days.

Colonel Ross: He did not mean to depreciate General Boyd but only to put him to his true standard. General Boyd had been a storekeeper and Judge Advocate.

Sentence: Suspension of 12 months and rendered incapable of ever serving in the 39th Regiment.

Later the Governor altered the court's sentence by reducing the suspension by nine months. The whole affair was an extraordinary clash of factions, echoing the greater political conflicts in England. In this age of influence a position of command in the Army was as valuable as a present-day directorship of a bank, and as commands were the gift of the Government, most generals were also politicians. The only credit from the incident goes to the men of the 39th, who apparently ignored it.

General Eliott, whose partiality in the affair affected his standing in the garrison, made himself even more unpopular with his officers by refusing to allow provisions consigned to individuals in the garrison by friends or agents in Minorca to be delivered to them, and by insisting that every article of food brought in should be disposed of by public auction. On 27 August he wrote to Lieutenant-General Murray, commanding in Minorca:

> The patrons of vessels are not allowed to bring anything of the provision kind for private persons, not even for the Government, everything is sold in public: before such regulations were made, at least one third of each vessel's cargo was employed for selfish purposes: on our situation nothing could be so mortifying.

As might be expected, Mrs Green had her own comment:

> The Governor has a few things sent as a Present from General Murray which he says he shall send to the Parade to be sold by auction and will not be a purchaser himself. The Governor has a declared dislike to having presents made to him. Indeed he is very little tried that way.

This policy, which the Governor followed throughout the siege, was of considerable importance at this time, as there had been no word from Consul Logie since the beginning of July, two months before. When at last a message did arrive, Eliott wrote to General Murray, from whose island whatever supplies there were now had to come:

The 'Cock of the Rock'. General Eliott during the Grand Attack, by
J. S. Copley.

Admiral Rodney

Sir Roger Curtis

M. D'Arçon

The Duc de Crillon

On the 30th ult [August] Consul Logie found the means of venturing me a letter to inform me that the Emperor of Morocco has decided in form, that he will give no protection to any of the Powers at War, and that they are at liberty to destroy each other in his Ports or on shore.

The British Grand Fleet was then cruising, in conspicuously safe waters, under Rear-Admiral Geary (of whom Kempenfeldt said, 'He is wholly debilitated in his faculties, his memory and judgement lost, wavering and indetermined in everything,') and the Combined Fleets of France and Spain were at Cadiz, where they had taken fifty-five British merchantmen captured in August. So there was no doubt which power would destroy the other.

September was the quietest month the garrison had experienced since the firing had started a year before. Six shots only were fired from the batteries. The rains were late, and the summer was intolerably long. When the news spread that they would no longer get the few cargoes of provisions from Barbary, the shopkeepers and bakers drastically cut the quantities of food on sale, and Mrs Green wrote: 'The poor Women and Children are round the Bakers' Doors every morning in vain waiting with their money. Though they have money they can't get bread.' This was the situation that existed before the arrival of Admiral Rodney and the relief. There were provisions in the town, but fear and greed prompted the merchants to eke them out, for the highest possible prices. None starved, but most suffered, and now there was a new danger. On 26 September the Governor wrote in a dispatch to Lord Hillsborough: 'The Garrison more sickly than usual. Much scurvy, many fluxes which have been fatal to a number mostly of the 72nd and 73rd Regiments.' Hunger, disease and boredom were the three potent enemies of Gibraltar in this winter.

D

CHAPTER VII

The utmost straits

BEFORE the grimness of the winter of 1780 descends on the Rock—
the bad conditions began to worsen from 2 a.m. on Sunday,
1 October—let us look at Gibraltar after a year of siege.

At first light the drums beat and the guards and workmen for the
day assembled on the Grand Parade. The moment a soldier opened
his eyes he could see Spain; there was never a moment's escape from
the feeling of encirclement. The men on night watch, from the pickets
at Bayside and Forbes to Rock Guard, up in the clouds, their clothes
damp, knew they had an hour or more to wait for their relief; an hour
to watch the Spanish Camp coming to life and to cook thin porridge
for breakfast. One morning the sentries at Rock Guard were amazed
to hear feminine voices and to see a party of ladies riding up the
rough track towards them on the King's mules, those patient creatures; they had come to picnic on top of the Rock. After the Parade
the Governor returned to the Convent and the Lieutenant-Governor
took a turn round the King's Bastion. Captain Leslie of the *Enterprise*,
now the Commodore, looked out at the Gut and wished he was at
sea, taking advantage of the westerly breeze and the fine day it promised. The Genoese gardeners filed out through Landport tunnel to
collect vegetables, and to sell information to the Spanish sentries who
sometimes came up to the Mill Tower. The fishermen put out in their
boats. The townspeople came out of their narrow doorways and
began to collect round the wickets that had been put up again in
front of the bake-houses. As the sun rose over the shoulder of the Rock
the officers in the batteries looked out hopefully for something to fire
at, whilst the gunners sat in groups, trying to forget that dinner was
still several hours away. In the lines below a work party was building

a covered passage, using the stones of the old Castle wall. The soldiers idled about, scratched their initials on the stones, caught lizards, diced, mended their uniforms, and got hotter and hotter as the sun swung overhead. Once they were ordered to fire their muskets at a deserter as he ran from the east side of the Rock towards the Spanish Lines and, though five hundred shots were fired, he kept on running and arrived apparently unhurt. About half the garrison were on these duties every day. In the town the bakers were closed again and women were gathered at the fountain on the Grand Parade. Some officers' wives were out visiting, genteelly stepping over the babies and puddles in the street. A Minorcan boat had crept into harbour the night before and there was much conjecture as to the price its cargo of tea would fetch when auctioned. In the gloom of the merchants' warehouses, among the barrels and crates bought from the merchant ships that came with Rodney's convoy, the Jewish shopkeepers bargained over a bag of flour or a handful of beans that they knew they would sell again for three or four times the price they were going to pay. They could hear the clucking of hens, or the rooting of pigs, that signified that the rich were, as usual, caring for themselves. At midday the heat dropped on Gibraltar like a stone, and the Genoese and Jews returned to their houses, closed their shutters and slept, like Spaniards, until four. But the dogs and the Englishmen, and the Scotsmen, and the Hanoverians, were out in the midday sun. Many of them were busy in the gardens that the Governor had encouraged them to build above the town, small patches of earth enclosed by stone walls, which by the end of the siege were producing enough vegetables to supply all their wants. Others were in their barracks, busy with the thousand trifles invented to fill a soldier's day, polishing, cleaning, mending and scrubbing, and sometimes stealing and lying: but the regiments, on the whole, were some of the best in the Army and there were few floggings and had been only two hangings in the garrison up to this time. The Governor always used to comment on the good behaviour and the good relations that existed between regiments and between the British and the Hanoverians in this first year. The Englishwomen were busy too, facing the task of cooking the slimy and unpleasant meat, the grey soggy fish and the yellow, and even moving, flour of their husbands' rations. In the Victualling Offices, and the Naval Stores, men were toiling in the thick atmosphere of rotten food, opening casks with no knowledge of what putrescence and decay they would find inside. Out in the open, in the garden of the Convent, General Eliott was talking to the captain of the Minorcan boat, asking for news, before entrusting him with his letter to General Murray. Outside Southport some sad women were laying a few wild flowers on the tiny graves in the Red Sands. Two soldiers carrying a comrade whose limbs were wasted with scurvy passed on their way to the hospital, where the wards were full of men, lying helpless, and unable to be helped by the over-worked surgeons and staff. At the New Mole there were more work-ing parties, transferring barrels of powder from the exposed maga-zines to some new buildings in the shelter of the rocks. As the sun dipped over Cabrita Point the senior officers, who had spent the day issuing orders, returned to their homes for an evening that could be nothing but quiet, or to dress for dinner with His Excellency, or for a game of cards at a meeting of the American Club (which was not a revolutionary body favouring independence but an association of officers who had served under General Wolfe: Colonel Green was the president). The junior officers, who knew quite well that the smooth running of the garrison depended on them, went to their messes and dropped exhaustedly into armchairs, complaining about the stub-bornness of their inferiors and the stupidity of their superiors. After a glass or two of brandy they planned campaigns that took them to the gates of Madrid and on one occasion they actually ventured out to break the windows of an old Jew's house. As it grew dark the wine-shops opened and the men came in for a glass of blackstrap, an in-flammatory mixture of wines, in the company of the successors of Minorca Moll. At night there was little movement but the slow tread of the sentries, and out in the harbour the Minorcan boat slipping quietly away. And, riding from post to post, the hooves of his white horse muffled in wool, old General Eliott, seeing that his fortress was safely shut up for the night.

At 2 a.m. on Sunday, 1 October, the enemy made a raid on the gardens in the Neutral Ground and tried to set the palisades at Bay-side and Forbes on fire. The pickets at the barriers fired their muskets and ran forward to throw off the burning materials hanging on the palisades, and discovered some ingenious machines made from twelve tubes loaded with balls and cartridges from which the fuses

had, fortunately, fallen out. They could not stop the Spaniards from
setting fire to the canes and huts in the gardens. In the morning it was
apparent that the attack was merely a diversion, as a new work had
been erected in the night by the Mill Tower, just over a thousand
yards from the Grand Battery. It appeared a makeshift construction
some thirty yards long and eighteen feet high, of timber, fascines and
sandbags, and the artillery were eager to try to knock it down. However, the guns in the Spanish Lines were raised and the batteries were
manned as if to meet and return the expected barrage, so the Governor decided against it. He judged the work to be so far advanced
from the enemy's lines as to be of little use to them. This sudden
activity was explained the next day when the Comte D'Estaing, who
had been out-manœuvred by Lord Howe off the American coast but
had later captured St Vincent and Grenada, visited the Spanish
Lines in the company of several high-ranking officers and spent three-
quarters of an hour looking at the Rock through a telescope. Out of
politeness the officers on the batteries refrained from opening fire, as
they did when General Alvarez visited his front line, which perhaps
explains why generals lived so long in the eighteenth century. On
the 3rd there were no distinguished visitors, and the batteries opened
up.

> The Governor was up at Willis's after Dinner and as we hear pointed
> one of the guns, which had the Good Luck to hit their new rais'd work.
> N.B. If this is not true I will mention it in my Journal as a mistake.
> N.B. A mistake.

There is no mistaking Mrs Green. The immediate result of the attack
was that the gardeners were reluctant to venture out again and in
any event the Spaniards had taken away most of the vegetables and
trampled much of what was left. The loss of this supply was a bad
blow to the garrison, already weakened by the onset of scurvy. Morale
was further lowered when two ships that had sailed for England the
month before and a sloop flying the British colours reversed, were
taken into Algeciras by Barcello's ships.

The scurvy had so far affected the garrison and the sailors that
many men went about their duty on crutches, and Captain Leslie
asked permission to take his ships away, which was refused by the
Governor. The disease rotted and wasted the men and there was no

cure, the doctors found, but juice of oranges and lemons, of which there was none in the garrison. However bravely the soldiers persisted in forcing their weak bodies to their posts, there is no doubt that this insidious enemy would eventually have defeated them, as it was to defeat the courageous garrison in Minorca. But there was a 'God Send'. On 11 October there was a heavy fog in the Straits and a small boat from Minorca stole into the harbour under its cover. The *padrone* told Captain Leslie that there were two other boats to the east of the Rock, and he ordered out the ships' longboats to guide them in. As the sailors rowed round Europa Point, there was no sign of the Minorcans, but dimly and in the distance they saw the shadows of ships passing through the Straits to the west. They lay on their oars in silence, until one vessel, coming nearer the Rock than the others, loomed out of the fog towards them. They laid alongside and boarded her. She was a Danish dogger, the *Vrow Helena*, and when they brought her in they found her cargo was oranges, lemons, raisins and figs. Denmark was a member of the Armed Neutrality, but this was no time for political considerations. Two hundred and sixty men had died from scurvy and many hundreds bore the effects of the disease. The lemons brought immediate relief and sick men left their beds within a few days. The juice was preserved with brandy, and continued to benefit the garrison for the remainder of the siege.

There appeared a new resolve on the part of the Spaniards to keep the garrison behind their walls and to cut off the small limits in which they strayed. General Alvarez informed the Governor on 11 October that there were to be no more parleys by land (a few days earlier Major Burke, the Town Major, had been out to look at the new work on the pretence of a parley) and on the 16th two gun-boats fired at Lieutenant Burleigh while he was out fishing, and his catch was a 26-pounder ball. This effectively stopped the small supply of fresh fish that came into the town. Towards the end of October, when the last of the salt cod had been scraped off the floor of the stores, a new scale of rations was introduced. There was no rice, butter was reduced to 2½ ounces a week, pease, oatmeal and wheat were cut by half, salt pork remained at a pound a week, but salt beef was reduced to half a pound, with one pound available to be bought, if a man could afford it. So the ration per day, if one can imagine it, was a cupful of oatmeal or pease, a slice of salt meat (weighing about four ounces) and a hunk of bread about the size of a small loaf, and these were in a state of decay and putrefaction. Mrs Green noted: 'The Beef is quite rotten and stinking—it seems to hurt everybody. The Troops are far from well, and to a Certainty are very weak and greatly fallen off in their Strength and likewise in their Spirits.' Every night the enemy extended their work near the Mill Tower, in spite of the firing from the batteries, until it began to take on the squat and ominous appearance of a mortar battery. Six men deserted from the garrison in the first week of November.

It was cold and it rained a lot. The young regiments, the 72nd and 73rd, were poorly equipped and short of spare clothing, and men began to die from fluxes and pneumonia. Their companions looked round for someone to blame for their critical and unpleasant situation. 'It makes every Body uneasy to find the Spirit of Dissatisfaction beginning to increase amongst the Troops,' wrote Mrs Green. In spite of constant firing from the batteries, the Mill Battery, as the garrison called the new Spanish work, was reinforced with timbers brought up from the Lines at the cost of many casualties among their men and mules.

The garrison fired over seven thousand shots at the Mill Battery, and the materials being brought up to it, yet the Spaniards did not return one shot from the land. Apparently they were still relying on the blockade to starve the Rock into submission, though the erection of the new battery argued their intention to open fire should another relief convoy reach Gibraltar. With this in mind, the Governor gave new orders for the disposition of the various regiments in the event of a bombardment. The blockade was increasingly effective, and two ships were taken in sight of the garrison early in November, one from Minorca and the other flying the British flag from the west. On the 12th a small armed merchant ship, the *Young Sabine*, beat the blockade and the attempts of five of Barcello's ships to board her, and came in, sails torn but flag flying. Her small cargo of cheese, hams and potatoes, and a few other necessities, sold at fantastic prices (potatoes, for example, at 1s. 6d. per lb.). As if out of spite, the Admiral sent over his gun-boats a few nights later and this time some of their fire was directed at the town. Two nights later the gun-boats came again, and in the Garrison Orders for 20 November there is this example of an early black-out: 'No lights to appear towards the Bay in any House

Barrack, Guardhouse, or other building after 7 o'clock at night.' In the meantime, the enemy had begun an approach from the Lines towards the Mill Battery, to enable their stores to be taken up under cover. In spite of the heavy fire from Willis's, the Spaniards not only completed this approach in a fortnight, but their workmen and sentries began to walk up to the gardens and take the vegetables still growing in full daylight. Lieutenant Burleigh was ordered to take his marksmen up to the front, but they were not fortunate enough to hit anyone.

December began with a storm and a flood of rain that brought small avalanches of earth, rubble and rocks down the Rock and into the streets of the town. Clothes, bedding, basements and casemates were drenched and, as there was barely any fuel left, stayed drenched. The blockade was temporarily weakened by the withdrawal of two frigates to the west, and a privateer, the *Anglicana*, got in. She sailed on the 3rd, with Lieutenant Gage as passenger, who carried a dispatch from the Governor to Lord Hillsborough: 'The troops bear short allowance cheerfully . . . We have lost this year by Death 260 and 20 Wolfenbuttel men deserted.' It was a politic dispatch, for as many British had deserted as Hanoverians, the rest were anything but cheerful, and there was no mention of the deaths among the soldiers' families and the townspeople. On the 5th the Governor ordered the remainder of the streets in the town, including the Grand Parade, to be dug up, and the visiting amongst the officers' ladies was reduced to a minimum. In any event there was little enough distraction for the garrison from the rain, the guns, the shortages, and the lack of news. 'Let me beg of you to send me any old newspapers you have, since July everything will be fresh to us,' wrote General Eliott to General Murray. And Mrs Upton, wife of an Ensign, was 'obliged to go to bed at 5 o'clock for want of light'. Some small ships came in from Minorca, taking advantage of the east wind, but it was not until 21 December and the arrival of the *Speedwell* cutter that the garrison began to anticipate the arrival of another relief. But they learned nothing from the Governor, who kept the dispatches brought in by Lieutenant Gibson, wounded in an engagement off Ceuta, to himself.

Our general information and private Intelligence lead us to believe that the Enemy does intend to make some very vigorous attempt to take the

Place, which however does not alarm us when we consider the great strength of it, and your zeal and abilities to avail yourself of that strength assisted by the Bravery and Perseverance of those under your command.

Almost as an afterthought Lord Hillsborough added, 'Provisions preparing, expected to sail early January.' The *Speedwell* also brought news of the imminent promotion of Colonel Ross to Colonel of the 72nd Regiment of which the Colonel promptly informed the garrison. The year ended on a note of expectancy. The garrison caught a spy; a privateer, the *Hannah*, came in with provisions on the 23rd and two Liverpool merchantmen arrived on Christmas Day, one carrying 300 barrels of flour; this last was an event that could hardly pass unnoticed by Mrs Green: 'This vessel may be placed among some of the God Sends that we have experienced since the Blockade and has put everyone in high Spirits.' She also noted the discrepancy between the amount of food stored in the town and the amount eked out at exorbitant prices by the shopkeepers to the poor families and townspeople. But she was a remarkably observant lady, and few if any of the crowd around the bakers' doors knew of the private stores accumulated in Gibraltar.

The year 1781 started joyfully for the garrison and the townspeople. When the carpenters started to erect landing stages and cranes in Camp Bay and Rosia Bay beyond the New Mole it was a sure indication that a convoy was expected. When they guessed the reason for making these arrangements for unloading beyond the range of the enemy's guns, very likely their joy was qualified somewhat. There were reports that the Mill Battery had been armed with eight 13-inch mortars. However, they had been living in the shadow of a bombardment for so long that they had forgotten the sun, and lost some of their fear of the dark. Suddenly, on 11 January, the relative advantages of their position became apparent. On that day the garrison were surprised to see two Moorish galleys being rowed towards the harbour under a flag of truce. They hurried down to Ragged Staff where the occupants were being landed: 110 British subjects from Morocco, including Consul Logie and his wife. They had to be helped ashore, and soon men and women who had little enough for themselves were hurrying to fetch food and clothes for their compatriots who had nothing but the rags in which they stood. Mr

Logie's story of the Emperor of Morocco's treachery was soon the common topic of the town, and the personal tragedies of each of the refugees were being told in the houses where they had been given shelter.

It had started when the Emperor, who had successfully blackmailed the British Government into fitting out his four frigates, found that he could no longer squeeze any presents out of Mr Logie. Though he had long enjoyed the support of the British, and the protection of the Navy, the Emperor was already considering Floridablanca's offers of friendship and a treaty when Rodney's victory in the Straits persuaded him that his old ally was still to be reckoned with, and he gave special attention to Mr Logie and continued to allow him to send over supplies to Gibraltar. Later in the year however, when the Spaniards renewed their offer and it appeared as if the British were about to be defeated, he allowed British ships to be taken in his harbours and their crews to be sold in his slave markets. Mr Logie stayed in Tangier, sending what food and information he could to the Rock until July, when he and the other British residents were made virtual prisoners in their own homes. In September the Emperor concluded the treaty with Spain, allowing them to farm the ports of Tetuan and Tangier for £7,500 a year and gaining the release of 100 Moorish prisoners, and permission to import grain into Morocco, where there was a scarcity due to the dryness of the summer. One clause of the treaty stipulated that the British Consul and subjects should be expelled from the Emperor's dominions. Early in October Mr Logie opened his door and found a party of the Emperor's Ethiopian soldiers who insulted him, spat in his face, and waved their daggers at him. Two days later he was summoned to the Emperor's camp at Sallee in the west of his kingdom. Captain Drinkwater gives this account of the incident:

After various questions relative to Gibraltar to which such answers were given as were least likely to please, the Emperor addressed himself to his troops, and a great mob that were assembled on the occasion, saying, 'the English were an avaricious, proud and headstrong people; they always attacked the head: but when people came to beg, they ought to crawl up by the feet. He had however deprived them of every benefit they formerly derived from his country'; concluding with ordering the Consul to be taken to Sallee. Mr Logie objected to this mandate, informing the Emperor he was ready to attend his camp; but that his Sovereign's service did not permit his trifling away his time in visiting towns.

It is difficult to cut off a man's head when he is standing upright, as many Britons were to prove in foreign courts, and Mr Logie returned to Tangier with the Emperor's assurance that the British would not be molested. The Emperor kept his word until 26 November, when orders came to prepare the boats belonging to the British for sailing, but these were later burned by a party of Spanish sailors with the connivance of the Emperor's guards. When the next order arrived, threatening all Christians, other than Spanish citizens, with slavery if they remained in Morocco after 1 January 1781, Mr Logie hurried to Tetuan to remonstrate that the British now had no means of leaving. He was not allowed an audience and whilst he was there he heard that his compatriots had been forced to leave Tangier and sent to Marteen, a poor harbour near Tetuan. They had been driven out of their houses and suffered the greatest indignities, and their property, worth some £60,000, had been confiscated. They remained, herded in this miserable place until 28 December, when the Consul, who had joined them there, was informed that the Emperor had handed them over as prisoners to Spain. They were driven on board the two galleys and transported to the Bay, where Admiral Barcello ordered them to anchor off the Orange Grove until he received orders from Madrid as to their future fate. They had no food, and the Admiral would give them none. For two weeks they were kept, crowded on the decks of the galleys, and only survived by the good offices of the French Chargé d'Affaires at Algeciras, who sent them provisions bought from his own pocket. On 11 January they were sent over to Gibraltar. The arrival of these pitiable people aggravated the fears of the garrison as well as increasing their detestation of the Spanish Admiral, as they realized the enemy fleet could blockade the Straits even more effectively with the use of the ports on the Barbary coast.

The weather remained stormy and Barcello's small ships were obliged to stay in the shelter of Cabrita Point, so it was that a brig from Madeira carrying seventy butts of wine came in on 16 January, and the *Tartar* cutter two days later. The latter brought news of war with the Dutch. But there was no sign of the expected convoy. Seven men deserted in this month, four from the advance guards and three by climbing down the back of the Rock. One of them was a well-known man in the garrison, a serjeant of the 56th Regiment, who left his wife and child in the town. He walked away from his post towards the Devil's Tower and his men would not fire at him; at the Tower, he stopped and looked back, as if undecided, but then he walked on towards the enemy. The garrison later heard that he hanged himself in the enemy Camp on the night he got there.

> From eve to morn their heavy works go on,
> And threat'ning batt'ries rise, 'midst show'rs of shot;
> Our Rock, like burning Aetna, red with flames,
> Whole vollies of destruction vomits forth;
> While death, with horrid grimace, hovers round 'em,
> And scenes of blood besmear their operations,
> Strew'd o'er with mangled limbs, and heaps of slain,
> With steadfast valour, fix'd determination,
> They labour and bring forward their advances.

Which is how Mr Ancell, the garrison laureate, put it. Early in February the navy's boats rowed round the Rock and discovered the broken bodies of two men who had attempted to desert by climbing down the cliffs on that side. The bodies were brought back and displayed on the Parade as a grim example of the price of disloyalty. Barcello's main force returned from the west, the cranes in the bays to the south swung creaking in the wind, and the garrison were more gloomy and depressed than ever. Private Gordon of the 73rd Regiment remembered that 'the beer was at the exorbitant rate of one shilling and sixpence a bottle', and Mrs Upton, that 'raisins pleased and satisfied my children when I had no bread to give them'. The shortage of bread was once more acute, and many of the bakers closed their shops altogether. Eventually all the bread was baked in one place, which opened at 7 a.m., with a large crowd round the door: 'A handkerchief was thrown in the window with the money in it, and no person was suffered to purchase two loaves', and the officers' wives, Mrs Upton among them, jostled with the soldiers' wives and the poor women of the town for their share. The other shortage, as before, was of fuel. Though Gibraltar is a few miles only from Africa, the winters can be bitterly cold, and Mrs Upton reminds us that fuel has more uses than one: 'Our clothes we washed in cold water, and put on without ironing—but when the rainy season came on, I suffered more from the cold than I ever did in the severest winter in England.' It is no wonder that, when a Spanish deserter reported that the sudden inactivity of the enemy's working parties was due to a proposition that had been made to Great Britain to buy Gibraltar for £6,000,000, some of the garrison were inclined to believe him. They felt as if they had been abandoned. Even the Governor began to feel this. When a privateer, the *Salisbury*, which had arrived through the blockade from Port Mahon on the 9th, left on the 17th, Consul and Mrs Logie sailed with her for England carrying a dispatch to Lord Hillsborough in which General Eliott had written: 'In case we are driven to extremes I am entirely at a loss—you will furnish me with Instructions how to act. This Fortress and so fine a Body of Troops are worth saving almost at any risk.' The old soldier was beginning to sense defeat, and not defeat in battle, which he might have borne, but slow strangulation, with the decision of when to cry 'enough' and stop the sufferings of his men and his people on his shoulders alone. Fortunately for Gibraltar and for Britain, General Eliott was a man of unusual fortitude and resolve, and at no time in the siege did this appear to better advantage than in these cruel months when he thrust his great nose and chin into every quarter of the garrison, as solid as the Rock itself. He ordered the Government ship the *Providence* to be broken up for fuel, and when a Minorcan ship arrived, in the prevailing east wind, he wrote angrily to General Murray:

I'm told you was so good to send me down Pigs. I take it as a kind token of your remembrance, tho' I dare not apply them to my own use, but they must be disposed of to the best bidder; an established rule made since the blockage from which not the Governor is excepted, as we are all embarkt on the same bottom.

And he ordered the regiments of the garrison to parade on review. The review took several days, starting on 26 February, as each regiment paraded for inspection, and then marched to its alarm-post, and fired several rounds over the parapet. In the evening, the officers of the regiment reviewed that day went to the Convent for dinner with the Governor. Though the regiments at that time were known by their numbers, or the name of the colonels who had raised them, many of the men in them were recruited from the same counties, and

they had all the pride in, and loyalty to, their regiment, that charac-
terized the Army when it was reorganized in the next century. The
12th Regiment, known later as the Suffolk Regiment, had fought at
Minden. The 39th, the Dorsets, had served in India. The 56th came
mainly from Essex, and the 58th from Northamptonshire. The 72nd,
the Royal Manchester Volunteers, was a regiment recruited for the
war. The 73rd, Lord Macleod's Highlanders, also recruited for the
war, were allowed to wear the kilt, and later became the Highland
Light Infantry. The Hanoverian regiments, Hardenberg's, Reden's
and De la Motte's, well-disciplined soldiers who had fought Britain's
wars in Europe (Hardenberg's fought at Minden side by side with the
12th), marched after, but no less proudly, than the rest. The Artillery,
Engineers and Artificers paraded separately, with the superior bearing of men who knew that the brunt of the defence of Gibraltar was
being born by them. As they paraded in their worn breeches and
tattered coats, their feet bound in rags, tramping through the mud of
the Grand Parade, to the beat of the drums, past the Cock of the Rock
on his white horse, the garrison must have gained some heart, and
the townspeople who watched them some confidence, that after all,
they were 'all embarkt on the same bottom'.

It was at this time that the officers of the garrison presented a
Memorial to the Governor.

That the officers of His Majesty's several regiments of foot, serving
under his Excellency's command, had been necessarily exposed to a
great variety of inconveniences since the commencement of the blockade, independent of the additional duties which they had been required
to discharge: That, in particular, their pay, which constituted their
chief, if not their sole support, had, at different times, suffered a great
diminution by the exorbitant rate of exchange: That every article of
clothing, and still more, those essential to life and health, were so advanced in price, that, with the strictest economy, their pay was totally
inadequate to the expences absolutely indispensible in their present
situation; a situation which, they apprehended, precluded them, in a
great measure, from participating with the officers at home in the exten-
sive promotions which had of late taken place in the army. They therefore
appealed to the paternal feelings, the justice and the humanity of his
Excellency; trusting that, through his recommendation and inter-
cession, such assistance and protection might be granted them, as their
situation and services deserved: They requested that his Excellency

would be pleased to lay their prayer, with all humility on their part, at His Majesty's feet.

General Eliott forwarded the Memorial to the Commander-in-Chief, Lord Amherst, but there was no reply, and for this, unjustly, the officers blamed the General. Another incident at this time hardly served to increase the officers' liking for their Commander, though it does show General Eliott in a new light. During March three officers of the 12th Regiment assaulted a Jew and were court-martialled. It was discovered, according to Mrs Green, that one officer, 'sold his Provisions over a year ago for ready cash—as the Provisions are curtailed the Jew required his money back—the officer refused and shut the Jew up and threatened him and fired his pistol without ball at him'. The Governor, who was always rather dis-gusted by what he called 'the rotten part of the town', took the Jew's part, and the officer was obliged to repay the Jew with double inter-est, and all three officers were fined 10 guineas each. Captain Spils-bury remarked, 'It is the first time they have found protection in this place.' But the incident was an indication of the growing antipathy of the garrison to the shopkeepers, and of the resentment in the army against the deprivations they were forced to endure. But in this cold, dry March, the army was well off. Though the weekly ration had been reduced again (the principal reduction being from 7 lb. of bread to 5 lb.), there was no bread at all for sale in the town. On 19 March the Governor noted: 'The Inhabitants begin now to feel utmost distress', and were living on 'the remains of a certain Species in the Naval Stores'. This was biscuit crumbs, the scrapings of the bins where the sailors' tack had been stored, which sold for 10d. and 1/- per lb. The most vivid picture of their misery comes from Mrs Upton:

> I cannot now recollect the distress of a poor woman, without feeling a pang at my heart which gives me a sensible uneasiness. She sat weeping at my door with two children, the one about seven years old, the other an infant which she suckled: after the former had repeatedly asked her for bread, she laid down her youngest child, and gave her breast to her other son, saying, Suck me to death at once!

The garrison had existed for fourteen months on the salt provisions left by Rodney, with a few supplies from Morocco, which were soon cut off, and occasional boatloads of luxuries from Minorca, which few could afford to purchase. The poor townspeople were on the edge of starvation, existing on the crumbs that their wealthier neighbours cheated them for. There was no word of the promised convoy and what news of the war filtered through, gave little hope that a fleet could be spared to escort it in safety to the Bay. Even the enemy's cessation of work on the isthmus seemed to argue that they expected the Rock to fall without their making any further effort. The Governor resolved on a last gamble to bring in supplies to support his resistance a little longer. For some time he had been in correspondence with General Murray in Minorca, and had learned that there was a British frigate, the *Brilliant*, stationed there under Captain Curtis. His own small squadron consisted of the frigate *Enterprise*, Captain Leslie, a sloop, the *Fortune*, and an armed vessel, the *St Firmin*. On 28 March forty invalids from the garrison were put on board the *Enterprise* and she sailed, with the *Fortune*, for Port Mahon. The *St Firmin* was to have sailed with them, but she fouled the New Mole, and had to stay. Captain Leslie carried this letter to General Murray:

Gibraltar, 27th March 1781.

Sir,

Enclosed I transmit copies of a letter from Captain Leslie, commanding the Enterprise, with my answer, by which Your Excellency will be fully informed of my reasons for concurring in the proposal to send the Enterprise and St Fermin to Mahon. This, though hazardous on my side, the exigency I hope will justify, as I will freely declare to you most secretly, that a very little time will reduce us to the utmost straits, and I fear 'tis reasonable to apprehend (however determined the intentions may be at home) that no convoy from Great Britain can with certainty be depended on, considering the various and important services our fleet must be called upon to perform in opposition to such armaments as threaten from every quarter. I have therefore ventured for a time to deprive this fortress of an essential part of its defence, trusting that (by throwing in a supply of provisions although ever so small) the advantage will overbalance the risk; this first step, I have taken; but, Sir, I must have recourse to you to render this step effectual for the public service, by requesting your influence with the naval commander to employ his whole squadron in coming down to our relief, and allowing such provisions as can be spared from the king's stores to be shipped on board the king's ships—taking under his convoy such trading vessels as will load with provisions for our assistance. By the character of Captain Curtis this service could not fall into better hands, as, by description, his ambition is to distinguish himself in the public cause. When the service is performed, there is not the least difficulty for any of the ships to take the proper opportunity of returning to Mahon. I hope and believe, both coming and returning the ships will be exposed to no danger as the enemy has only three bad sailing frigates and five xebecks to the eastward, one xebeck and several gun-boats in our Bay. . . . This appears to me a practicable scheme and liable to no great danger for the squadron; at all events it is to be wished some attempt may be made for the national honour as well as the preservation of this garrison. These proposals, Sir, I lay before you for consideration, desiring you would please totally to change, alter, amend any or every part, and substitute whatever else may better conduce to this great end with the utmost expedition, on which our existence depends.

All the Governor's hopes, and they were little enough at the end of March, were pinned to the mast of the *Enterprise* as she cleared Europa Point and headed east. The garrison knew nothing of his plan, and Mr Ancell thought that the ships had gone to help his comrades in Port Mahon; they still looked for their relief to the west.

As it happened, for once the garrison was right. On 1 April Barcello's cruisers were called in to Algeciras, and the next day, the enemy were busy at the Mill Battery, laying mortars. On the 3rd Mr Ancell was in raptures:

The garrison are noisy with tumultuous joy, occasioned by the arrival of a cutter last night from the West, who brings the captivating and enlivening intelligence of our fleet being on their passage for the Mediterranean. We seem to be another people—the very atmosphere is changed—no depression of spirits; every countenance is adorned with satisfactory smiles—a social greeting of friends and acquaintances, with overwhelming extacy, accost each other, 'Dear friend, all our wants will shortly be supplied.'

The cutter was the *Resolution*, and to assist the joviality carried a cargo of rum, sugar and coals, the ingredients of a good hot punch. In the middle of it all the *St Firmin* sailed (an unlucky ship, one of Rodney's prizes, whose captain had died of drink some months before) and was taken by two xebecks coming from the east. When the *Resolution* sailed, Colonel Ross went with her to England.

The Spaniards were busy preparing several ships, which the garrison suspected were for use as fire-ships, and on the next night four boats were sent out to attempt to cut out a sloop and burn two other vessels which were anchored some way out in the Bay level with Cabrita Point. Lieutenant Burleigh, who had put the idea to the Governor, had command over the thirty men in the boats. The night was cloudy and rowing with muffled oars they approached within a few hundred yards of the enemy ships, when a sudden gap in the clouds revealed them in the moonlight. Those who were watching from the Rock held their breath, but the Spaniards took no action, and the boats returned, but less silently than they had left, as everyone was blaming the other for their failure. Captain Witham undoubtedly had something to say. The next day the enemy were again busy in their batteries, and they withdrew their ships under the guns at Cabrita. On the evening of the 7th the *Eagle* cutter fought her way in from the Barbary coast, and the captain said he was surprised not to find the Fleet in the Bay. It was impossible to ignore the preparations the enemy were making along their Lines and in the Mill Battery, and on the 8th General Alvarez and a suite of officers visited the advance works. Yet, when the relief of a year before arrived, they had made the same preparations, and there had been no bombardment. In the general joy at the approach of relief from the sea, the garrison failed to appreciate the threat from the land. On the 9th they discovered that all Barcello's ships, apart from two xebecks and the gun-boats, had left their stations in the Bay. The apprehensive activity of Admiral Barcello's ships delighted the garrison, who had for so long seen them masters of the Bay. On the 11th they saw a felucca come speeding round Cabrita, signalling to Algeciras, and in the evening there were many lights and beacons on the hills to the west. Nobody went to bed, and about midnight a cutter flying the British flag came in to the New Mole, and to the officer of the guard's challenge, her captain, Captain Trollop, answered, 'From the Fleet.'

CHAPTER VIII

A most desperate stroke

AT the beginning of March 1780 Horace Walpole wrote in his Journals: 'The error of this reign has been to haul into dispute undefined questions.' This was an astute diagnosis of the ills caused by the government of King George III through his creatures. There were no clear-cut issues facing the politicians at home, or the generals overseas (except General Eliott in Gibraltar, General Murray in Minorca, and General Eyre Coote in India, where old wars were being re-fought). In America the whole conduct of the war was obscured by clouds of indecision, as the Government blew hot on subjugating the rebellious colonists, and cold on paying for it to be done. Sir Henry Clinton, an unstable man at the best of times, was further confused by being both Commander-in-Chief and Peace Commissioner. No wonder he persistently pressed Lord North to accept his resignation. No wonder Lord North did the same to the King. In England the country was divided as it had not been since the Civil War. Walpole continued:

Alas! it is unhappy that by the enormities of the Court, and the incapacity of our present Governors, the nation should be forced to enter into discussions, the very attention to which doubles our danger; for when the Opposition think of nothing but vanquishing the Court, the Court can think of nothing but defending itself at home. No plans can be formed for abroad, nor does either side think of attaching or defending the country from France. Everybody felt the danger we were in last summer from the incapacity of the Commander-in-Chief and of the chief Admiral. Great information was collected from Lord Amherst's neglect of Plymouth, and a charge against him was threatened in Parliament—yet all is as much forgotten as if events of the last war.

The best men were in the Opposition; no Whig admiral, and they included Barrington, Howe, Keppel and Kempenfeldt, would now serve under the Earl of Sandwich; no good general could survive long under the barrage of contradictory orders emanating from Lord George Germaine. In April the famous motion 'that the influence of the Crown has increased, is increasing, and ought to be diminished' was carried in Parliament. And this at a time when England was at war with the American Colonies, France and Spain, was opposed by the Armed Neutrality, was threatened with a rebellion in Ireland, and was without an ally in the world. She only remained undefeated through the weakness of her enemies. Washington conserved his army above New York, waiting for the French aid, or the British blunder, that would enable him to move decisively. The Court of France sent her fleets on irrelevant and costly expeditions to capture West Indian islands. The Court of Spain trifled with Richard Cumberland, and waited hopefully for the surrender of Gibraltar. The failure of the armada of 1779 had been too expensive to risk again. The position was stalemate.

Then in May 1780, Great Britain made a move. Sir Henry Clinton and his second-in-command, Lord Cornwallis, moved south and took Charleston. Clinton then returned to New York. This division of forces had been urged by Lord George Germaine, who believed that the Southern States were full of loyalists who only needed a little encouragement to mobilize and march north. He was wrong in this as he was in everything else. But it seemed like a victory at the time. As if to redress the balance, there occurred in the next month the Gordon Riots, which paralysed the Government in everything except their desire for revenge. This was pursued and resulted in twenty-five executions (seventeen boys and girls under eighteen, and three under fifteen were hanged) and the acquittal of Lord George Gordon. In August the combined enemy fleets captured the East and West Indian convoy and carried it into Cadiz. In September Parliament was dissolved, and the King's party embarked on an election campaign notorious for the amount of money spent on bribing voters. In the same month Admiral Darby, who had succeeded the debilitated Admiral Geary, managed to avoid meeting the French fleet returning to Brest in triumph from Cadiz. The reporter in the *Annual Register* remarked: 'It was reported that the hostile fleets were for some days so near each other, that it was a matter of some care and nicety to prevent their being entangled in the dark.' In October news arrived of Cornwallis's victory at the Battle of Camden, and Walpole wrote:

On the news from Clinton in the preceding week (of the landing of 6,000 French troops on Rhode Island) everybody had declared the American war must be given up. This new success was likely to revive the King's obstinacy—as all advantages had done to the involving us deeper in ruin. . . . Lord Cornwallis's victory had given the Ministry, and they hoped the nation, spirits; and as they could not hope any further success, they opened the session.

The Opposition had been stunned by the Gordon Riots, shocked by the elemental power of the mob that was starkly revealed, and the Government carried the motion to continue the war for another year.

So far, no one had spared a thought for Gibraltar, but on 2 November Lord Hillsborough wrote: 'Provisions preparing expected to sail early January.' General Eliott received this dispatch six weeks later by the *Speedwell*. However, his Lordship's expectations were not fulfilled, as on 20 December Great Britain declared war on the United Provinces, and on 8 January the French invaded Jersey. Now, while war with Holland meant little more than a licence to seize Dutch colonies and the French were expelled from Jersey by Major Pierson almost single-handed, neither the British Government, nor the Opposition, nor the people, felt safe unless the Grand Fleet was cruising in the Channel. Moreover, due to the lack of a single purpose, the Spanish fleet was in Cadiz, and the French fleet was in Brest, and while the Grand Fleet lay between them, not only could they not unite without the risk of being engaged separately beforehand, but they could not detach any ships to sail to the West Indies, or the American coast, where Rodney and Hood had a moral, though not a numerical, superiority. So the relief of Gibraltar had to wait on the necessity to keep the Grand Fleet in home waters. Through January and February the Fleet lay in the Channel and the garrison and people of Gibraltar starved, and there seems to be no reason connected with the conduct of the war why this state of affairs should not have persisted longer. What persuaded the Government to send Darby and the Grand Fleet to the Mediterranean was not the few outspoken words they received from General Eliott, nor the determination to save the Rock at all costs, but the pressure brought to bear by the merchants of London, who insisted that the Grand Fleet should be used to escort their trading ships, some three hundred of them, bound for the East and West Indies, which could not wait any longer. When the Fleet finally sailed on 13 March, Walpole was indignant:

> The grand fleet which had been so long preparing sailed this week to relieve Gibraltar, twenty-eight ships-of-the-line &c. This was a most desperate stroke; as large a French fleet was at Brest, and another Spanish as large at Cadiz. If they joined or enclosed ours, the odds were great; if they did not, the Channel was open to the French: we had no ships at home, nor a camp formed; and Portsmouth, Plymouth again, Newcastle, and many other parts of the island, were exposed to invasion.

As it was, Darby was delayed off the coast of Ireland, waiting for the ninety-seven victuallers with supplies for Gibraltar, which were coming from Cork. He narrowly missed the French fleet under the Comte de Grasse, which sailed from Brest on the 22 March headed for the West Indies. The French were more concerned with their own affairs in that area than with the Spanish attempt to recapture the Rock. Having collected the victuallers, Darby returned to the Channel to shepherd the merchant fleets out to the open sea, before proceeding to the Straits. There was still the Spanish fleet. The French ambassador in Madrid, M. de Montmorin, wrote to the Comte de Vergennes: 'The Spanish fleet returned to Cadiz on the 27th. I must confess I am more easy knowing it to be there than if it was in the Straits.' Don Luis de Cordova lived not to fight another day. But the Spaniards were very angry with the French, claiming that they had again betrayed them. Darby and the Fleet arrived at the mouth of the Straits on 11 April, and Captain Trollop in the *Kite* sped ahead into Gibraltar.

Everyone became very wise after this event, exactly seven months after, when the French fleet under de Grasse was the decisive factor in the surrender of Cornwallis and his army at Yorktown. The extreme view was expressed by John Sinclair in his pamphlet 'The Propriety of Retaining Gibraltar Impartially Considered' published in 1783: 'The author indeed is of the opinion that the possession of

America has been sacrificed to the retention of Gibraltar.' This view was certainly current at the time, and was reported in the *Annual Register* (1782). However, it hardly bears examination, as there was no guarantee that the Brest fleet would sail, and no certainty that it could have been intercepted, and had the relief been delayed, not only would Gibraltar have been lost, but its loss would have released Spanish men and ships to undertake more active measures in the West, so ensuring the loss of America, and possibly Jamaica as well. However, the best argument, or at least the one that carried the most weight, was that the detention of the outward-bound convoys to the Indies would have been destructive to commerce, and ruinous to the merchants of the City of London. And it was these gentlemen the garrison should have cheered, when Captain Trollop answered, 'From the Fleet.'

CHAPTER IX

Damnation to the Enemy!

NOBODY in Gibraltar went to bed that night. As the sky began to lighten on the morning of Thursday, 12 April 1781, the Line Wall was crowded with onlookers from Orange's to the South Bastion. Merchant and fisherman, rich and poor, the few fat and the many thin, madam and missus, trooper and serjeant, drummer and ensign captain and colonel, were all as one in their joyful anticipation of seeing the British flag once more flying in the Straits. The Governor and General Boyd were riding down towards the New Mole to greet the ships' captains and supervise the 500 men who were to unload the stores there and in Rosia and Camp Bays. The invalids in the Naval Hospital were gazing out of the windows to the west, and the only eyes not strained in that direction belonged to the guards and gunners on duty on the North Front. At first, there was nothing to see in the Gut but a thick roll of white mist. Captain Drinkwater was there:

> As the sun, however, became more powerful, the fog gradually rose, like the curtain of a vast theatre, discovering to the anxious Garrison one of the most beautiful and pleasing scenes it is possible to conceive. The Convoy, consisting of near a hundred vessels, were in a compact body, led by several men of war: their sails just enough filled for steerage, whilst the majority of the line-of-battle ships lay-to under the Barbary shore, having orders not to enter the Bay, lest the Enemy should molest them with their fire-ships. The extasies of the Inhabitants at this grand and exhilerating sight are not to be described. Their expressions of joy far exceeded their former exultations.

As the first ships approached the Bay, fifteen enemy gun-boats rowed out from Algeciras and, when they reached Cabrita, opened fire, supported by the battery on the Point. Almost contemptuously, a ship-of-the-line and two frigates swung towards them, and after a few shots, compelled them to turn and row for the shore. As the British warships came on, the crews of the gun-boats jumped out and ran to hide among the rocks, leaving their craft empty, and at the mercy of the Navy. The ships swept past in a lordly manner, disdaining to destroy the 'bum-boats', as they called them, much to the later regret of the garrison, who were to learn how much damage the 'bum-boats' could do. But now there were no regrets. The British flag flew magnificently over the Bay, and at 10.45 a.m. the first of the victuallers dropped anchor off the New Mole.

In the meantime those on guard on the North Front had watched an unusual activity in the enemy's forts and batteries. The guns were elevated, and the long sponges and rammers could be seen projecting above the ramparts. Any doubts they may have had of the enemy's intentions were violently dispelled when, at the precise moment the leading ships of the convoy dropped anchor, the Spaniards opened fire.

At first the garrison could not believe it. For eighteen months they had lived under the threat of bombardment, and now it was happening. The first cannonballs and shells crashed against the Rock, and fell like hail into the town, beating down roofs and walls, maiming and killing those unfortunate enough to be in their paths. For a brief moment the smiles stayed fixed on their faces, though their hearts had stopped. Then they beat alarm, panic and confusion. Stricken with fear, the townspeople struggled to fly to the south, whilst at the same time the soldiers fought to get to their alarm-posts and obey the call to arms being drummed out from every quarter. Mrs Upton was caught up in it:

> Our house was one of the nearest to the Spanish lines. I seized my children and ran with them towards Montague's Bastion, which I knew was bomb-proof. An officer of the 58th Regiment met me saying 'For God's sake Madam. Where are you going? Do not you know that you are going nearer to the enemy's fire? Stoop with your children under this covered way.' Six and twenty pounders without number went over my head.

It was in these first few minutes that most of the casualties occurred that day. Mr Ancell noted: 'A shell which exploded in the Prince's

lines wounded an officer and tore the Serjeant's hand off on duty
there . . . three men killed in King's lines; one killed at Southport by
a piece of a shell that burst in the air. Several houses are on fire.'
Those inhabitants unwise enough to return to their houses also
suffered, but most, realizing the uselessness of locking doors when
cannonballs were breaking down the walls, fled out of Southport and
across the Red Sands to the rocks behind the South Barracks, where
they could not see the town, but where, from the continuous roar of
explosions, they could guess what havoc was being wreaked on their
property and possessions. A small ship was sunk by the watering-
tanks, but the New Mole and the Bays were beyond the range of the
Spanish guns, and the remainder of the convoy anchored off these
places, waiting to be unloaded.

At the first salvo General Eliott wheeled his horse round and
galloped back to the town to the Grand Battery where he could
command the garrison in the event of an assault. General Boyd went
to the King's Bastion to prepare the troops there for the same contin-
gency. But there was no assault, nor, once the men were under
cover, many more casualties. The enemy were firing blindly at the
town, and were also sighting on the British batteries, which had
opened on them from the first shot. The barrage was maintained at
a tremendous rate, as if to make up for the months of inactivity,
until shortly after one o'clock it began to slacken, and then stopped
altogether. The officers in the batteries peered out through the
embrasures to discover the reason for the sudden cessation. In the
afternoon sun they saw the Spanish artillerymen sitting back, eating,
smoking, and even sleeping. They were taking their siesta.

In the welcome pause allowed by this inviolable Spanish custom
the garrison were able to estimate the number of guns that the enemy
had brought into action. The Black Battery, behind Fort St Philip,
mounted 14 guns, with 12 bearing on the garrison. Fort St Philip itself
mounted 27 guns, 11 bearing on the garrison. The Infanta's Battery,
to the east of the fort, mounted 7 guns. Next to the Infanta's, the
Prince's and Princess's Batteries mounted 14 guns each. Fort St
Barbara mounted 23 guns, but only 6 bore on the garrison. In
positions between these gun batteries, and in the St Carlos Battery
(which the British called the Mill Battery) the enemy had some 50
mortars, of 13-inch calibre, all of which bore on the garrison. This

formidable array of artillery, comprising 114 heavy pieces, had hurled several thousand cannonballs and shells into the town and at the batteries on the heights above, with devastating effect on the first, but fortunately little on the second. The inhabitants, who took advantage of the respite to hurry back to collect what valuables and possessions they could carry away, found the streets littered with cannonballs and the fragments of shells, and the bricks, slates, windows and doors of shattered buildings. And through the gaping holes torn in the walls of the merchants' store-houses they could see heaps of provisions that had been denied them and kept back to force prices as high as possible. The people had no time except to wonder, and then hurry back to what shelter they could find in the south. The merchants collected what they could, but balanced against their own lives, these goods, which had weighed so heavy against the lives of their neighbours and protectors, were light, indeed, and were left to the Spanish bombs.

The barrage started again at 5 p.m. and continued, without a break, throughout the night. Those who had found cover, like Mrs Upton in Montague's Bastion, stayed under it:

> This was no time for the indulgency of pride, distinction, or even delicacy. The soldiers who were off duty, in their blunt, honest way, endeavoured to cheer my spirits saying: 'Never fear madam, if the d— Dons fire to eternity they will never take the old rock nor the good souls that are upon it.' I admired their courage, but could not eat any dinner with them agreeable to their kind invitation.

That evening Ensign Upton arrived at the Bastion with a curtain, which he hung round one of the soldiers' beds. Mrs Upton particularly remembered 'the disagreeableness of lying near an hundred private soldiers'. Mrs Green, and all the journalists of the siege, left the pages for these early days of the bombardment blank, or jotted brief notes about the firing and unloading. In retrospect, particularly when the pages were being prepared for publication, they expanded, and Mr Ancell excelled himself. Here he is on Friday 13th:

> One minute a shot batters a house about your ears, and the next a shell drops at your feet; here you lie prostrate, waiting the mercy of the explosion: If you escape unhurt, you are perfectly stunned, and almost suffocated with an intollerable stench of powder and composition: On

every hand slaughtered objects lie before you, harrowing up the tender feelings of the soul; one loses an arm or leg, another cut through the body, a third has his head smashed, and a fourth is blown to pieces, with the bursting of a shell. Thus in a moment do they launch into eternity, probably without time to utter the ejaculation, 'God be merciful to me.'

A detachment is ordered to march, to reinforce a part of the works considered too weak for a strong attack, or to relieve another who have stood twenty-four hours facing an inveterate foe; probably before they reach the post, my comrade falls by my side, and with a tender regret gazes on me, while I push forward to the battery or guard, and leave him to groan out his last accents, weltering in blood!

A husband is called upon for duty, the service demands his immediate presence, nor dare he stay to take his farewell, by imprinting an affectionate kiss; the thundering Mars, envious of his felicity, raises the javelin for destruction, and levels his commiserating partner, while he is absent; not satisfied with lopping off so material a branch of happiness, but extends his decisive commands over the tender offspring. On his return (O sensibility) what a ravaging scene is presented to his view! let imagination conceive; a wife that soothed his every uneasiness, and softened the rigours of his fate, is alas! no more—His dear beloved children that prattled with a thousand innocent and engaging smiles, and lisped forth their duteous accents, that tended to dissipate the heart corroding cares of life, and promising to be a comfort in his aged days, are now reduced to a lifeless lump of clay. Will not his heart break forth in exclamation, 'Oh! my beloved wife—my charming Harry, my amiable Polly; not suffered to kiss those lips while warm, nor to press you to a bosom to which you was ever dear.'

In fact, the numbers of killed and wounded amongst the garrison were remarkably few compared to the number of balls and shells falling around them. The Governor's list from 12–19 April gave 3 Serjeants and 20 Rank and File killed, and 3 Officers, 5 Serjeants, 1 Drummer and 69 Rank and File wounded. The enemy's rate of fire was computed variously to be between 3,000 and 5,000 shots every twenty-four hours. On this Friday, when it was evident that the bombardment was not to be followed by an assault, another 500 men were sent south to assist with the unloading, whilst 150 more were detailed to carry powder and balls up to the magazines on the hill, which were becoming exhausted by the high rate of fire maintained by the gunners. At the same time the sick in the town were conveyed to the Naval Hospital. As parties of men moved through the town going about these duties, they could not help seeing the private stores of the merchants, the butts of wine and spirits in the cellars of the wine-shops, the terrified chickens and pigs that had escaped from their pens, revealed by the collapsing walls of the houses, and many determined to return that night to take advantage of this profusion. They remembered the long months of famine, when the same merchants had, with helpless shrugs doled out meagre portions of these same provisions for prices that would have bought ten times the amount elsewhere, and determined to take their revenge.

Saturday 14th, and if some men came on duty unsteady, and with their pouches and pockets bulging, the officers looked the other way. The enemy fire continued unabated, and their gunners were firing accurately at the batteries, their shots reaching Green's Lodge, and even as high as the Royal Battery, which was only a little way below the Rock Gun. The Governor ordered the garrison guns on the hill to hold their fire and to be withdrawn from their embrasures to minimize the damage of the enemy's barrage, and perhaps rid them of his attention. General Eliott was fortunate not to be standing by his study window when a shell exploded outside shattering it. In the south the unloading continued at a tremendous pace, and the stores were piled up where they were landed. Admiral Darby had orders to sail for the Channel with the first east wind, and the victuallers were anxious to return with him. The soldiers and sailors, working incessantly, managed to unload ten ships a day. The enemy's gun-boats made an attempt to attack the ships at anchor, but were easily driven off by the Navy, who again disdained to pursue them. The inhabitants, who had now spent two nights in the open, were busy erecting what shelters they could on the site of New Jerusalem, and were issued with tents from the garrison stores. Many of them were bargaining with the ship's captains for a passage to Great Britain when the convoy would leave. In the town, few left the cover of the casemates and bomb-proofs. There was scarcely any order amongst the regiments, as, in the confusion of the first attack, men had run for the nearest shelter, and now they were reluctant to move. The Governor ordered the guards to change during the afternoon, when the Spaniards took their rest,

and during these hours the officers managed to assemble their men
into their proper quarters; for the moment, the families who had
taken refuge with the troops were left where they were, though Mrs
Upton and her children were moved from Montague's Bastion to
King's Bastion. She did not appreciate the change: 'The room I
was put in smelt very disagreeably: I enquired the cause and was
told a man was killed in it, not an hour before, by a ball which
entered in at a hole over the door.' Many enemy shells had fallen
without exploding, and the Garrison Orders for the 14th record the
name of the brave man who had to deal with them: 'The Regiments
to send all Blind Shells and Shott that fall near their quarters to the
Laboratory and delivered to Serjeant Gribble.' So far, the only
soldiers who had ventured from their shelters into the town had been
those whose duty had led them through the streets, and who had
returned to loot the previous night. This evening, however, the
Spaniards started to fire incendiary shells, which soon started fires
near the Spanish Church, and each regiment sent a detachment in
to help put out the flames. With the shells dropping about them
revealing more and more of the hidden food stores, and opening the
wine-shops so that the liquor spilled out and ran down the gutters,
discipline was forgotten, the fires were left to burn, and the troops
split up into bands, looting, and drinking, and barricading themselves in holes and cellars. Some were caught and dragged out by
their officers, but, the candle not being thought worth the risk, most
were left to riot among the exploding shells, in a burst of luxuriance.

The town is deserted by all but the soldiery, who now are left to commence merchants, wine-men, butchers, bakers &c. Here a shell blows
off the roof of a wine-house, the troops haste to partake of the consuming
spoil, regardless of life or limb, they drink briskly round, 'Destruction to
the enemy.' Here are parties, boiling, baking, roasting, frying, &c.
Turkeys, ducks, geese, and fowls, become the diet of those, who some
days ago were eagerly soliciting a hard crust of bread—Every pig they
meet, receives a ball or bayonet, and this is performed with an unconcern and calmness scarce to be credited, amidst a heavy fire, disregard-
ing the supreme jurisdiction of the mighty God of War. Thus they roll
in plenty at the hazard of their lives, nor can the precautions and
vigilance of the officers prevent them from profusely enjoying the
varieties of a town once flourishing and peopled, brilliant in commercial

and military affairs: From Water-port to South-port houses are blazing, and shot battering down those that will not burn.

So wrote Mr Ancell. In Captain Drinkwater's account, he reveals the sympathy that the officers had for their men, after all, they had endured the same hardships, and been forced to pay the merchants the same exorbitant prices.

It did not appear through all their intemperance, that these irregularities arose from any cause so much as a spirit of revenge against the merchants. A great quantity of liquor &c. was wantonly destroyed, and, in some cases, incredible profusion prevailed. Among other instances of caprice and extravagance, I recollect that of roasting a pig by a fire made of cinnamon.

The officers were less pleased when their men failed to appear the next morning. Mrs Upton woke up on Sunday the 15th: 'The first object I beheld in the morning was a man lying dead by the door. He died, I am told, of intoxication.' Captain Spilsbury noted: 'Such a scene of drunkenness, debauchery and destruction was hardly ever seen before.' And in General Boyd's Log Book, an account of the siege kept for the General by his clerk, which starts on 12 April, there is this wonderful entry for the 15th:

This day the Emissarys of Wickedness seems to sport with great wantonness, Robery, Moroding, Housebreaking and shoplifting by the Soldiery (a scene never known to be practic'd by the besieged only by the besiegers after a storm who are generally allowed a small space of time to plunder) enforced by Drunkenness: that it appears Death is not regarded and that plunder and all sorts of debauchery are the chief Ensigns of Glory and Fame by the Commonality.

How the 'commonality' felt appears in a letter from a soldier, who 'took a cheerful Glass and with a hearty zeal for the King and Country, drank "Damnation to the Enemy", swearing with the utmost unconcern fire away ye Buggers'. Never was there such a loyal mutiny as that of the men of the Gibraltar garrison who strayed into the ruins of the town, and were reluctant to come out again.

When the Spanish guns stopped firing at one o'clock on Sunday afternoon the Governor issued orders for the regiments to change their quarters. The Hanoverian brigade, apart from the unloading party and the Artillery the most sober men on the Rock, were moved to the bomb-proofs under the Grand Battery. The flank companies of the 12th, 39th and 56th Regiments were ordered to occupy Montague's Bastion, the Galley House, and the rooms in Waterport; the remainder of these regiments were sent to the south to encamp behind the South Barracks. The 72nd Regiment was allotted the King's Bastion. The 58th and the 73rd Regiments were quartered in the South Barracks. These dispositions were made so that the best troops were left in the town, and those whose discipline was suspect were moved south out of temptation. The only drawback was that many men were too drunk to quit their hide-outs and others refused to do so; also, there was nothing to stop a man slipping out of his quarters at night in search of loot. In an attempt to put an end to the debauch, a party of officers went into the town armed with axes and began to stave in barrels and crates, so that the streets ran with wine and brandy and tea and sugar and flour in a waste that at any other time would have been madness. There were still casualties. Mr Ancell recorded them faithfully:

> A corporal had his head shot off as he was calling from a window to a man in the street. A soldier was so miserably torn by a shell that he could not be known only by his dress. A Genoese youth, endowed with every grace and amiable qualification, and on the point of nuptial celebration, was unfortunately killed, to the irremovable grief of his enamoratto. A shot killed two soldiers, one of whom was brushing his shoes for guard.

The unloading of the convoy was carried on day and night. As soon as the Governor knew of Admiral Darby's orders to sail at the first opportunity, he wrote asking him not to leave the victuallers at the mercy of the gun-boats. The Admiral replied, 'You must be very sensible in what situation everyone is till the return of the squadron', but offered to leave two frigates and two cutters if the wind changed before the unloading was completed. General Eliott inspired considerable respect in Admiral Darby, as he had in Admiral Rodney, and when he asked for as much powder as the Fleet could spare to be landed for the use of the garrison (the Government had apparently forgotten this requirement) the Admiral replied:

> It is the noble defence you are preparing to make which has induced me to stretch this supply to the utmost . . . happy am I in doing every-

thing in my power for the Service of the Garrison on which are fixed the Eyes of the whole World.

Two thousand two hundred and eighty barrels of powder were collected from the warships much to the gratification of the Governor, whose decision to stop firing from the hill batteries was partly made as an economy in powder.

On the 16th the gun-boats came again and tried to attack the unloading parties at the New Mole, but they were soon driven off by the warships. The enemy were firing from the land as much as ever, and General Eliott narrowly escaped when a shell landed on Columbia's Battery, from where he was observing them. As all the officers' quarters in the town had been destroyed, the gentlemen now lived in barracks with their men, and this contributed considerably to the restoration of order. The women and children were now moved out of the town, and sent south. Mrs Upton was delighted, as the King's Bastion 'was so crowded with soldiers it was impossible to procure either a bed or platform', though later she was to regret changing this shelter, which was at least bomb-proof, for a tent in 'Captain D—t's garden'. She left the town in the middle of the bombardment, 'My husband carried little Charlotte, while my son Jack ran by my side', and never returned to it. The next day the enemy gunners performed the prodigious feat of hitting the Rock Gun, some 1,400 feet above them. The fleet had brought news of promotions in the garrison, and three Colonels, Ross, Green and Picton, were appointed Brigadiers. It was on this day that the Spanish Church, which had survived the capture and earlier sieges of the Rock, caught fire. The Lieutenant-Governor, General Boyd, was at hand, and directed the salvage of 300 barrels of flour stored there. Captain Drinkwater mentions the fate of these barrels:

> Many casks of flour were brought into the King's Bastion, and piled as temporary traverses before the doors of the southern casemates, in which several persons had been killed and wounded in bed. These traverses, however, did not continue long; for the men, when the spoils in the town became scarce, considered those barrels, which the Enemy's shot had pierced, as lawful prizes. The contents were soon scooped out and fried into pancakes, a dish which they were very expert at cooking; and the upper casks, wanting support from below, gave way, and the whole came to the ground.

E

The unloading of the victuallers had been carried on so expeditiously that, by 18 April, only six days after the convoy had arrived, the majority of them were ready to sail. Several merchantmen, which had sailed with the fleet in the hope that their cargoes would fetch a good price in Gibraltar, could find no purchasers among the merchants on the Rock and lay in the Bay waiting to return to England having wasted their journey. The Gibraltar merchants were more concerned with leaving the desolation of their homes and stores than with bringing in more goods to be destroyed by the bombardment or pilfered by the troops. This day the Navy revised their opinion of the 'bum-boats', which scored several hits on the warships before speeding back to the shelter of Algeciras. The daring raids of the gun-boats, and their success, raised some criticism in Parliament of Admiral Darby when he returned, one member suggesting that it was the superior quality of the Spanish gunpowder that enabled their boats to lie out of range of the British ships and to fire at them with impunity. The Admiral replied:

> That if such a fact existed he made no doubt it would have been reported to him. Sir John Ross had performed the service in the Bay of Gibraltar, but had not made any complaint of the quality of the powder. No argument could be drawn from the fact of the gun-boats reaching our frigates; each of them carried a very long gun, an 18- or 24-pounder, and it was the length of the gun, not the superior quality of the powder, which enabled their shot to take effect. Our guns were shorter and would not carry so far. The gun-boats in a calm operated against our frigates by means of their oars and were secure from pursuit; but as soon as a breeze sprung up, they were easily beat off.

On 20 April Admiral Darby notified the Governor of his intention to sail that day. The moment the news spread through the garrison, the officers' families who had procured passages home hurried to the New Mole to join the crowds of Jews and the Genoese, some of whom had given their life's savings to the ships' captains to take them away from the Rock. There is no record of how many sailed, but, as the writer of Boyd's Log Book remarked, 'they flock off by all Vessells that sails from hence as so many disturbed Swarms of Bees', and when the Spaniards eventually captured two of the vessels they found 141 of these unlucky people aboard them. It might therefore be reasonable to assume that at least half the population left Gibraltar, leaving little more than a thousand in the sparse shelter of the rocks to the south. There had not been time to unload the colliers which had sailed with the fleet and these were scuttled by the New Mole, and some transports which carried ordnance were brought inside a boom at the same place. By six o'clock in the evening the Fleet was under way, and the gun-boats came out to salute them with a few parting shots. In General Eliott's dispatch to Lord Hillsborough there was no mention of the riotous behaviour of his troops, and he concluded: 'We are not likely to want anything till this attempt of the Enemy's takes some certain direction.'

CHAPTER X

These infernal spit-fires

THE town was destroyed. The streets were barely discernible under
the rubble, dust and smouldering timbers. The gutted craters of
houses shook under the continual bombardment, which, now the
Fleet had gone, seemed to be intensified. There was scarcely a building recognizable between the Grand Battery and Southport, except
the Convent and the Lieutenant-Governor's house, which he refused
to quit. These last two buildings were kept constantly in repair,
though General Boyd spent most of his time in the King's Bastion,
and General Eliott eventually had a tent pitched beyond the Red
Sands; both used to sleep in their houses. Yet, the town was full of
soldiers. Drunk soldiers, dead soldiers, but above all, soldiers looking
for something to steal. The disposition of the regiments had been
changed, and those who had spent the first week of the bombardment
in the south unloading the convoy, were now making up for lost time.
The riotous jollity of the early days was gone, replaced by a desperate
determination to find something of value before everything was
pounded into dust by the Spanish Coopers (as the garrison called the
shells that fell around them). Men fought over a trinket, and those
who could find nothing in the town, began to pilfer the Government
Stores in the Victualling Office.

A Soldier for want of Plunder, swore to his comrade that he'd have
the first thing that offer'd in order to keep his hand in practice, so
went in search, and at last he found the skeleton of a French Lady
the property of a Surgeon in the Garrison, which he took off until
stopt by our Guard, when the Skeleton found refuge until an opportunity served to send her to the owner and the Soldier got clear.

Boyd's Log Book recorded this story. And in a letter to Lord Amherst, which must have cost him much to write, General Eliott at last gave his account of the sack of Gibraltar.

May 7th 1781.

My Lord,

I must not conceal from you the scandalous irregularity of the British Regiments composing this Garrison ever since the Enemy opened his Batteries; except Rapes and Murders, there is no one crime but what they have been repeatedly guilty of and that in the most daring manner: altho' many have been tried and convicted before General Courts Martial of the most henious offences yet only one has been condemned to death, notwithstanding I have strictly informed them to proceed with vigour in consideration of the circumstances we are in: but I have not been able to gain the least ground neither in their judicial proceedings nor by urging the officers to double their diligence and attention to Military Oeconomy: things are so bad that not a sentinel at his post but will connive at and assist in robbing even The Kings' Stores under his charge, they are constantly detected, but scarce ever receive adequate punishment.

I must declare that the Hanoverians have committed no public outrage and I believe but few private, having maintained apparent good order despight of the most dissolute examples.

I have no reason to suspect that any care is wanting at the Post next the Enemy; the soldier is wakeful when the fumes of liquor are evaporated.

On 26 April the General had issued this Garrison Order: 'Any soldier found sleeping on his Post or taken plundering will if convicted be immediately executed' and on 4 May there is this entry in the Orders:

The criminal John Wild of the 58th Regiment to be executed at guard mounting tomorrow at the storehouse where he committed the robbery with a label on his [body] on which is to be wrote the word *Plunderer*, the body to remain hanging until sunset when it is to be taken down and buried by a party of the Regiment, all the 58th Regiment not on duty to attend the execution and form in front of the Guards.

Unfortunately this example did not deter the looters sufficiently, as, in any event, they risked their lives by going into the town.

The bombardment was also doing considerable damage to the batteries at Willis's and the stones dislodged by the constant hammering of missiles against the Rock fell into the lines below. The Castle was hit many times, but the shots rebounded from its massive walls like tennis balls. Whilst parties of engineers were detailed to repair the batteries and clear the lines, another party had a most important duty to perform on 21 April. The garrison flagstaff on the Grand Battery, a permanent temptation to the enemy artillery, was knocked down, but it was only minutes later that the colours, more glorious for being tattered, were nailed to the stump. However, it was not possible for the enemy to maintain the high rate of fire. Some of their guns were damaged, and the timbers beneath them were shaken and dislodged by the constant jarring. The garrison noted about this time that the number of shots was reduced to about a thousand a day, which might have been expected to provide some relief. As was the manner of the day, as one side slackened its fire, so the other increased its fire, and the Governor ordered the hill batteries to open up whenever they saw the enemy's work parties attempting to make repairs on their batteries.

There was no relief as the gun-boats, which could not now be prevented from lying off the Rock for as long as they wished, came over on 23 April and fired 300 times at the heaps of stores and the soldiers' tents in the south. Mrs Upton wrote: 'A woman, whose tent was a little below mine, was cut in two as she was drawing on her stockings. These infernal spit-fires can attack any quarter of the Garrison as they please.' To make matters worse for those under canvas, the weather at the end of April and beginning of May was atrocious, with heavy rains that poured down the side of the Rock, sweeping away the small banks of earth, and filling the ditches the men had made to protect their tents, and drenching the occupants and their bedding and clothing. As the troops were on duty often two nights out of three, there was little sleep for those who returned to find their beds no more than muddy puddles. They, and the families and townspeople who were existing in a group of tents above the Naval Hospital erected by Major Hardy and hence called Hardy Town (though the garrison called it Cowards' Retreat or the Female Camp), were less protected under these circumstances than the stores, which the Governor had ordered to be covered by the sails of the colliers sunk by the New Mole.

On 27 April the provisions that the Governor had requested from General Murray in Minorca arrived: twenty-five sail, escorted by the

Brilliant, Enterprise and *Minorca* frigates, the *Fortune* sloop, and accompanied by three privateers. On his arrival Captain Curtis of the *Brilliant* succeeded Captain Leslie as naval commander in the Bay. Another officer to join the garrison at this time (he arrived with Darby's fleet) was Lieutenant Koehler of the Royal Artillery, at the start of his unusually chequered career.

Admiral Barcello had temporarily abandoned the blockade of Gibraltar. There was no point in maintaining it, with stores for two years landed on the Rock from the convoy, and a further 1,000 tons from Minorca. Instead, he concentrated on harassing the encampments in the south with his gun-boats, and mortar-boats, of which he now had a squadron of twenty or more. General Alvarez persisted with the bombardment of the town, though there was little purpose in it. A few men of the garrison were wounded each day, and, as they became accustomed to the firing, and careless or contemptuous of it, the numbers increased. The writer of Boyd's Log Book was fascinated by the occasional meetings of cannonballs and men, and recorded them with gusto: 'Two men killed one of which was in the office easing Nature when a Ball took off his head and left His Body, the only remains to finish Nature's cause.' Men were close to nature, and therefore to death, in the eighteenth century. An execution was as good as a play. The fate of unfortunates, like Lieutenant Cunningham of the 39th Regiment who walked about for a fortnight after having been struck by a shell splinter and suddenly fell dead on Waterport Guard, was of consuming interest. The journals are filled with arms, legs, heads and other parts of the human anatomy (Boyd's Log Book: 'A canon ball shot him through the middle and dash'd his privities against the wall'), so that there hardly seemed enough in the garrison to go round. In fact the casualties from the opening of the enemy guns to 4 June, when the barrage had slackened to about five hundred shots a day, were 1 officer, 7 serjeants, 1 corporal, 1 drummer and 53 privates, dead or died of wounds, and 8 officers, 1 surgeon, 1 surgeon's mate, 16 serjeants, 15 corporals, 5 drummers and 201 privates wounded. As the enemy had by this time expended an estimated 56,760 cannonballs and 20,134 shells, they had a poor return for their efforts. Not every casualty was caused by enemy action:

A dead shell fell on Landport cover'd way, a Gentleman on that duty desirous to see what the shell contained ordered one of the Artillery to break it, who took up a cannon ball and struck it with all his force until at last the Shell being roused up . . . exploded.

The story is from Boyd's Log Book. There were many blind shells, which perhaps explains the garrison's relatively few losses, and when these had been opened by Serjeant Gribble, less forcibly, they were found to contain sand mixed with the powder, and the garrison were duly thankful to the thief in the enemy's laboratory.

On 2 May two small boats arrived from Algiers without opposition, and unloaded their cargoes of sheep, wine and brandy. A strong guard was put on the last two items. That evening a lucky shot from the garrison exploded the magazine in the St Carlos Battery (the Mill Battery) and put it out of action for several days.

Fires continued to break out in the town, spreading among the timbers of the ruined houses, and on the 6th the Governor ordered that any materials of this nature not removed out of range of the Spanish guns were to be confiscated. The house-owners resented this order, suspecting that it would be interpreted as an official licence to loot, and complained about it bitterly after the siege. There is no record that anything was salvaged, and it was soon followed by another order forbidding the removal of any property from the town.

Those inhabitants who remained were leading a very miserable existence in Hardy Town. They had little enough shelter from the thunderstorms that hung about the Rock, and they were driven from it almost every night by the visits of the gun-boats. The garrison tended to think their fate a cruel, but just, retribution for their greed. Boyd's Log Book expressed this view:

> The Spanish shells discovered many private and valuable stores which were hoarded up by Jews and Genueses in order to mass their fortunes by extortion; but their little alls are now distroyed and themselves as lost sheep obliged to brooze upon the Rocks under the shelter of hutts, caves, cliffs and tents at a place the Military call Cowards retreat, which lies out of the line of land-fire: But when the Gun-boats appear, it is shocking to behold them half-naked running to Cracks and Corners to save their lives, such is the disolation of these unhappy inhabitants.

Their 'disolation' was increased on the 7th when, after the garrison had fired some four hundred times at the gun-boats without hitting them once, General Eliott was angry:

There would be no end of expending ammunition, if we fired every time they came, and while they were at so great a distance: in future no notice to be taken of the gun-boats, unless they approached within the distance of grape.

Captain Drinkwater was near enough to hear him say it. The General was perturbed about the gun-boats. He wrote to Lord Hillsborough: 'Till lately I did not conceive the mischief our situation unavoidably exposed us to whilst the Enemy is at liberty to cannonade and bombard us with impunity from the Bay. Our whole rock is open to their random fire.'

On 12 May the gun-boats, accompanied by mortar-boats, came as usual a little after midnight. Some of their shots went over the Rock, so they must have approached near the shore, but the garrison guns stayed silent. After that, they attacked every night, when the weather was calm. Mrs Upton remembered:

> Every time the gun boats came I dragged my poor children out of bed and stood leaning with them against a rock. The third night I was here, a ball struck the rock against which I leaned and covered us with dirt and stones! In a few minutes after, a shell burst so near us, I had scarcely time to run out of the way.

Worse was to come. On 23 May,

> About one o'clock in the morning, our old disturbers the gun-boats began to fire upon us. I wrapped a blanket about myself and children, and ran to the side of a rock.
>
> They had the temerity to advance so near, that the people in our ships could hear them say, Guarda Angloise . . . Take care, English!
>
> Mrs Tourale, a handsome and agreeable lady, was blown almost to atoms! Nothing was found of her but one arm. Her brother who sat by her, and his clerk, both shared the same fate.

This was Mr Israel, a Jew who was respected by the garrison. In all, seven people were killed and thirteen wounded that night. There was considerable resentment that the gun-boats had been allowed to approach so close to the shore without being fired on, and the Governor revoked his previous order. Many families, who had thought that they would be safe in the south, now decided to leave Gibraltar at the first opportunity, and on 27 May, when seventeen of the ordnance ships and transports left behind by Admiral Darby sailed for England escorted by the *Enterprise,* they took passages on them. Mrs Upton and her children were among them.

In the meantime the Spaniards kept up the barrage from the isthmus. There had been two deserters from the garrison: one was shot dead by a sentry, but the other reached the Spanish Lines. As a result of the information he gave the enemy, they lessened their fire on the town, and began to batter the positions on the North Front. Their gunners were now so practised that they succeeded in hitting the Rock Gun several times. The rioters in the town took this opportunity for a peculiar form of amusement. Captain Drinkwater described the scene:

> When the soldiers were engaged in a succession of irregularities, a party of them assembled in the Spanish Church, to carouse and be merry. In the midst of their jollity, the image of the Virgin Mary was observed in the ruins by one of the party, who instantly proposed, as a piece of fun, to place her Ladyship in the whirligig. The scheme seemed to meet with general approbation, till one, wiser than the rest, stopped them with a remark, that it would ill become them, as military men, and particularly Englishmen, to punish any person without a trial. A court martial consequently sat, with mock ceremony; and her Ladyship was found guilty of drunkenness, debauchery, and other high crimes, and condemned to the whirligig, whither she was immediately carried in procession. The Governor (who, notwithstanding the firing, regularly attended the parade) at guard-mounting discovered the poor Virgin in confinement; but expressed his disapprobation of the action, and ordered her instantly to be removed to the White convent, where by the bye, she was by no means exempt from further insult and disgrace.

The whirligig on the Grand Parade was a wooden machine resembling a large bird-cage which could be revolved. It was used for the punishment of 'Lewd Women guilty of capital Crimes' (Boyd's Log Book).

There was a lot of gossip amongst the soldiers who went on guard on the North Front about the possibility of an assault from the land. A Walloon deserter had said that an attack was being planned on Landport and the Red Sands, and the news soon spread round the garrison. The advance guards at Forbes and Bayside barriers had been withdrawn when the bombardment commenced, and there was considerable excitement when Mr Ancell reported this story on 21 May:

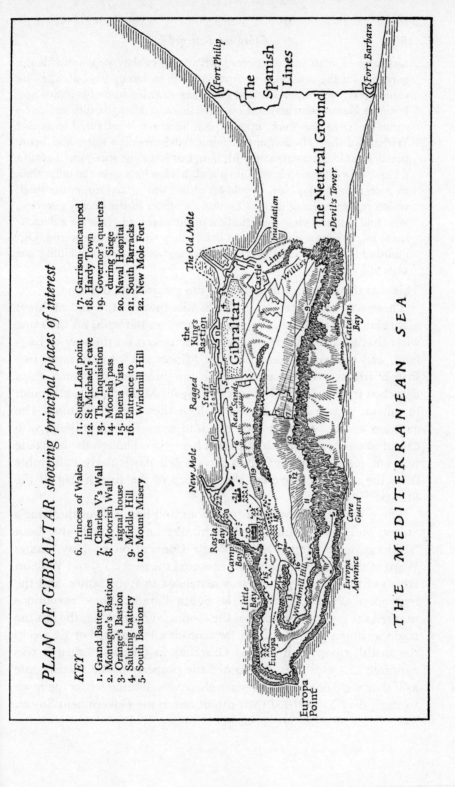

PLAN OF GIBRALTAR *showing principal places of interest*

KEY

1. Grand Battery
2. Montague's Bastion
3. Orange's Bastion
4. Saluting battery
5. South Bastion
6. Princess of Wales lines
7. Charles V's Wall
8. Moorish Wall signal house
9. Middle Hill
10. Mount Misery
11. Sugar Loaf point
12. St Michael's cave
13. The Inquisition
14. Moorish pass
15. Buena Vista
16. Entrance to Windmill Hill
17. Garrison encamped
18. Hardy Town
19. Governor's quarters during Siege
20. Naval Hospital
21. South Barracks
22. New Mole Fort

Last night a man was discovered advancing in slow steps towards the garrison, on the road leading from Bayside to Landport, but when he came pretty near the advanced guard, he crawled upon his hands and knees; a Hanoverian serjeant on duty there, challenged him before he came as far as the work, upon which he made a retreat. Lieutenant Witham of the 58th Regiment, immediately made a sally, and being pretty nimble, soon came up with him, but just as he was going to make a blow, he unfortunately fell into a shell hole, which gave the other time to push thro' to Bay-side. A gold laced hat was picked up on the road, which makes us imagine that he was an officer in the enemy's service, who had come to view the situation of the place, and how far a detachment might advance in the night before they would be discovered. Our guards in the lines fired pretty briskly, and was very near killing our own officer.

This was the only assault made on the garrison at the time.

There was some activity in the Straits towards the end of May: a Russian fleet sailed through to the West on the 27th, on the same wind that took the *Enterprise* and the victuallers on the way to England, and two vessels came in from Minorca. Two days later, two British frigates, that had escorted the nineteen ordnance ships detached from Admiral Darby's convoy for Minorca, sailed through in pursuit of two Dutch frigates, which they eventually took. The garrison heard later that they ran into some French cruisers, who captured one of the British ships and her prize. Though the blockade was not renewed, the garrison always felt particularly vulnerable from the sea, and regretted the absence of the British flag in the Straits.

There was more looting of provisions and liquor from the King's Stores, and the criminals Sam. Whitaker and Simon Pratts, both Artificers, were hanged at the White Convent on 29 May. James Ward of the 58th Regiment was executed the next day, and William Rowls of the same regiment was sentenced to 1,000 lashes, and the sentence was carried out on the South Parade. These executions marked the end of the worst of the looting and drinking, though the trade in stolen goods went on for months afterwards. For six weeks the British troops had treated Gibraltar as they had when it was captured in 1704. They had looted the property of the townspeople as if they were enemies, and when there was nothing left in the town to steal, they had turned their attentions to the Government Stores.

(The casks of rum landed from the convoy were buried in different parts of the Rock to avoid their being stolen.) The officers were at first reluctant to punish the offenders severely, as they felt that the Jewish merchants, the 'hard hearted hucksters', deserved to have their stores and homes plundered, and it was only the firm action of the Governor that restored order in the garrison. General Eliott was more concerned for his men than he ever was for the townspeople, or even his officers and, when a Ragusan ship was driven under the garrison guns and obliged to surrender on 31 May, he wrote that it was likely to be condemned as a prize, and suggested that the garrison and the Navy should share the prize-money, and that the officers should relinquish their part to the private men.

June was opened by the gun-boats, which continued to give the garrison little rest. On the 4th the garrison celebrated King George III's birthday by disturbing the enemy's siesta with a 66-gun salute fired at the St Carlos Battery. The Spaniards retaliated by putting two shots through the Royal Standard that had been run up on a new flagpole on the Grand Battery. On the morning of the 9th the Rock resounded to an enormous explosion from the Spanish Camp. Those of the garrison who were not on duty hurried to find a vantage point from where they could see, at the foot of the Queen of Spain's Chair, one of the enemy's magazines burning furiously. The whole Spanish army was drawn up under arms before the Camp, and they counted thirteen regiments and a body of cavalry. General Alvarez and his suite were seen riding down from San Roque to the scene of the disaster. The exploding shells in the magazine prevented the Spaniards from making any attempt to put out the fire, which burned for three hours and destroyed a considerable quantity of the enemy's ammunition and powder. The garrison were delighted, though they could not discover the cause of the fire.

The gun-boat attacks were persistent and disquieting, and though the garrison worked well enough by day, repairing and strengthening the batteries and beginning to clear the streets of the town, the nightly disturbances, with their mounting toll of casualties, were becoming intolerable. The gunners on the King's Bastion and the Line Wall risked the premature explosions of their shells by cutting the fuses so that they would explode in the air above the boats, but there was no defence against the gun-boats until two transports left behind by Admiral Darby for the purpose were cut down and fitted to carry four heavy guns each, to serve as advance guard-boats. Towards the end of June the first of these, the *Vanguard*, was towed out and moored off the New Mole. At the same time a 13-inch sea-mortar was mounted on the end of the Old Mole, and six cannons were laid in the sand behind the Mole, with the intention of firing across the Bay at the Spanish Camp. The distance was a little over three thousand yards, and a sceptical crowd gathered on the morning of the 28th, to watch the Artillery fire six rounds from each gun. To cheers, all the shot went home, and all but two of the shells landed and exploded in the Camp. There was a lot of confusion in the enemy's Camp and a battalion that was on parade scattered three times as the garrison fired. In this month, 141 inhabitants and soldiers' families, taken prisoner when two of the transports that sailed with the *Enterprise* in May were captured in the Straits, were returned to Gibraltar. A soldier, who had hidden some watches he had stolen in a cannon, returned to collect them to find that they had been fired at the gun-boats. The garrison suffered forty casualties when a shell hit a tree in the Picket Yard and killed that number of sparrows, who had lived there through thick and thin.

It was very hot. The enemy bombardment slackened, until they fired no more than thirty rounds a day. Odd things began to happen. Boyd's Log Book for 3 July:

> Three women were flogged thro' the camp for buying and receiving stolen goods from the Plunderers, one of them was an honest Midwife who will be of great loss to the Garrison if she is sent out as order'd, for in general, we Marry and breed faster than ever known in peacable times: the second was a highland woman without a word of English and the third an Irishwoman who had enough to spare for her two fellow sufferers without leaving herself short of Blarney in the least.

These three unfortunates, according to an account sent to the Secretary at War, who might have been surprised to receive it, were Mrs Drake, belonging to the Artillery, Mrs Mitchel and Mrs Clarke, and they were accused of receiving a little soap. Their punishment was to be 'stripped to the waist and to receive One Dozen lashes on their bare backs with the cat of nine tails by the hands of the Common Hangman, having at the same time a label apprising their crime, pinned to their respective breasts'. The garrison presumably went on marrying and breeding as fast as ever. Four days later the Artillery mounted a pair of stag's horns on the Queen's Battery. The next day, Captain Witham went off to the Jewish cemetery and started to dig it up for a garden. Garrison Orders for 19 July: 'It is particularly recommended that the men with burdens walk slow.' Three days later, a major and the Adjutant of the 72nd Regiment fought a duel with three pistols each, and missed with all six. And by the end of the month the enemy were firing only three shots a day, but no more and no less than three shots; the garrison began to call them the Father, the Son and the Holy Ghost, and to suggest that the Spaniards were trying to convert them with this magical number. On the 26th the cat from Willis's was killed by one of them. Brigadier Ross, who had returned to Gibraltar with Admiral Darby, sailed off in a small boat for Faro.

These dog-days were spent by the saner members of the garrison working on the hill batteries, and moving quarters, as the regiments in town were relieved by those encamped in the south. The enemy marched off several regiments in the direction of Cadiz, and replaced them with militia, and Admiral Barcello's squadron was reinforced until it comprised 1 line-of-battle-ship, 1 frigate, 7 large xebecks, 5 smaller row-galleys, a sloop, 10 fire-ships, 2 bomb-ketches, 12 gun-boats and 4 mortar-boats. Something was evidently in preparation. The Government in London thought that they knew what it was.

Lord Hillsborough to General Eliott, 17 July 1781:

> Extract of authentic Intelligence received from one of His Majesty's Ministers at a foreign Court . . . Certain advices are received that twelve thousand Men were to be embarked at Cadiz on the twenty sixth of June and were intended to be sent against Gibraltar. This was conjectured from the immense quantity of ammunition of War on board the Fleet compared with the small quantity of Biscuit and other Provisions. Amongst other Articles indicating the Purport of the Ex-pedition there is an almost incredible number of small Baggs to be filled with Earth in order to render the Morass before Gibraltar proachable for the Spanish Army. The Duke de Crillon is to command the Attack which is to be made at once on all sides.

However, before this important but incorrect information reached the Rock, the garrison had seen a huge enemy fleet of seventy sail pass the Straits towards the east. The object of the attack was not Gibraltar, but General Murray's brave garrison at Fort St Philip, Port Mahon, Minorca.

It was the hottest summer that Captain Spilsbury of the 12th Regiment had experienced on Gibraltar, and the 12th had been there for ten years. The gun-boats called on 1 August, rowing between the *Vanguard* and the Rock, and they were supported by the land batteries which enfiladed the King's Bastion and the Line Wall. The garrison retaliated by firing into the Spanish Camp from the Old Mole. Two days later the second guard-boat, the *Repulse*, was towed out and moored south of the *Vanguard*. These boats now mounted nine guns against the enemy, and several times managed to keep the gun-boats at bay. During the day the enemy religiously fired their three shots, unless the officer on duty in the British batteries took it into his head to open fire, in which case the barrage was invariably returned. The provisions landed in the south had been stored away in preparation for the autumn rains, but presumably in some confusion. Garrison Orders, 5 August: 'The ration of provisions as last week, except that no oil will be issued till further orders, and half a pound of cheese will be delivered for the four ounces of butter, in lieu of the quarter of a pint of oil.'

On 7 August the ship carrying Lord Hillsborough's letter arrived from the west. It was in the morning, with a haze in the Gut, that the signal flags were out in the enemy's watch-towers, and a sail was seen hanging in the still air against the African mountains. Fourteen gun-boats were rowing out from Algeciras, and Captain Curtis sent out Sir Charles Knowles with three longboats to reach the ship before the enemy, and take off any dispatches for the Governor. At the same time he ordered the *Vanguard* and the *Repulse* to be towed out to help her in. The garrison collected to watch the battle. The British sailors pulled hard, and Sir Charles reached the ship first, and returned with a package for General Eliott, and the information that the ship was the sloop *Helena*, armed with fourteen small guns, becalmed, but drifting slowly towards the Rock. The gun-boats easily outstripped the cumbersome hulks, and came within range of the *Helena* when she was still over four miles out. Lying a few hundred yards off, they began to rake her rigging and decks with grape and round shot. The *Helena* answered with a broadside and musket fire, but appeared lost when a xebeck and several galleys came out to support the gun-boats. Captain Curtis and his odd armada, rowing against the current, did not appear to be moving at all. But the crew of the *Helena* fired briskly at the twenty vessels attacking her, and prevented them from coming in to board her, until, at last, the *Vanguard* and *Repulse* were swung round, and optimistically fired a broadside. At that moment there was a little breeze from the west that lifted the *Helena*'s torn sails, and brought her gently towards her rescuers. The enemy, many of whom had been seen to fall, turned back for Algeciras, towing some of their boats, witness to the accuracy of the *Helena*'s gunners. The garrison cheered as she came in, and were pleased to learn that, in spite of the damage to her masts and rigging caused by the high elevation of the gun-boats' cannons, she had lost only one man killed and two wounded. Captain Curtis, who returned a little later, wrote to the Admiralty: 'The bravery, the coolness, and the judicious conduct of Captain Roberts, do him infinite honour; his officers and men deserve the highest commendation.' General Eliott wrote to Lord Hillsborough:

> The particulars of Captain Robert's (of the Helena) gallant behaviour and his ship will no doubt be transmitted to you by Captain Curtis, but as he (Captain Curtis) is not a man to speak of any transaction so highly redounding to his own honour, on my part it is an indispensable duty to inform your Lordship that his zeal for the service is scarcely to be paralleled in forwarding every operation that can in any way contribute to our comfort or defence.

The old General rather liked the young Captain. This was as good as saying that the garrison, or rather the officers of the garrison, did not. Captain Drinkwater was a good barometer of the opinions of the Officers' Mess, in other words he was a man seeking promotion and fortune among men seeking promotion and fortune, and he left this account of Captain Curtis, who was better at the search than any of them:

> A man of insinuating manner and pleasing address—thereby ingratiating himself much with his Superiors. His conduct to Lord Howe whilst acting with His Lordship on the American Station was so fawning and obsequious that in an American caricature of him he was exhibited as a dog keeping Lord H's *posteriors*—with the motto 'What a Cur-tis.'

After long service, Captain Drinkwater finished life as a Colonel, and left a little clue to his own character in these words about General Eliott: 'Altho' he never assisted Colonel D in *his* professional Views, He was on other occasions very friendly and generous to *others.*'

The hot days passed, with the regular visitation of the Father, Son and Holy Ghost, and the warm nights, with the less welcome visits of the gun-boats. Two vessels came in from Faro, with fruit, onions, salt, and rumours: rumours that the Combined Fleet of the enemy was cruising off Cadiz; rumours that 10,000 Spaniards and 15,000 Frenchmen had landed on Minorca; rumours that Great Britain had ceded Minorca to the Russians, who were sending a fleet to its assistance. On 19 August the *Kite* cutter arrived from England with duplicates of the dispatches brought by Captain Roberts, so the rumours were neither denied nor confirmed. The slow trickle of deserters was renewed, and four pressed sailors rowed over to the enemy from the *Repulse*. On the 25th Garrison Orders recorded an odd incident, perhaps provoked by the heat.

> On the night of the 23rd inst. some pigs the property of Lt. Col. Cochrane of the 58th Regiment were wantonly maimed in a most barbarous and savage manner, and one of them carried off. A reward of 50 dollars upon conviction is hereby offered to whoever shall discover the Person or Persons who were guilty of the above outrage.

Whenever there was trouble the 58th were usually involved in it. Four days later, during an attack by the gun-boats, occurred one of those incidents that fascinated the garrison and Captain Drinkwater:

> In this attack a wounded matross was killed by a shell in the Hospital. The circumstances attending this man's case are so melancholy and affecting, that I cannot pass them over in silence. Some time previous to this event, he had been so unlucky as to break a thigh: being a man of great spirits, he ill brooked the confinement which his case demanded, and exerted himself to get abroad, that he might enjoy the benefit of the fresh air in the court of the hospital: unfortunately, in one of his playful moments, he fell, and was obliged to take to his bed again. He was in this situation, when a shell from the mortar-boats fell into the ward, and rebounding lodged upon him. The convalescents and sick, in the same room, instantly summed up strength to crawl out on hands and knees, whilst the fuse was burning; but this wretched victim was kept down by

the weight of the shell, which after some seconds burst, took off both his legs, and scorched him in a dreadful manner: but, what was still more horrid, he survived the explosion, and was sensible to the very moment that death relieved him from his misery. His last words were expressive of regret that he had not been killed on the batteries.

As General Eliott had said, they were all embarked on the same bottom and, in that century, bottom was another word for courage.

The garrison were to need bottom. On 23 August Mr Ancell noted: 'The enemy are diligently employed in lengthening their approaches on the isthmus,' and added:

> Thus Albion's sons defy the hostile foe—
> Dare ever to be free and spurn at danger:
> From shore to shore they steer with conqu'ring arms!
> With Britain's royal ensigns spread abroad;
> On which the wond'ring nations, gaze with pleasure,
> While George's enemies are struck with dread—
> Ye hectoring Dons, the British standard view,
> That bids defiance to your fleets and armies;
> Nor let ambition lead you on to woe,
> But stop! before we work your overthrow.

CHAPTER XI

Which way do the wind blow?

IN the spring of 1781 the United States and France were exhausted by the war. In January the Pennsylvania line of Washington's army mutinied, returning to their station only after Congress had agreed to discharge half of them, and to redress the grievances of the remainder. In April Washington wrote to Colonel Laurens in Paris:

> If France delays a timely and powerful aid in the critical posture of our affairs, it will avail us nothing should she attempt it hereafter. Why need I run into detail, when it may be declared in a word that we are at the end of our tether, and that now or never our deliverance must come.

But France was falling deeper into debt with every day, and the minister who might have saved her, the financier Necker, was dismissed by Louis XVI. The last gesture made by the French Court to American independence was the fleet commanded by the Comte de Grasse which sailed to the west in March. Spain, hovering ponderously on the verges of the war, sent an army to Minorca in June, captured Penascola, and bombarded Gibraltar, hoping, like an elderly matador, to collect an ear without too exhausting a faena. The Dutch fought a drawn battle off the Dogger Bank with a British squadron under Admiral Hyde Parker, and took no further part in the struggle.

Great Britain was in no better case than her enemies. She was everywhere on the defensive, her armies were scattered, and her navy trying to cope with too many tasks, with no direction as to which should receive priority. In the same month that Washington wrote desperately to Laurens, General Clinton, Commander-in-Chief of the Army in America, wrote to Lord George Germaine:

With the 10,000 men I requested I should not have had a doubt of success. But in my present reduced state and prospects I dare not flatter myself with any; and if the French should be still reinforced, Your Lordship will, I am persuaded, judge our situation to be even critical. For, with regard to our efforts in the Chesapeake, Your Lordship knows how much their success and even the safety of the armament there will depend upon our having a decided naval superiority in these seas.

Clinton had asked Lord George for 10,000 more men, was promised 4,000, and finally received one sick regiment. America was only one battle-ground. Sir John Fortescue, historian of the British Army, summed up the general situation at this time:

Clinton fencing with Washington at New York: Cornwallis fighting a desperate action at Guildford: Rawdon stemming the American advance for a few days: Campbell helpless and deserted at Penascola: West Indian commanders fighting a treacherous population and a deadly climate: Murray still defiant at Minorca: Eliott proudly disdainful of perpetual bombardment at Gibraltar: Goddard trying desperately to fight his way to Poonah: Popham snatching Gwalior by surprise: Carnac plucking himself by sheer daring from Scindia's squadrons: Flint making mortars of wood and grenades of fuller's earth at Wandewash: Lang indomitable among his starving sepoys at Vallore: lastly of Coote, shaken by age and disease, marching about raising his beleaguered colleagues.

Had he been historian of the Navy, he might have added: Rodney under fire in Parliament for the private spoliation of St Eustatius; Parker seeking retirement after the bloody battle with the Dutch; Darby avoiding action in the Channel; Arbuthnot replaced by Graves at New York for conspicuous inertia; Hood dodging de Grasse amongst the West Indian islands; Johnstone taken by surprise at St Iago; and lastly Kempenfeldt fuming about the state of the Navy in the *Royal George* that was to be his tomb.

In London the Court, when it was not being scandalized by the drunkenness and venery of the Prince of Wales, heard with alarm the worsening reports from America. Yet when the news of the final catastrophe was received, it so shook the administration that one of its pillars, Germaine, turned and attacked the other, Sandwich, in Parliament. The surrender at Yorktown on 19 October 1781 of Lord

Cornwallis and 7,000 men, was the culmination of the attempt to subdue the Colonies, by 'liberating' the southern states. One of the delusions under which George III and his ministers laboured was that the citizens of Carolina would return to their loyalty to the crown once the Continental Army had been driven out of the state. So after Cornwallis's successes, Lord George coloured Carolina red once more, and encouraged the General to push northwards to Virginia, to join forces with General Philips and Benedict Arnold, whom he thought were at Chesapeake, still burning tobacco factories. But General Clinton had already withdrawn part of these forces to meet the threat of an attack on New York. Cornwallis came to Chesapeake Bay, and Washington, having gained his objective by threatening New York, marched south. The situation of the British at Yorktown was not desperate until de Grasse arrived at the mouth of the Chesapeake with 4,000 troops and 24 sail-of-the-line. The British fleet of 19 sail-of-the-line and 2 50s, under Admiral Graves and Hood, failed to do more than 'brush' the French, who completed the blockade of Yorktown, and within a few weeks the siege was over. In the meantime, the Continental Army returned to Carolina, and drove the British back to Charleston.

Yorktown was virtually the last action of the war in America. Those American loyalists who had rallied to the British were shamefully abandoned, in the notorious tenth clause of the capitulation terms accepted by Cornwallis, and were hounded down by the revolutionaries. The British held out in Savannah, Charleston and New York, whilst the Americans waited for another French fleet to help them continue the attack. It never came, because in 1782 the North Ministry fell, and negotiations for peace were begun.

The ripples made by the disaster barely reached Gibraltar. Yet Yorktown, and the long series of unsuccessful campaigns that ended with it, depressed and angered the people of Great Britain, so that General Eliott's achievements on the Rock were a hundred times brighter by comparison. The Gibraltar tradition, the great attachment the people of England felt for the distant fortress, which was of small profit to them otherwise, sprang from the circumstance that it was held, whilst almost all else was lost. By the same mark, once the war in America was over, and France had fulfilled her obligations under the treaty of 1778, her arms could be turned against Gibraltar in accordance with her promise in the Convention of Aranjuez. French troops were already engaged with the Spanish in the siege of St Philip's Castle in Minorca, and it was felt that only the reduction of this place, and Gibraltar, could bring the peace France needed.

CHAPTER XII

Password Denbigh—
Countersign Steady

IN September 1781 General Alvarez, 'qui avaient fait tant de bruit dans les gazettes de Madrid' (Bourgoing), and a considerable racket against the walls of Gibraltar, began to open the siege in form. The blockade had been broken by the reliefs of Admirals Rodney and Darby; the bombardment had flattened the town, but had had little effect on the garrison except to make them 'skip as merrily about as we would at a game of crickett between Middlesex and Surrey' (A Soldier's Letter). The procedure for assaulting a fortified town had become a ritual since the days of Vauban; the attackers first dug a line of trenches parallel to the part of the fortifications they considered the weakest, within range of the walls, but sufficiently far to be able to withstand the defenders' barrage; after a bombardment, they threw up an advanced work, which they joined to their lines by a covered way, and from which they developed further works into a second parallel; from here, if it was required, they proceeded to a third parallel, and a fourth, until their guns were near enough to batter a breach in the fortress walls; they then assaulted the breach and took the fortress. This relatively simple exercise was complicated by the necessity to protect the parallels from being outflanked, and elaborated by the prerequisite of erecting a bastion to face a bastion, a ravelin to meet a ravelin, and a curtain to cover a groyne, until it became the science that obsessed Uncle Toby, and blinded many otherwise competent generals. This was the procedure adopted against Gibraltar in the sieges of 1704 and 1727 with prodigious lack of success. It was impossible to dig a trench on the isthmus deep enough to protect troops without the bottom of it filling with water, and so the approaches had to be built up on the sand; the batteries on the Rock dominated the ground below and the works required for an assault were literally under the muzzles of the garrison's guns. To protect the men from guns so high above them, the works had to be eighteen feet high, and this entailed long and sustained efforts by the enemy engineers under fire, not only to throw them up, but to repair them when they were knocked down. No matter how near the enemy approached, the only way into Gibraltar was the funnel between the Rock and the Bay, the terrible 'bocca de fuego', the Mouth of Fire. In 1705 the enemy actually reached the curtain wall at Landport, before being forced to retreat, but since then the Inundation had been dug, Willis's batteries established, and the Grand Battery over Landport tunnel built. In 1755 Colonel James considered the Rock impregnable, and since then Colonel Green had added many improvements, which Captain Drinkwater described as 'all so singularly contrived and of so formidable a nature, that all direct attacks by land, henceforward, may be considered as quixotism and insanity'. As no one can accuse General Alvarez, who had been sitting in San Roque for two years already, of being either quixotic or insane, the decision to commence preparations for an assault from the land presumably came from his superiors, and in all probability from the King in Madrid. The General's opinion of the venture becomes apparent later. The garrison took it very seriously.

At first there was little to apprehend. September was sultry, and the trinity of shells arrived daily like a benediction. Some of the inhabitants had returned to the town to live in cellars, or makeshift shanties among the ruins. The only disturbances occurred when Captain Witham was on the batteries. He always answered the three shots, provoking the enemy guns to retaliate, and in Captain Spilsbury's diary there is the entry: 'Captain Witham at the batteries. An almost incessant fire was kept up.' When they knew Witham was on duty, the inhabitants stayed out of the town. On the 12th the Spaniards startled the garrison in the evening by suddenly firing a grand salute. It was not a Saint's Day, which by now the garrison knew, or an annual celebration, so they guessed, correctly, that the Duc de Crillon had had some success in Minorca. They had strong sympathies for the British garrison there, 2,700 men facing a reported

25,000, though General Eliott had not responded to General Murray's request for troops: this was fortunate, as the few he might have spared would have made no difference against the overwhelming strength of the enemy, and would have been sorely missed in the garrison, where 1,000 men, apart from the guards and artillery, were at work every day. Four days later they knew that their own trials were about to begin again.

On the night of 15 September the enemy built up three banks of sand in a zig-zag from the west end of the St Carlos Battery (the Mill Battery) towards the Bay. In spite of the heavy fire from the garrison on this new work, they brought up more materials at night, and reinforced the sand with casks and timbers. As a diversion, the gun- and mortar-boats were sent over at night to fire on the batteries on the North Front, and some of their shells falling into the lines from the side, and from behind, caused several casualties. During the day some two hundred Spanish workmen were employed in the new work, and were subjected to a constant barrage from the garrison batteries near the Bay. The enemy replied from St Carlos and the Lines often to effect, as Mr Ancell recorded on the 19th:

> Between nine and ten o'clock last night, a shell fired from St Carlos, entered a house, leading down from South-line-wall Guard, where Majors Mercier and Vignoles, of the 39th regiment, and Captain Burke of the 58th regiment (Town-Major of the garrison) were sitting at a table, which fell upon the latter's thighs, and smashed them. The rubbish which dropped from the ceiling wounded the two Majors, and extinguished the candle, so that all the light they had was from the fuze of the shell. Major Vignoles having put his hand over the table, found Capt. Burke in a gore of blood, upon which he exclaimed to the other, 'Oh! Burke's killed'. They then as hastily as they could, owing to their wounds and being in the dark, retreated to the door, which they had scarce accomplished, when the shell burst, and tossed the Town-Major from the place where he had fallen, to another part of the room, part of his flesh was blown up to the ceiling, and the walls besprinkled with his blood. In this mangled situation he was taken up, and carried to the Naval Hospital, where he shortly after expired. As the men were carrying him, he entreated in a languid tone, which indicated to a speedy dissolution, that they would kill him, and put an end to his misery.

The next day Captain Foulis of the 73rd was appointed Town-Major. The *Helena* and *Kite* sailed for England, carrying invalids, and the Governor's dispatch telling of the activities on the isthmus. The garrison and the enemy were now firing seven to eight hundred rounds at each other every day, but the troops on both sides were inured to the bombardment, and scarcely bothered to take the smallest precautions, so the lists of casualties began to lengthen. Even the few cows that browsed on the slopes of the Rock used to go and sniff at any shell that fell near them.

Ten years after the siege an account of it was published written by a certain J. Heriot, and a copy bought by William Booth, who had been one of Colonel Green's lieutenants (his wife had a piece of the small cow for roasting). When he read Heriot's account of the events of 1 October, describing the appearance overnight of a new enemy battery about thirty yards long and eighteen feet high, he took a pencil and wrote in the margin: 'I saw the Engineer marking out this Battery and made the first report of it and had the thanks of General Eliott for doing so,' which was an odd thing to do, and appears even odder when there is no mention of Mr Booth, apart from his share of the small cow, in any of the journals, letters, dispatches or diaries, that confirms his claim. However, the new epaulement was real enough, to the west of St Carlos Battery, in front of the zig-zag the enemy had erected previously. Brigadier Green (Mrs Green had returned to England in June with Charlotte, and unfortunately died a year later from the effects of a chill she caught in a bomb-proof shelter during the gun-boat attacks) gave it as his opinion that the new battery was intended for mortars to shell the camp in the south, but he was wrong, as the Spaniards mounted six 26-pounder cannon there, for battering down the walls. That was some time later, as the enemy appeared in no hurry to start their assault.

The garrison had ample time to prepare for the attack, and different sections used it to their own advantage. The serjeants of the various regiments went to the hospital to learn how to apply tourniquets; the master of the *Flying Fish* that came in at the end of September sold his cargo of tea at one guinea per pound; a soldier tried to desert by swimming across the Bay and drowned; the Governor ordered the batteries to slacken their fire to save ammunition; and the crew of the cutter *Speedwell* which was lying in the harbour, planned to seize the ship, take it to Algeciras and sell it to

the enemy, and return to England rich, if dishonourable; the plot
was betrayed and the ringleaders imprisoned.

On the night of 4 October the enemy opened their parallel,
running from the St Carlos Battery to the east. It was not a very impressive parallel, being made of casks with sand thrown over them,
but they persisted with it, until it stretched some sixty yards across
the isthmus. The Governor wrote to Lord Hillsborough: 'The want
of able soldiers to compleat the Regiments, also a strong reinforcement to the Garrison becomes now a most serious consideration.'
With the garrison's fire reduced to fifty to a hundred shots a day, the
enemy pressed on with their works near the Bay, and on the morning
of 16 October the garrison saw that the zig-zag work behind the new
battery had been enlarged until it was itself a battery, with six embrasures already opened. They now had the St Carlos Battery
mounting 8 13-inch mortars, the new St Paschal's Battery mounting
6 26-pounders and 2 13-inch mortars, and the zig-zag St Martin's
Battery mounting 12 26-pounders, grouped 1,200 yards from the
Grand Battery, and the beginnings of a parallel; the Governor was
persuaded by Colonel Tovey of the Artillery to allow him to open a
concentrated fire in an attempt to destroy the new works before they
were brought into action. The regiments were busy changing quarters on 21 October, so it was decided to commence the barrage on the
afternoon of the 22nd. A tremendous volley was opened at four
o'clock and kept up through the night. Several fires were started on
the works, caused by inflammable shells and a few red-hot shots
falling amongst the piles of fascines and timbers behind them. The
garrison had great hopes of seeing the new batteries reduced to
shapeless heaps, but at first light they were discovered to be in much
the same condition as the afternoon before, in spite of the 2,000 shot
and shells that had been fired at them. The thick banks of sand
fronting the works could not be knocked down, and there was an
endless supply of sand which was used to put out the fires that were
started. It seemed to the garrison that the enemy had discovered an
infallible way of approaching as near as they wished. Three men
deserted, and spirits were further depressed when an English cutter
was taken attempting to enter the Bay. On the 30th of the month the
Unicorn cutter managed to come in on a strong breeze with four boats
from Faro, carrying fruit, which was immediately bought by the

Governor and sent to the hospital for the sufferers from scurvy. The rest of the cargo sold for some of the highest prices paid during the siege, as if the garrison had decided that it might not have much more use for money, whereas a pound of onions for 2s. 9¼d., or a pound of tea for £2 5s. 6d., or a pound of sugar for 17/–, could at least be enjoyed before the enemy attacked.

The insidious infliction of scurvy became inevitable as the men had little to eat but the salt provisions from the Government Stores. There were other diseases, and Captain Spilsbury noted on 1 November that two men of the 58th had died of spotted fever and one of the 12th had shot himself. The next day the gun-boats attempted to attack the camp above the Naval Hospital, but were driven off by fire from the *Vanguard* and the *Repulse*. The *Fortune* sloop, which had also been cut down and carried five 26-pounders, was anchored south of the *Vanguard* after this attack: the garrison were no longer able to retaliate against the Spanish Camp, as the Governor had ordered the ordnance on the Old Mole to be directed against the threatening batteries on the isthmus.

General Eliott was scarcely ever seen by the garrison during these early days of November. He was closeted in the Convent with Captain Curtis. He appeared at the questioning of one Antonio Juanico, a sailor on one of the Portuguese boats who was suspected of spying, and he saw Brigadier Green, but only to take one of the Brigadier's precise plans of the enemy's works, before returning to his study. He came out on the 12th to greet Brigadier Ross, who arrived on the cutter *Phoenix* to take over command of the 72nd Regiment. The Brigadier was lucky, as the *Phoenix* came in unopposed. The same day a second cutter was taken by the enemy and sailed to Algeciras in triumph. It is unlikely that either Ross, Eliott or Curtis was watching.

In the meantime the garrison was working and sleeping under fire, and exchanging stories of marvels, like the shell splinter that flew three miles and landed in the sea off Buenavista, and escapes, like this one told by Mr Ancell:

Last night a shell fell under the platform of a tent where two corporals were asleep, when the intollerable fume and stench of the composition awakened them, nor could they imagine from whence the smoke proceeded. The shell lay burning under the boards, when they opened the tent door to let in the air, to prevent being suffocated, at that instant it exploded, and blew them some yards, without receiving any injury, they shortly recovered from their surprize, and turned their eyes to the place where the tent had stood, but the bedding, blankets, tent-poles, &c. could not be seen, they being torn to pieces, and scattered in many places. In this naked situation they began a search for their wearing apparel, but only found the cuff of a coat in one place, part of a sleeve in another, and their shoes parched to a cinder. Thus forlorn they began to console each other, when corporal R–ho–n exclaimed, 'D—m it, I don't care for the loss of my cloaths, but all my money is gone,' he having about fourteen rials in his pocket when he went to bed.

General Alvarez was not obeying the Rules of War. His half-hearted parallel did not have the redans required to protect it from the flanks. His new batteries were guarded as if they were behind the Spanish Lines, and not 1,000 yards from the enemy. His casual sentries allowed deserters to slip past them into the beleaguered garrison. He was behaving as his predecessors before Gibraltar had behaved, which had led the French Marshal Tessé to complain in 1705, 'The general spirit of the Spaniards, even of the most zealous, is to foresee nothing.' The French did not suffer from the feeling of inferiority that a Spaniard felt in the shadow of Gibraltar. 'As solid as the Rock' was a Spanish saying long before it was an English one. After two years in the insignificant town of San Roque, gazing at the huge vertical peak, watching the red ants of his enemy swarming at its base, it is hardly surprising that General Alvarez approached his task of reducing the famous fortress by assault with diffidence and reluctance. When he saw the stretcher-loads of mutilated men carried back to his Camp from the forward batteries, he decided to risk as few men as possible in guarding them. He disobeyed the Rules, and paid the penalty for it, as the Rules told him that one of the things to be expected from the defenders during a siege was a sortie.

It is not known when General Eliott first contemplated making a sortie, because he took good care to keep it a secret. William Booth said he knew, and made this claim, in pencil, for posterior fame:

General Boyd had heard, thro' Lt Seward of the Royal Artillery, my opinion of the practicability of the Sortie—and after consulting with me on the subject, he went out as far as the Devil's Tower to see if what I had asserted was true—Viz. that of the approaches being without any work whatever to flank them and that their Batteries in the Rear must of course strike the reverse of their own works—this was found to be true. The Sortie was very soon after made and the troops found themselves completely covered from the fire of the Enemy's guns by their high and advanced Parallels—My assertion was 'that we could get under the enemy's approaches clear of their fire, those lines not being flanked by anything'.

But anyone could have seen that, and the appearance of General Boyd, now seventy-one years old, doddering out to the Devil's Tower might have wrecked the whole plan. The only thing to be said in support of Mr Booth's assertion is that he made it in pencil in the margin of a book, which is where often the most revealing and heart-felt comments appear. At a guess, General Eliott conceived the idea of destroying the enemy works by hand, after Colonel Tovey had failed to knock them down on 22 October; it was from about that time that he started to have long and private talks with Captain Curtis every day. Wherever the idea originated, it germinated into a precise plan after 20 November, when two Walloon deserters came into the garrison. One of these was a corporal, and he described the new works in detail, pointed them out to the Governor from Willis's and, more important, he described the number and position of the guards. The garrison knew none of this, as both deserters were kept locked up in the Convent. This was fortunate, because on the 22nd a soldier of the 58th went over to the enemy. General Eliott's secretiveness served the garrison well on this occasion. Nobody suspected that any plan was afoot until the gates were shut after the evening gun had fired on 26 November. Then the garrison discovered that the wine-shops were closed. The news spread quickly from the few who could read to the majority who could not:

EVENING GARRISON ORDERS

Gibraltar, Nov. 26 1781

Countersign, STEADY

All the grenadiers and light infantry of the Garrison, and all the men of the 12th and Hardenberg's regiments, officers, and non-commissioned officers now on duty, to be immediately relieved, and join their regiments: to form a detachment consisting of the 12th and Hardenberg's regiments complete, the grenadiers and light infantry of all the other regiments, (which are to be completed to their full establishment from the battalion companies) one captain, three lieutenants, ten non-commissioned officers, and a hundred artillery; and three engineers, seven officers, and twelve non-commissioned officer overseers; with a hundred and sixty workmen from the Line, and forty workmen from the artificer company. Each man to have thirty-six rounds of ammunition, and a good flint in his piece, and another in his pocket. No drums to go out, excepting two with each of the regiments. No volunteers will be allowed. The whole to be commanded by Brigadier General Ross; and to assemble on the Red Sands at twelve o'clock this night, to make a Sortie upon the Enemy's batteries. The 39th and 58th regiments to parade at the same hour on the Grand Parade, under the command of Brigadier General Picton, to sustain the sortie if necessary.

At 7 p.m., the Stores opened to issue tools to the workmen, and inflammable materials to the engineers and artillery. Private Gordon of the 73rd remembered:

A call came about 8 o'clock for the grenadiers and light infantry picquet of the 73rd regiment to turn out. When I came to the door of the picquet room, C.B. of the royal artillery bid me adieu! being surprized at the strangeness of such an address I asked him in haste what he meant? He told me . . . you are going to burn the Mill Battery.

The garrison was very excited. Two regiments, the best companies from the others, a strong force of artillery and workmen, and, it was later discovered, 100 sailors (Captain Curtis's contribution, and commanded by Lieutenants Muckle and Campbell), in all over 2,000 men, was an impressive force to detach for a sortie. The hours before midnight were spent by those who were to go out in the quiet preparation of their equipment; there was an atmosphere of unreality, and men confused hours with minutes, were ready too soon, or sat about, unready, too long. Their comrades who were to stay, fussed about them anxiously, lending their clothes, their flints, their equipment, so that they too might be in some way part of the expedition. In the meantime General Eliott had assembled the Field Officers together, to give them his orders. There were to be three columns. (See opposite page.)

At 2.45 a.m. on 27 November the right column began to file out of the fortress. The moon was down, there was the faintest movement on the water of the Bay, and the huge Rock, their friend and protector, towered silently above them, black against the blue-black sky. They

LEFT COLUMN. LIEUT.-COL. TRIGGE

	Officers	Serjeants	Rank & File
72nd Grenadiers	4	5	101
72nd Lt Infantry	4	5	101
Sailors with an Engineer	3	3	100
Artillery	1	4	35
12th Regiment	26	28 (2 Drums)	430
58th Lt Infantry	3	3	57
	41	48 2	824

CENTRE COLUMN. LIEUT.-COL. DACHENHAUSEN.
MAJOR MAXWELL

	Officers	Serjeants	Rank & File
39th Grenadiers	3	3	57
39th Lt Infantry	3	3	57
73rd Grenadiers	4	5	101
73rd Lt Infantry	4	5	101
Engineers with Workmen	6	14	150
Artillery	2	4	40
56th Grenadiers	3	3	57
58th Grenadiers	3	3	57
	28	40	620

RIGHT COLUMN. LIEUT.-COL. HUGO

	Officers	Serjeants	Rank & File
Reden's Grenadiers	3	7	71
La Motte's Grenadiers	3	7	71
Engineers with Workmen	4	6	50
Artillery	1	2	25
Hardenberg's Regiment	16	34 (2 Drums)	296
56th Lt Infantry	3	3	57
	30	59 2	570

The right column to lead and march through Forbes barrier, for the extremity of the parallel; keeping the eastern fences of the gardens close on their left. The centre immediately to follow, marching through Bayside barrier, and directing their route through the gardens for the mortar-batteries. The left column to bring up the rear, marching along the Strand for the gun-batteries. No person to advance before the front, unless ordered by the officer commanding the column: and the most profound silence to be observed, as the success of the enterprise may depend thereon. The 12th and Hardenberg's regiments to form in front

F

of the works, as sustaining corps; and are to detach to the right and left as occasion may require. The reserve to take post in the farthest gardens. When the works are carried, the attacking troops are to take up their ground in the following manner. The grenadiers of Reden's and La Motte's behind the parallel; the 39th and 73rd flank companies, along the front of the fourth branch; and the 72nd grenadiers and light-infantry, with their right to the fourth branch and left to the beach.

came through the ruins of the town, across the Picquet Yard, and through the damp hole of Landport tunnel, across the bridge over the ditch, and under the lines and batteries, where the gunners watched them, invisible behind the rocks. Reden's Grenadiers led the column, Hanoverians, chosen for their sobriety and discipline, and for the Governor's pleasure in preferring them to the British. Now the Inundation was on their left, and the palisades of Forbes barrier before them. They had marched in silence, but the opening of the barrier betrayed them to some Spanish sentries on the edge of the gardens. The sentries challenged, fired, and ran. Colonel Hugo, the time for silence past, shouted at his grenadiers to form an attacking line, and pressed forward at a run towards the parallel. He found it unguarded, occupied it, and the engineers and workmen who had followed began to knock down the casks, level the sandbanks and fill the ditches. This party advanced so fast that they lost contact with a company of Hardenberg's Regiment, who missed their way, ran through the gardens, and suddenly found themselves facing the long sloping parapet of the St Carlos Battery. Here they were fired on by the Spanish guard alerted by the sentries. The top of the parapet was some eighteen feet above them, and the sloping bank was pitted with shell holes from the garrison's fire. The enemy fired their muskets again. The Hanoverians could only retreat or charge. They charged, gained the top of the parapet, and saw the Spanish guards running back below. The drop from the parapet to the trenches was nearly twenty-four feet, but they scrambled down and formed up to the right of the Mill Tower, prepared to meet a counter-attack. The centre column meanwhile had advanced through the gardens to-wards the firing and, coming to St Carlos, which was their object, they occupied it. Colonel Dachenhausen was with the 39th flank companies and, seeing figures in a line by the Mill Tower, he ordered his men to fire on them. Several of the Hanoverians were hit before the countersign was shouted, and they were sent to join their regiment to the right. The artillery found eight 13-inch brass mortars in St Carlos, which they spiked, and the engineers prepared to set fire to the fascines and platforms in the battery, whilst the British grenadiers moved forward and occupied the Centre Guard-House of the enemy. The left column, under Colonel Trigge, advancing between the Inundation and the Bay, met some resistance, but the 72nd flank companies attacked and took St Paschal's and St Martin's, driving the enemy in flight before them. There the artillery spiked eighteen brass 26-pounders, and two 13-inch mortars. The attack had met with complete success all along the line. The infantry formed up to repel a counter-attack, and the engineers began to dismantle the batteries and set the heaps of timber on fire. As the flames began to light the isthmus, the artillery opened up from Willis's on the Spanish forts and Lines.

Now the men could see each other and, flickering like a mighty tongue of flame, their Rock, reflecting the light of the fires. They could see the flashes of the guns in the Spanish Lines as they fired uselessly above their heads. And, if they were near St Carlos, they could see a stout senior officer with a sword slung over his shoulder, who looked remarkably like General Eliott, standing on the enemy works. The old Cock of the Rock had come out with the sortie, and now stood, in the best of humour, surveying the ruin of the Spanish batteries. Captain Curtis was there too, near the Governor, who just then turned to the troops nearest him: 'Look round, my boys, and view how beautiful the Rock appears by the light of this glorious fire' (Ancell). The batteries were well alight when Brigadier Ross came across the Governor. General Eliott was in a talkative mood:

Eliott: What do you think of the business, is it not something extraordinary that we have gained the Enemy's works so easily?
Ross: The most extraordinary thing is to see you here!

The Brigadier, who was disgruntled at the possibility of having to share the glory of the success with anyone, stumped off, and missed a scene that would have annoyed him even more. The Governor was to have not only the glory but the legend. Captain Witham, who had previously captured a young Spanish lieutenant, Don Vincente Friza, by waving a linstock at him, now approached the Governor

with the keys of the enemy magazine, which had been taken from a
Captain of the Artillery wounded in the first charge. This unlucky
officer was lying in the ruins of St Carlos, near the body of a Highlander, whom he had wounded, and who appeared to be dead, and
who had wounded him. When the time came to set St Carlos on fire,
he refused to be moved, though General Eliott himself went down to
try to persuade him. He answered the General's insistence: 'No, Sir,
no, leave me, and let me perish amid the ruins of my post.' After he
was dead, someone remembered that he had cried out: 'At least one
Spaniard shall die honourably.' The detachment had now been on
the isthmus for an hour, and the enemy had made no attempt to
retaliate, apart from firing grape shot, which had a shorter range
than balls, and caused some slight casualties. Their troops were
drawn up, but remained as spectators throughout the foray. A small
body of cavalry, some forty strong, appeared on the right flank of the
detachment, and General Eliott ordered two companies of Hardenberg's to wheel to face them, but there were too few to attack. At
3.45 a.m. trains were laid to the powder magazines, eighteen
Spanish prisoners were escorted to the garrison, the wounded were
taken back, and the detachment prepared to retire. The plan was that
the 12th and Hardenberg's should remain in their positions until the
flank companies, artillery and workmen had returned through the
barriers, and then retire themselves, the 12th through Bayside, and
Hardenberg's through Forbes. Everything went well until Colonel
Hugo and his regiment found the barrier at Forbes locked, and
nobody there to open it, and were obliged to hurry round the
Inundation to follow the 12th in through Bayside before somebody
locked that, and they were left out on the isthmus. As the last few
men were returning to the protection of the Rock, rising like a
steeple into the grey of morning, they heard the screams of a man
from the line of fires behind them, but not for long, for then the
powder magazines blew up with terrific force. It was five o'clock in
the morning and the sortie was over.

The detachment paraded and were counted. Four privates had
been killed; and one officer, Lieutenant Tweedie of the 12th, and
twenty-four other ranks had been wounded. One man was missing,
a highlander of the 73rd, the man who had fought the Spanish captain and died only when the magazines exploded. Of these, Harden-

berg's regiment had two killed and twelve wounded, but whether from behind or from the front did not appear in the records. One soldier of the 73rd had lost his kilt.

The mystery of the sortie is—how many Spaniards were there in the batteries at the time? There is no doubt that it was a great success; the patient work of months was destroyed in under an hour, and the morale of the garrison was given a fillip which it has never lost. But was the success due to the good generalship of the Governor and the bravery of his troops, or to the incompetence of General Alvarez? There are three estimates, all made shortly after the sortie. On 28 November General Eliott wrote to Lord Hillsborough:

> The force of the enemy in their lines consisted of 50 or 60 cavalry and 600 infantry composed of Spanish and Walloon Guards, Artillerists, Cassadores, and other Light Troops, besides the usual body of Workmen carrying their arms . . . The vigorous efforts of His Majesty's Troops on every part of their extensive front were irresistable and the Enemy after a scattering fire of short duration gave way on all sides and abandoned their stupendous works with great precipitation.

He added, carefully omitting his own part in the affair,

> Brigadier General Ross had the Chief Command and conducted the attack with so much Judgement . . . as highly contributed to the general success . . . Captain Curtis accompanied as a volunteer and distinguished himself by his discernment, assistance and personal efforts.

This carefully phrased dispatch suggests that the 600 men in the Lines were those who abandoned their stupendous works, but the Spanish Lines were 600 yards behind the works, and not a man, apart from the body of cavalry who ventured out for a short time, stirred out of them. Mr Booth spent the early hours of that November morning sitting above Landport tunnel, ready to send out more workmen if they were needed. He commented on Heriot's estimate of 410 Spanish guards: 'Very true, but what could 410 men do against upwards of 2,000, a third of the garrison or rather more, but a sortie should never exceed that number according to Vauban's system.' He then becomes involved with Vauban's system:

> It is certainly unusual to attempt a Sortie at a distance of 900 yards, and therefore the Spaniards might have thought himself secure but their own approaches were so improperly guarded, having no banquette or

any redans to flank their works, which naturally would lead a General like Eliott to take advantage of such material neglect and therefore deviate from the rules of Attack as they had from those of Defence.

On the subject of the General's appearance on the isthmus he added:

This in my opinion was wrong and contrary to the Rules of War, for a Governor was never known or suffered to go out of his Garrison with a third part of his Army—what would have been the consequence had the 14,000 men advanced in time?

The only officer who was known to have gone out with the sortie, and whose journal is usually accurate, was Captain Spilsbury of the 12th Regiment. Captain Drinkwater's History tallies remarkably closely with Spilsbury's journal, and gives this estimate:

Only two officers and sixteen privates were taken prisoners; and little opposition being made, very few were killed in the works. The guard, from the best information, consisted of one captain, three subalterns, and seventy-four privates, including the artillery.

Perhaps the most reasonable supposition is that there were Booth's 14,000 in the Spanish Camp, Eliott's 650 in the Spanish Lines, and Drinkwater's 78 in the advanced batteries. If this was so, it reveals the awful discrepancy between the magnitude of General Alvarez's command and the paucity of his talent for it. His was the peculiarly Spanish failing, which led Marshal Tessé to write: 'I would not trust a Spaniard, however brave, with the defence of a steeple; they fight duels, but as a body, and for their country, is an idea which never enters their heads.' The brave Captain of Artillery, who died at his post, had already written his report for the night, in which he said 'nothing extraordinary had happened'.

There were two sad postscripts to the sortie. One is in Boyd's Log Book: 'Colonel Tovey of the Royal Artillery died this morning and left an amiable Daughter with a handsome fortune.' And written over the line in another handwriting is: 'Married Lt Lindly 73rd 2 days afterwards.' The other is the unhappy fate of Baron Von Helmstadt, Ensign in the Walloon Guards. This young nobleman was twenty-two years old, and captured during the sortie. Captain Drinkwater begins his story:

The Baron was dangerously wounded in the knee, and not without many intreaties submitted to amputation. When the surgeon first informed him that an operation was absolutely unavoidable, he resolutely opposed it: amputation, he said, very seldom succeeded in Spain; besides, he was then betrothed in marriage to a lady, and would rather risk his life than present himself before her with only one leg. The Governor, being told this determination, immediately visited the Baron, and used every argument to persuade him to comply. His Mistress, the General said, must undoubtedly esteem him the more for the honourable wound he had received in the service of his country; and, as to the operation being fatal, he might almost assure himself of a certain recovery, since, in the many similar cases which had occurred in the Garrison during the siege, our surgeons had been generally successful; and, to convince him by ocular proof, ordered several mutilated convalescents into the room. This generous attention of the Governor had a powerful effect on the Baron, who no longer able to resist his importunities, at length consented to the operation.

Mr Ancell ends it.

29th December. This morning early, died in the naval hospital, Baron Helmstadt, taken prisoner at St Carlos, on the 27th of last month, and who since had a leg amputated, owing to a wound he received by a musquet ball in that action. The corpse was dressed in full uniform, according to the Spanish custom, and the General and principal officers, walked in solemn procession, to the New-mole, where a flag of truce waited to convey the body to the Orange Grove: A band of music playing a dirge, and a company of grenadiers, escorted the decorated bier to the water's edge, and upon the corpse being lowered into the boat, the latter fired three vollies in honor of the deceased. The coffin had all that art and ingenuity could invent, to render it elegant, which must sensibly please the enemy, when they consider the respect paid by the Governor to this fallen officer. He was young, handsome, and on the point of nuptial celebration with a beautiful lady, born in the province of Andalusia, and who during his sickness, had furnished him daily (by flags of truce) with wine and other refreshing diet which this garrison could not afford; but the day before his departure, she came half-bay over, hearing of his dangerous situation, to visit him, and take her last adieu! but the Adjutant General who went out to receive the flag of truce, assured her she could not be permitted to land until the Governor's pleasure was known, and the next day he would wait on her with his Excellency's commands; instead of which she received the lifeless trunk of him on whom her every wish and happiness was founded.

Sortie Day is still celebrated in Gibraltar. The men who went out did not know whether they would meet tens, hundreds or thousands of the enemy; it was their day, and still is.

Garrison Orders. 27th November, 1781.

> The bravery and conduct of the whole detachment, officers, seamen, and soldiers, on this glorious occasion, surpasses the Governor's utmost acknowledgement.

CHAPTER XIII

We shall give time enough

THE victory at Yorktown, for which even General Washington gave
the credit to the Comte de Grasse, was considered in France and on
the continent of Europe to mark the continuing decline of British
power throughout the world. The Courts of St Petersburg, Berlin,
Vienna, Paris and Madrid were of the opinion that it was only a
matter of time before Great Britain would sue for peace, and in
Madrid, Charles III and Floridablanca were hoping to seize
Minorca, Jamaica and Gibraltar, before negotiations were started.
They called on France to honour the many compacts and treaties
between them, and to help repay Spain for the losses she had sustained in their long, and up till now unrewarding, alliance. French
ships were to clear the way to Jamaica, and French troops to serve
with their Spanish comrades in the sieges of Minorca and Gibraltar.
Minorca was the first object of their united efforts.

It was doomed. In January 1779 General James Murray, who had
served as a Brigadier under General Wolfe, wrote to Lord Weymouth:

> The two British regiments look more like ghosts than soldiers. The
> invalids and drafted men are quite worn out, and in a siege would be
> useless. If in March I can muster fourteen hundred able rank and file
> fit to go through the hardships of a siege, we shall be stronger than our
> present condition promises.

And in March, when he was expecting to be invaded by French
troops numbering 24,000, he wrote to General Eliott on Gibraltar:

> I am as well prepared for them as I may be. If we are really invaded
> here and your neighbour at Cadiz will allow us to send a superior Fleet

to that of the French into the Mediterranean I think they may repent their visit here, for in that event, I judge the whole of the invading Army must be made prisoners and their Fleet destroyed with the bargain, I am confident weak as we are that we shall give time enough for succours to arrive.

Murray was a brave and able commander, who would have remembered the fate of Admiral Byng, and not expected Minorca to be sacrificed for Gibraltar a second time. However, General Eliott risked censure by retaining the 73rd Regiment brought to the Mediterranean by Admiral Rodney, and in June 1781 he refused Murray's request for help, saying that as the Spaniards had returned few prisoners to him, he could not spare any men. Yet only a few months before Murray had been encouraging privateers to run the blockade to Gibraltar, and in April had sent a large supply of provisions from his stores on the island. There is no doubt that General Eliott acted wisely, as, when the attack did come, the enemy were so superior in numbers that 1,000 more men would have made no difference to the result, and would have suffered the same huge losses as Murray's own regiments.

In July 1781 the garrison of Gibraltar saw the invasion fleet sailing to the east and, in August, 8,000 Spanish troops were landed on Minorca, commanded by the Duc de Crillon. The fleet, under Admiral Cordova and de Guichen, sailed back to Cadiz, de Guichen returning to Brest and being avoided by Admiral Darby; they left a squadron to blockade Port Mahon, commanded by the Spanish Admiral Moreno. In fifteen hours, which was as long as they took to march across it for Murray could make no resistance, this army had occupied the island and its three ports, and the British garrison had retired behind the massive walls of Fort St Philip, three miles from Mahon. There were the 51st and 61st Regiments, two Hanoverian battalions, and a number of seamen landed from the ships that had been at the island: in all, 2,700 men, though many were already sick. Fort St Philip was immensely strong, built on a peninsula at the entrance of Port Mahon, but its strength was also its weakness, as the passages, casemates and strong-points in its star-shaped walls were underground, dank and unhealthy.

Louis de Berton des Balbes de Quiers, Duc de Crillon, who had more names than talents, was sixty-three, a veteran of sixty-eight actions and twenty-two sieges, or so he claimed in his Mémoires which are at times more surprising than Baron Munchausen's, and a Frenchman who joined the Spanish Army when Spain entered the Seven Years War. He was a descendant of Henry IV's general, Crillon le Brave, but his own suffix ought to have been Crillon la Bave. In his account of the assault on Minorca, he wrote that the British had 7,000 men and, 'La valeur Espagnol remplacera ce qui nous manque de force.' 'La valeur Espagnol' was again in evidence, when, arriving outside Fort St Philip, Crillon sent a message to General Murray offering to let him name his own price for surrender. Murray rejected the bribe indignantly, and Crillon set about besieging the fortress. He was joined in September by 4,000 French troops commanded by Baron de Falkenheim, but this reinforcement did not stop Murray from making a sortie and capturing twenty-two prisoners, and almost surprising Crillon himself. The prisoners were sent to Gibraltar, so Admiral Moreno's blockade was as ineffective as Crillon's siege.

What defeated Murray and his garrison was the same enemy that threatened the garrison of Gibraltar, the scurvy. It appeared in December, and soon gained a terrible ascendancy over the stricken soldiers. No vegetables could be grown in Fort St Philip, and there was no friendly port near enough which could send ships through the blockade with supplies of fruit. To make matters worse, Lieutenant-General Draper, the second-in-command, argued openly with Murray about the conduct of the defence. The only hope for Minorca, and the dying garrison, was the British Fleet, and the Fleet in the winter lay in harbour, whilst Lord Sandwich fought engagement after engagement in Parliament. The men accepted their suffering and triumphed over it for seven weeks. Day after day they dragged themselves from their stinking cells to mount guard; some had to be carried to their posts; others became too weak to be moved and lay waiting to be claimed by death. On 1 February 1782 there were 760 soldiers able to answer when the roll was called. In the next two days 100 of them were carried to the hospital. Without the daily guard of 415 men there could be no defence of Fort St Philip, and on 5 February General Murray capitulated. Of his original force, only 600 had strength to crawl out of the fort between the ranks of the victors, and they were so wasted and drawn that it was reported the

enemy wept at the sight of them. General Murray had held out for
nearly six months, and he had given time enough for succours to
arrive, only there were none sent. As a postscript to the Spanish
capture of Minorca, and as an example of Russian interest in the
Mediterranean, the cession of Minorca by Great Britain to Russia
was suggested before its fall, with the condition that the Russian
Fleet should come to its assistance. General Potemkin, who has been
credited with it, was not the first, or the last, Russian to cast his eyes
to the south, and his net in the Mediterranean.

The threat to Jamaica was made following the capture of Minorca.
The plan was to concentrate 50 Spanish and French ships-of-the-line
and 20,000 Spanish troops from Cuba, at Dominique (Haiti), and to
invade Jamaica in March or April 1782. An important part of this
force was to be the French fleet under the Comte de Grasse. De
Grasse had left the Chesapeake in November 1781 and, stopping at
Martinique to augment his force to 29 ships and 6,000 troops, he
sailed to take Barbados. The wind was against him, and he turned on
St Kitts, anchoring off Basse-terre in January. He was followed
there by Admiral Hood with 22 ships, who enticed him out of his
position blockading the harbour, and occupied it himself by a superb
manœuvre. The British garrison of St Kitts, General Fraser and 700
men, had retired to Brimstone Hill and, as Hood had taken or sunk
the French ammunition ships, there seemed little doubt that they
could hold out. However, the planters of St Kitts, seeking to in-
gratiate themselves with the French, who occupied the rest of the
island, seized the artillery and ammunition intended for the British
garrison and handed them over to the enemy, who at once employed
them against the positions on Brimstone Hill. Fraser was forced to
surrender on 12 February, and Hood extricated his squadron only by
a deft escape under cover of night. Nevis and Montserrat fell to de
Grasse, and he recovered the islands of Demarera and Essequibo. On
25 February Rodney arrived from the east with twelve ships, and
joined Hood off Antigua. De Grasse sheltered at Martinique, whilst
the British Fleet put in to Gros Islet Bay, St Lucia. Early in April the
French fleet sailed, Rodney followed, and on the 12th fought the
famous action of the Saints, during which he broke through the
French line, scattered their ships, and in the subsequent pursuit, in
which Hood was more active than Rodney, captured the flagship

Ville de Paris, and de Grasse. This ended any aspirations the enemy entertained to Jamaica, though the assembled Spanish force sailed off and captured the Bahamas. When the new ministry recalled Rodney, it was fortunate that operations in the West Indies had otherwise ended.

The war in the west was over. There were left the distant conflict in India, and the central drama of the siege of Gibraltar.

CHAPTER XIV

Half wore out

THROUGH the winter of 1781–2 neither the Governor nor the garrison of Gibraltar had the slightest idea that the war in America was virtually over, or that the overtures of peace were being heard in the capitals of Europe.

In the days following the sortie they watched the fires burning among the mounds of sand, which had been too great for them to level; in the Spanish Camp they saw the execution of several unfortunates, as General Alvarez exacted the penalty for his own incompetence; on the isthmus, at night, they heard the Spaniards fire at the crack of cooling timbers, anticipating another attack, and during the daytime they watched the enemy's cavalry cavorting about out of range of the guns. At first the enemy appeared stunned by the audacity of the sortie, and made little attempt to put out the fires, or to salvage materials from the ruined batteries, but early in December parties of workmen were seen collecting brushwood on the hills behind the Camp, and a strong guard was mounted in the Centre Guard-House, which, being made of stone, the garrison engineers had been unable to demolish. The artillery kept up a steady fire on this position from the hill batteries, but the Spaniards seemed determined to establish themselves there in order to have an advanced defensive post in the event of any future expedition from the Rock.

But the garrison were in no case to attack, and as December passed they became progressively less able to defend themselves. Within a few weeks, hundreds of men were struck down by scurvy. It is difficult to find the exact strength of the garrison as none of the figures tally, and it was the custom to add fictitious names to the regimental rolls so that their pay might be converted to the use of the Colonel. Taking Captain Drinkwater's figures as the most reliable, the desperate situation of the garrison becomes apparent:

LOSSES SUSTAINED BY THE GARRISON 21 JUNE 1779–
2 NOVEMBER 1781

Total strength 21 June 1779	5,382
73rd Regiment joined January 1780	1,052
	6,434
Total strength 26 November 1781	5,952
Killed, died of wounds, discharged, deserted	482

NUMBER OF MEN AVAILABLE FOR GUARDS, PICKETS,
WORKING PARTIES, ETC.–26 NOVEMBER 1781

Total strength 26 November 1781	5,952
Estimated number of officers, staff	265
„ „ „ artillery	480
„ „ „ engineers	89
„ „ „ sick and wounded	591
	1,425
Number available for guards, etc.	4,527

DAILY DUTIES. 24 HOURS

Guards	933
Pickets	600
Working parties	1,000
	2,533

Over half the garrison were on duty every day and several nights a week, and if the cooks, orderlies, batmen, hospital attendants, clerks, drummers, corporals and serjeants are taken into account, the proportion was considerably greater. Furthermore, the disposition of the regiments in two locations, north and south, made it impossible for the duties to be shared equally; those quartered in the town bore the main burden, and many of their men were kept out of their beds six and seven nights at a time. On 29 November 1781 there were 467 scorbutic men in the Naval Hospital; on 20 December there were

603. Besides these unfortunates there were the wounded and those suffering from other ailments. (In an indent sent to Lord Hillsborough to be forwarded to the Medical Contractor for the Army, these items figure prominently: 'Glauber Salts 50 lbs, 1 doz bone nippers (we find them very useful), Stump caps 4 dozen, Stump pillows 4 dozen', suggesting that whatever the affliction was the surgeon either washed it out or cut it off.) The threat of scurvy was greater because it resulted from a deficiency common to all the garrison. At any time, the men, who were falling by tens, might fall by hundreds.

When the *Unicorn* cutter sailed on the night of 12 December, she carried the Governor's dispatch reporting the success of the sortie, and a postscript saying that he had sent a boat 'to Algiers for lemons'. When the *Phoenix* sailed the next day, he wrote: 'I cannot help informing your Lordship that the Scurvy gains ground with great rapidity within these few days in the most alarming manner.' The garrison had to have a fresh supply of citrus juice in order to survive until the new season's vegetables were ready for consumption. Ships were still able to enter and leave the Bay providing the wind stayed favourable for them, but Barcello's gun-boats lay under Cabrita ready to snap up any vessel becalmed or unable to outsail their oarsmen. On 7 December a cutter was taken whilst the garrison looked on helplessly, and four days later the boat returning from Algiers ended her journey in Algeciras. In the meantime the enemy kept up a smart fire from the isthmus, and managed to knock down the garrison flag again: it was flying ten minutes later. The officers of the garrison presented another Memorial to the Governor, which was received in silence.

On the night of the 19th two ordnance ships, the *Henry* and the *Mercury*, arrived, having taken twenty days for their passage from Portsmouth. In the morning the garrison heard the news of the surrender at Yorktown, and were doubtless relieved that General Eliott had succeeded Lord Cornwallis as Governor of their Rock. The same post informed them that His Majesty had been pleased to advance Brigadiers Ross and Green to the rank of Major-General. On the next day Major-General Ross set off in a small boat to Faro, and thence to England, to receive the approbation of his countrymen for his brief but glorious visit to Gibraltar. The garrison were becoming accustomed to the sudden disappearances of Major-General Ross, who commuted between Whitehall and Main Street in his own private campaign for promotion. Brigadier Picton, a leading light in the Lieutenant-Governor's party, whom Captain Drinkwater found 'very tall, dignified and rather pompous', had been left behind, both in the sortie and the race for promotion, and the party was mortified. The year ended on a note of mortification. The young Baron died, lists of dead and wounded, all different, were copied into journals and letters, the works destroyed in the sortie were slowly being repaired (during which many enemy workmen were mortified), and the scurvy spread gaunt black fingers over the garrison, in the most terrible mortification of all.

> While peaceful flocks in verdant meadow, graze,
> Supply their wants, and slumber at their ease;
> Now skip and sport, and each contented feed,
> And one by one are destined to bleed.
> But here—'midst hardships, soldiers ne'er repine,
> But with the pomp of war sit down to dine;
> To feast upon an ounce of salted beef,
> Which at the most affords but small relief;
> No sparkling wine to animate and cheer,
> No pint, nor pot, of British home-brew'd beer,
> But pickled beef and water is our fare;
> Coop'ed up like pastur'd sheep, within the walls,
> And one by one cut off by shells and balls.
> Here two or three together meet for mirth,
> And seat themselves behind a bank of earth;
> Here bread and water cheerfully goes round,
> And grass, got on the rock, for sallad found;
> Sometimes brown toast and vinegar supplies
> The place of punch and crowns our festive joys,
> Thus happy in our sports each other cheer,
> In God we place our trust, nor danger fear,
> With heart and hand, the walls and batt'ries man,
> Live hard, fight, watch, do all that Britons can!
>
> (Ancell)

The new year started fine. The garrison goats were feeling the spring.

Garrison Orders, 1st January 1782:

Password, Windsor. Countersign, Grub.

No goats to be allowed to stray during the Night, or to feed in the daytime without some person to take care of them on pain of Confiscation and Disobedience of orders.

During the day Corporal Martin and a matross earned themselves five guineas each from the Governor for saving the life of Mr Rodgers, an Artillery officer who was pinned down by an enemy shell in Willis's. The General told the Corporal that 'he should equally have noticed him for relieving his comrade'. A ship, the *St Philip's Castle*, came in from Minorca on the 4th, carrying twenty-two Spanish prisoners taken by General Murray in his sortie, and letters from the old optimist, who was gallantly keeping 12,000 troops of Spain and France at bay from the clammy and disease-ridden casemates of Fort St Philip. On the 10th the ship returned east. About this time the spy, Antonio Juanico, taken from the Faro boat in December was found guilty and condemned to be hanged on 4 February. On the 12th the *Henry* and the *Mercury* set sail to the west. The Spanish officer, Don Vincente Friza, and four prisoners taken in the sortie, were put aboard the *Henry*, whilst several townspeople and families took passage on the *Mercury*. The *Henry* carried a long dispatch from the Governor to Lord Hillsborough. 'The scurvy does not increase,' he wrote, and asked for 'molasses, essence of spruce, rice malt, bornea tea, powder sugar, Rob of Lemon, Portable soup, and strong red wine.' He added:

Having observed amongst the packages landed from the Ordnance ships that some are marked Gun boat Stores gives me to hope that some assistance of that nature is preparing to be sent us. . . . When it shall be thought proper to send a reinforcement or recruits from England to this Garrison I beg that Carpenters Joiners Wheelwrights Sawyers or any of that Tribe to the amount of an hundred may be drafted from the Regiments at home.

The enemy fire had slackened considerably and they were seen exchanging guns in the Lines. (A deserter had reported that they had used three sets of guns since the start of the bombardment.) The garrison engineers took advantage of the lull to caisson the embrasures of the batteries at Willis's with timbers from the broken colliers sunk off the New Mole, hence the discovery of the shortage of 'any of that Tribe'. The caissoning was done behind a large canvas screen, which apparently deterred the enemy gunners from firing on the working parties climbing about the front of the Rock. On the morning of the 16th, with the wind blowing from the north-east, two cutters were seen trying to make for the Bay. The enemy saw them too, and sent a frigate, a xebeck and several gun-boats out after them. The cutters, unable to proceed against a headwind, tacked away towards the east, drawing the Spaniards after them. It is interesting to note that the ships were in sight for the whole day, as an indication of the difficulty in passing the Straits when the wind was in the opposite direction.

The sun continued to shine, and the enemy to work on the redoubt they had erected round the Central Guard House, and the garrison to fire on them. Captain Spilsbury, who was a keen observer of the more curious incidents in the garrison, has an enigmatic entry in his journal for 17 January: 'Lt. B— Ingineers, out of his senses'. Could this be Lieutenant William Booth, already claiming credit for the sortie? Three days later the regiments changed quarters, giving some relief to those from the town who encamped in the south. There was no relief for the Royal Artillery, who continued to fire away at the workmen on the isthmus. The Spaniards were working on the St Carlos Battery, and many were injured trying to put out the fires the garrison gunners started among the fascines brought up in the night. But the same men who had before worked slowly and without enthusiasm, now braved the fire and restored the batteries with great energy, as if to wipe out the shameful memory of the sortie. On the night of the 28th the two cutters which had been chased eastward came round Europa Point to the New Mole, having left their pursuers out in the Mediterranean and, shortly after, a third cutter came in from the west. These three, the *Viper*, the *Lively* and the *Dartmouth Tartar*, were welcomed in the garrison as an indication of the growing interest in England in their fate; the story of the sortie had drawn people's attention to the small Rock, where British troops were having considerably more success than they had had in the huge continent of America. The congratulations of the ships' captains did not prevent them from charging exorbitantly for the provisions they carried. Tea was back to a guinea a pound, hams were 3s. 2d., corned beef 1s. 8d., cheese 4s. 10d., butter the same, port wine was at the disgraceful price of £1 14s. 5d., per dozen, and a sheep sold for £14 1s. 0d. Towards the end of January the enemy copied the engineers at Willis's and put up a large canvas screen in the hope that, if the garrison gunners could not see their workmen, they would not fire at them. The garrison gunners knocked it down.

Stunted February, never a very satisfactory month, saw the surrender of General Murray and his scarecrow garrison in Minorca, the collapse of the King's blind autocracy in England, and the continuation of the long endurance of the Gibraltar garrison, as they lay on their Rock, grey, dusty and indomitable. 'Everything Military is carried on with the same order and regularity as in the greatest Splendor of Peace and Plenty; altho' the Soldiers are half wore out with hardships and low provisions', the writer of Boyd's Log Book wrote with pride, longing, and a touch of exasperation. The enemy finished work on the St Carlos Battery, and began to repair St Martin's, and to open their parallel to the east. On the 4th the Governor pardoned Antonio Juanico, and there was a God Send (though General Eliott deserved some credit for it) when three vessels arrived from Portugal loaded with oranges and lemons. The effect of these fruit on the sick was again remarkable and the number of scorbutic men decreased. Early in the month the artillery began to practise with a new gun-carriage invented by Lieutenant Koehler. This strange man requires some introduction, as he became a firm favourite of Governor Eliott's, and Captain Drinkwater wrote that the General declared that 'he was the only true friend he had ever found in his life'. Koehler was an abstemious man, with a brusque manner, and his contempt for his fellow officers undoubtedly attracted the Governor to him. He was a good artist, and his watercolours were occasionally used to illustrate the dispatches sent to Lord Hillsborough. He was also a clever engineer. One of the problems that faced the artillery on the Rock was that the type of gun-carriage in use could not be depressed sufficiently to fire downwards at a target at short range. They had improvised a means of propping up the back of the carriage, but that meant that it was fixed permanently in that position, and the shot had to be rammed upwards, with the gunner exposed in the embrasure. Lieutenant Koehler's gun-carriage was based on the simple expedient of two planks; the

lower one, with a groove down the centre, was hinged at the front to
a normal carriage, and could be lifted at the back and fixed, at any
height, between two slotted upright posts by a horizontal bar between the slots; the upper plank, to which the barrel was fixed, had a
spindle eight inches in diameter at the centre which lay in the groove
of the lower plank, allowing the gun to recoil without moving the
whole carriage, and also to swing to one side to be loaded. If the gun
was required to be fired at elevation, it was simply turned round, and
the carriage reversed. The invention contributed to the accuracy and
speed of the artillery later in the siege.

The enemy squadron worked its way back from the east on 15
February, but too late to stop two ships coming in from England. On
the 17th a cutter, the *Flying Fish*, fought her way in, and the next day,
in the early hours, a brig was sighted from the Europa Guard. When
challenged, her captain answered 'From Cork', and was told to come
to anchor at the Mole. Being an Irishman, the captain took his ship
towards the Old Mole, until he realized he was running straight at
the enemy's guns, whereupon he ran her aground on the Spanish
side of the Mole. He and his crew were brought off by the navy, and
the Spanish gunners fired away at the brig all day from the Black
Battery and Fort St Philip without making a single hit. Mr Ancell
heard what the captain said when he came ashore and reported:
'By J— us, he intended to run his ship up to his merchant's store-
house, having heard when at Cork, that we had burnt all the Spanish
batteries and spiked up their guns, and that he imagined he might
anchor in any part of the bay with safety', whereupon the garrison
felt that they ought to apologize to him for his ineptitude.

The efforts of the enemy gunners to hit the brig from Cork amused
the garrison, until they succeeded. Any diversion from the routine of
parades, guarding the lines, dragging powder and shot up the hill,
picket duty, drinking in the dark, or taking the long walk to Hardy
Town to find that the men encamped in the south were there first,
was absorbing, and when Bombardier Campbell walked into his
casemate and announced that a cannonball had just grazed his nose,
the story received greater currency than it might have been expected
to merit. The interesting question was: when would Bombardier
Campbell fall down dead? There was little doubt that he would, as the
rush of air behind the ball would have injured his brain; that

Bombardier Campbell did not appear to realize this, only added a macabre piquancy to the game. He was treated with the utmost consideration by his own regiment, and inquired after sympathetically by the others, for days, for weeks, until he was still walking about long after the most optimistic estimate of his chances had expired. Then they called him a fraud and forgot him.

On 20 February the *Lively*, *Viper* and *Dartmouth Tartar* sailed for England. They carried the news that the scurvy had abated considerably due to the administration of the lemons and oranges sent in from Portugal, but that Major-General Green was seriously ill, and requested leave to return home. The Governor added that the batteries the enemy were erecting on the ruins left by the sortie were near completion, but that he had 'all reason to believe the Enemy's loss must be considerable as our Artillery is remarkably well served— in my opinion far exceeding that of the Spaniards'. But the Artillery looking out were by no means pleased to see thirteen new embrasures in the sandbanks pointing at them. On the 23rd there was firing in the Straits and, after beating off an enemy frigate, a ship came in. To the surprise of the garrison, it was the *Mercury*, which had sailed, they thought, for England on 12 January. The families who had sailed with her were not so much surprised as angry to find themselves back on the Rock, which they could hardly have mistaken for the white cliffs of Dover. The Governor, as close as ever, had arranged with Captain Heington of the *Mercury* that he should put in at Lisbon to buy fruit and wine for the garrison, and return as soon as he could. In order to ensure that no word reached the enemy, the passengers were embarked and kept in ignorance of the plan, so much so that when Captain Heington tried to persuade them to change ships at Lisbon they refused, and so came back to Gibraltar in the belief that the Captain was mad or they were dreaming. They were in time to see the Spanish ships dressed over-all in Algeciras, and hear the *feu-de-joie* from the Camp and Lines, as the forces before Gibraltar heard the news of the surrender of Fort St Philip and the British garrison to the Duc de Crillon. The next day several Spanish vessels came into the Bay from the east to reinforce Barcello's squadron. The month ended with the arrival of an ordnance ship, the *St Ann*, carrying the parts of two gun-boats, and advice that a second ship, the *Vernon*, was sailing for the Bay. General Eliott held a field day, and reviewed the regiments at Windmill Hill; the officers dined with him at the Convent afterwards, according to Boyd's Log Book, wearing their hats.

The mad hatters were followed by the March hares, or rather rabbits, which were seen running about Misery Hill and Sugar Loaf Point, which they shared with the apes. There was no road up the hill in the south, and only the roughest track to St Michael's Cave (the British called it St George's Cave, but the old name stuck). The animals on the Rock lived mostly among the trees and shrubs which were inaccessible on the high cliffs south of the Signal House. They had been hunted up to this fastness by the troops. Elsewhere on the Rock the hot spring sunshine brought out all sorts of creatures that had survived the bombardment and made their homes in the ruins of the town and under the rocks and cliffs of the lines and batteries. There were centipides and scorpions and snakes, big hairy spiders and green lizards. Colonel James, writing of the latter, called them skinks: 'They hide under flat stones, or in the holes of old walls and ruins; these were the salamanders of the Ancients.' The garrison lived in very much the same way: in torn and dusty uniforms, with haggard sunburnt faces, with the same slow sureness as the lizards, until the moment came to strike, they hid under the stones and in the holes and called themselves the British Salamanders.

On 1 March the Spaniards sent over an officer under a flag of truce, who told the garrison what they had feared, but expected, that the Minorca garrison had surrendered on 5 February. The next day the artillery set fire to the new 13-gun battery, but, as Mr Ancell wrote: 'The foe manifested a valour, and in an intrepid manner, jumped upon the glacis, pouring baskets of sand upon the flames, when after much difficulty and danger they got it put out.' The energy and courage of the Spaniards on this occasion, and on many others at this time, excited the admiration of everyone who witnessed it. They were all soldiers and courage was common coin amongst them. After the fall of Minorca, and these exhibitions of bottom on the part of their enemies, the garrison regarded them with new respect and caution, which were the foundation of their later defence. One instance of this was that the batteries now fired at the Spanish General whenever he appeared in the Lines, which was a higher compliment than their previous polite restraint. There was also good reason for their extra attention towards the enemy. At the end of February the Spanish Camp had been increased by forty tents and, on 6 March, sixty more were pitched and parties of workmen were landing stores, and building a road from the beach. The garrison was by no means idle, and the bridge across Landport ditch was pulled down. By the New Mole, the ship's carpenters were laying the keel of the first gun-boat brought by the *St Ann*, and meeting some difficulties. It was Captain Spilsbury who recorded them: 'Our people don't agree about the head and stern of our gun-boats.' They had to wait for an expert to come from England before carrying on the work. Both sides kept up a smart fire, and many men were seen to fall in the Spanish works; the garrison had fewer casualties, perhaps because of the activities of two boys of the Artificer company, Richardson and Brand. These two had such sharp eyesight that they could see the flight of a shot from the moment it left the gun. They took turns in watching out whenever a party of workmen was on the hill, and warning the men when a shot or shell was coming towards them. Captain Drinkwater, with a particularly macabre incident to recount, mentioned one of them:

In the course of the day [25 March] a shot came through one of the capped embrasures on Princess Amelia's battery, took off the legs of two men belonging to the 72nd and 73rd regiments, one leg of a soldier of the 73rd, and wounded another man in both legs: thus four men had seven legs taken off and wounded by one shot. The Boy who was usually stationed on the works where a large party was employed to inform the men when the Enemy's fire was directed to that place, had been reproving them for their carelessness in not attending to him; and had just returned his head towards the Enemy, when he observed this shot, and instantly called for them to take care: his caution was however too late; the shot entered the embrasure, and had the above-recited fatal effect.

On 21 March the *Vernon* at last arrived having had a turbulent voyage during which, escorted by a frigate, the *Success*, she had met a Spanish frigate of forty guns from Algeciras; after a fight, the Spaniard struck, and on board her Captain Pole of the *Success* had found her papers in which there was a full description of the *Vernon*, and information that the enemy had thirty ships out looking for her. On seeing some sails in the distance, the Captain had burned the Spanish frigate, and sent the *Vernon* on alone to Gibraltar. Towards evening she entered the Straits, and found herself surrounded by enemy ships. Fortunately it was dark, and she managed to escape by sailing with them, so that they supposed she must be one of them, until the opportunity came to tack and head for the Rock. Some hours later, the ships that Captain Pole had seen came in, the *Cerberus* and *Apollo* frigates, and four transports carrying the 97th Regiment, and the Colonel, Colonel Stanton. The *Vernon* brought ten gun-boats and the assembly expert and, with the new regiment, it would have been a strong reinforcement, except that the 97th were sick, and of its 700 men 100 and more died within the next few months. During the last days of March the enemy completed and armed the batteries around the Mill Tower and extended the parallel to the east, finishing in a redoubt in the centre of the isthmus, which the garrison later learned was called the Mahon Battery. On the night of the 31st the gunners on the Rock managed to set it on fire, and the Spaniards had to knock part of it down to prevent the flames spreading to the parallel. The garrison fired more times during March than in any month since the beginning of the siege: 3,657 shot, 10,362 shells, 733 rounds of grape, 56 carcasses (incendiary bombs), and 45 light balls; yet the enemy were in a stronger position before the North Front than they were at the time of the sortie. It was discouraging. Yet they had survived the attack of scurvy, and several ships had come in with lemons and oranges; they were well provisioned, and had received reinforcements of a regiment, twelve gunboats, guns and ammunition; there were no longer the problems caused by the inhabitants and families, most of whom had left; and the men were only 'half wore out'. That was quite encouraging.

CHAPTER XV

A simple military artist

WHILST the siege was proceeding in this relatively undramatic way since the sortie, events were conspiring to make Gibraltar the cockpit of the world's attention. The British campaign in America frittered out, and with it the last of George III's pretence that the Americans were still his subjects. Peace was the word in fashion: in Great Britain, where the loss of America ensured the return to Parliamentary government; in France, where the treasury was exhausted; in Holland, where the Government turned its coat only to find it threadbare on both sides; and in America, where a new people was anxious to experiment with independence—but not in Spain. Charles III had entered the war with definite objectives: one, Minorca, had been gained, but the other, Gibraltar, remained obstinately out of his grasp. For two years and eight months the Spaniards had tried to regain Gibraltar by blockade, by negotiation, by bombardment, and the French had shown little interest in their efforts. Now, however, the Rock began to appear to the diplomats in the courts of Europe as it did to the soldiers of General Alvarez, a massive stumbling-block on the road to peace; for, by the Convention of Aranjuez, France was bound to stay at war until her ally recovered her lost fortress. As it was apparent that Spain would not capture the Rock by herself, the French Government, with not a little reluctance and complaint and shrugging and contempt, found themselves obliged to direct the vast power of her armies and navies, her military flair and genius, against Governor Eliott and his small garrison. At the same time Great Britain, which had lost an empire, a handful of West Indian islands, her foothold in Florida, and the finest port in the western Mediterranean, was determined to hold on to her Rock.

Not George III, not his ministers—but the people, saw Gibraltar as a symbol of national pride and independence which stood a yard off Selsey Bill, instead of 1,000 miles away and a few yards from Spain.

When, at the beginning of 1782, the strategists at Versailles turned to their maps of Gibraltar, their gazettes, and their Vaubans, it became apparent to them that the siege had been undertaken without any plan. This was not strictly true, as the Spaniards had a heap of plans, but had not adopted any of them. As early as 1774, the Colleges and Military Seminaries in Spain had been instructed to suspend all studies but those concerned with the attack on fortified places by land and sea. In the years following, and particularly after the failure of the bombardment, they had invited the leading military experts in Europe to submit their plans for the reduction of the fortress. Now that the French demanded a plan, and were prepared to assist in it, Minister Floridablanca uncovered the piles of paper, diagrams, models, projections and elevations, and held a competition; and the prize was the greatest imaginable for any strategist, to see the mights of France and Spain turning his statistics into men, his diagrams into machines, his words into bullets, and ultimately his obscurity into glory. The attack of Gibraltar was a nice exercise, and produced some nice projects.

There were simple plans: to provide every soldier with a ladder; to dig a mine under the great north cliff and blow it up; to pile up stones behind the Lines until it became a question of opposing a mountain to a mountain, when, presumably, another plan would be required; to raise the height of the isthmus by moving the Queen of Spain's Chair, until the troops could run along it and take the Rock from above. There were fantastic plans: to build a thousand cork horses, complete with saddles and reins, and equip a squadron of maritime cavalry, who would ride across the Bay, and take the Rock (perhaps by mere surprise); to replace the guns and mortars with vast syringes, powered by fire engines, which would throw twenty hogsheads of water a minute onto the Rock, and wash the defenders into the sea; to use the syringes to shoot vinegar instead of water, which would dissolve the limestone of the mountain and leave the defenders on a strip of sand level with the isthmus. There were magical plans; to poison the air around Gibraltar without affecting the Spanish Camp; to hurl bombs containing one magical mixture

from mortars containing another; to fly over the defenders in a balloon and pour down bucketfuls of a drug that would give them con-
vulsions. There were other airborne plans: to carry a gun battery by
balloon and fire down onto the defenders' heads; to send over 200
men in 100 balloons, though there were no instructions as to what
they should do when they got there. There was a magnificent plan:
to land engineers on the east side of the Rock, who would, un-
observed by the defenders, dig a tunnel straight through to the other
side, through which the Army would march one night, and arrive,
drums beating and flags flying, on the Grand Parade. 'This project,'
wrote the author of 'Conseil de guerre privé sur l'événement de
Gibraltar en 1782', who refers to all the plans, 'was so great that all
others must give it pride of place.' The author also produced a plan,
and it won the prize.

Jean-Claude-Eléonor Le Michaud d'Arçon described himself as 'a
simple military artist'. He was born at Besançon in 1733, and had
achieved some distinction as an engineer with the French army. In
March 1780 he sent the Spanish Ambassador in Paris a detailed
mémoire outlining his project for taking Gibraltar. In this *mémoire*, he
first mentioned a machine 'incombustible et insubmersible' which,
he claimed, would enable an attack to be mounted from the Bay
against the weakest part of the defences. The machine was the hulk
of a ship, large enough to mount fifteen 24-pounders, and plated
with green wood reinforced with old cables to resist the penetration
of ordinary shot, and with a system of pipes that would spray water
on the outside for the extinguishing of red-hot shot. As it was required to do the minimum of sailing, the hulk could be heavily
plated until it was as strong as a land battery; and the fire-extinguishing apparatus would obviate the danger that would threaten an
ordinary man-of-war. It would be, in fact, a floating battery. Ten of
these batteries would be anchored within range of the Line Wall, in
which, after eight or ten days, they would open a breach. Then 150
sloops carrying 50 men each would advance, and land the troops who
would make the assault. This was M. d'Arçon's first plan for the
capture of Gibraltar.

The plan was favourably received by the Spanish Ambassador,
M. d'Aranda, and the French Ministry of War, and at the end of
July 1781 d'Arçon was sent to Gibraltar to make a detailed study of

the fortress. By this time he had elaborated on his first idea, and had invented a network of pipes which would cover the side of the battering-ship, behind the plating, and through which water would be pumped 'like the blood in the veins of an animal': if a shot should penetrate the wood and enter the ship, it would cut one of the pipes, and the water would flow out exactly where it was required and extinguish the ball. He was also working on a project for a quick-firing match, so that all the guns on the batteries could be fired simultaneously, and he had invented the first landing-craft, with flat hinged bows, to take the place of the sloops. At Gibraltar he made a painstaking survey of the ground and decided that the New Mole should be the point for the assault, whilst the land batteries engaged the defenders' guns in the bastions on the Line Wall, and the gun-boats and mortar-boats supported the floating batteries. The plan was then submitted to the committee in Madrid, which approved it, the French and Spanish Courts ratified their decision, and it began to be put into action with a briskness that was entirely un-Spanish, and emanated from the small energetic French engineer. Ten ships destined to be converted into floating batteries were collected at Cadiz, and d'Arçon went down to see them. The Spanish Court appointed the Duc de Crillon to command the attack.

This was unfortunate because the Duc de Crillon also had a plan, or so he claimed afterwards. (It is probable that every general had one, and Crillon was the obvious choice after his success in command of a combined force in Minorca.) Crillon claimed that King Charles had promised that if he succeeded in Minorca, he would be allowed to follow his own plan for the siege of Gibraltar. What this was does not appear in his Mémoires, but there was one project which in-volved the sacrifice of three or four large ships by running them aground and then using them as a landing stage for the troops, who would be ferried across the Bay under cover of gun-boats, which were neither incombustible nor insubmersible, and which nobody cared for very much. However, whatever the General's plan was originally, it became confused with the Chevalier d'Arçon's inven-tions, much to the annoyance of the latter, as we will see later.

So, in March of 1782, with d'Arçon at Cadiz, and the Duc de Crillon still at Minorca, secret preparations were in hand for the annihilation of Governor Eliott and his garrison.

CHAPTER XVI

Preparations uncommonly vast

GENERAL ELIOTT heard about the enemy's secret plans on 1 April from an informer named Chicardo, who had arrived in a small boat from Portugal. Chicardo reported that the Spaniards had commandeered twelve ships at Cadiz, and were lining them with cork and cables for an expedition against Gibraltar in the summer. On the same day, through an ironic coincidence, grates for the heating of shot were issued to the batteries on the North Front. The grates were not put in use, and the garrison continued to fire cold shot, particularly at a deserter, who was seen running from Landport towards the St Carlos Battery. He fell just short of the battery and was dragged in by the Spanish guards. In the night a Spanish deserter came over to the garrison, and reported that the Englishman had died shortly after being taken into the battery: he estimated that the enemy had suffered almost 1,000 casualties, half of them fatal, whilst repairing the advance works. This was little consolation to the garrison when, on the 9th, they saw two new regiments joining the Spanish Camp, fresh troops in new uniforms, one white and one blue; and two days later they heard from the patron of a boat from Portugal of the preparation in Cadiz of floating batteries, lined with cork and oakum, of a French engineer of renown, and of the imminent arrival of the Duc de Crillon with his victorious army, and Admiral Don Bonaventura Moreno, who had commanded the Spanish navy at Port Mahon, with ten line-of-battle ships, and a fleet of gun-boats and mortar-boats.

Several ships a day arrived at Algeciras or the Orange Grove with stores for the Spanish Camp. The enemy were particularly employed in moving materials from the Camp to the Lines, and their fire slackened to 100 rounds a day. April 12 was the anniversary of the opening of the barrage, and the garrison had been locked up in Gibraltar for almost three years; not only that, but the enemy were about to launch an attack which, from what they saw and heard, would be far greater than anything they had so far experienced. Yet the news that caused greater concern among the officers and rattled the glass in the Convent windows was brought in by the store-ship, *Antigallican*, which came in on the 20th after a brush with Barcello's cruisers. Lord North had resigned on 20 March and the new Cabinet was led by the Marquis of Rockingham, Lord Shelburne and Charles James Fox; General Conway replaced Lord Amherst as Commander-in-Chief. General Eliott's guardian angels were out of office, and General Boyd smiled as he took the air at the King's Bastion. The lower orders in the garrison were indifferent, as they stood neither to lose nor gain, and more interesting things were happening on the Rock itself. 'A Soldier of the 12th Regiment (for Sodomy) stood two hours in the Pillory, fix'd near the gallows and received 500 lashes from the Common hangman and then sent on board the Provost Ship,' Boyd's Log Book recorded on 19 April, and two days later Captain Spilsbury remarked: 'A picquet was demanded from the 97th, but they could not furnish it. So much for young Regiments.' The garrison also had something to watch in the harbour, when the first of the British gun-boats was launched, and fired its 18-pounder out into the Bay. The expert had sorted out the problems of the ships' carpenters, and several more of the boats were nearing completion. The squadron under Captain Curtis had been withdrawn behind a boom of masts and chains in the shelter of the New Mole, and it was hoped that the gun-boats would be used to assist vessels that were becalmed as they came into the Bay, and fell prey to the enemy boats and galleys.

Though the scurvy had now so far abated that on 9 May there were only thirty-three scorbutic men in the hospital, there were still occasional fatalities from illness: 'Serjeant Clanes of the 39th Regiment died this morning of a Decay and another Serjeant's wife dressing for his funeral dropt down dead' (Boyd's Log Book). The Governor wrote home for a further supply of portable soup. The letter went with the *Cerberus* and *Apollo* frigates, which sailed for England, escorting the transports and ordnance ships that had arrived in the last two

months. They were unfortunate enough to meet an enemy squadron
in the Gut, consisting of two frigates and three xebecks, which took
three of the unarmed British transports and carried them into Algeciras. On 9 May the garrison also had their first glimpse of the battering-ships:

> This forenoon arrived from the westward, one line of battle ship, con-
> voying eight large store-ships or Indiamen. From the appearance of their
> rigging and sides, which is dry and shabby, and having but a few hands
> on board, we cannot imagine from what part they have arrived or what
> occasion brought them in here. (Ancell).

They were not kept wondering for long. The ships were hauled close
to the shore at Algeciras, and parties of workmen began to unrig
them. They were the famous cork ships, or junk ships, as the garrison
called them, and Mr Ancell added, 'Most people think they are more
fit for fire-wood than attacking a fortress.' A Portuguese boat slipped
in the next night carrying 30,000 oranges, and her captain reported
that the Emperor of Morocco had once more opened his ports to
British shipping. This news, though welcome, was of little importance
at this stage of the siege, when the garrison could look across the Bay
to see the Spanish Camp growing almost daily and the hulks at Algeciras being prepared for the attack. General Green, who, though not
fully recovered from his illness, felt obliged to remain at his post,
turned his attention to the batteries along the Line Wall, and those
facing the Bay in the south, and ordered palisades to be erected along
the foot of the Wall. The work was carried out under a blazing sun,
and the heat brought out the usual rash of odd incidents. Captain
Spilsbury noted on the 16th: 'One 12th making belief to shoot a girl
in Camp the firelock went off and shot her dead', and three days
later three men of the 58th, attempting to desert down the precipices
on the east side of the Rock, fell to their deaths one after the other
from a rope too short to take them to the bottom. On the 25th a
Serjeant in the 97th stabbed himself and one 12th, drunk, fell down
the hill and fractured his skull.

On the 16th three British store-ships came in, avoiding the cruisers
at Cabrita Point by hoisting French colours until they were within
reach of safety, and landed powder, shells, bedding and timber. The
enemy in the meantime were busy with the hulks, cutting gun-ports

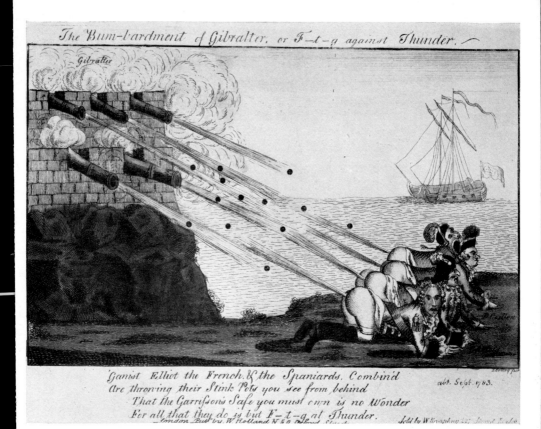

The Bum-bardment of Gibralter, or F—t—g against Thunder.

Gibralter

'Ganist Elliot the French, & the Spaniards, Combin'd
Are throwing their Stink Pots you see from behind
That the Garrisons Safe you must own is no Wonder
For all that they do is but F—t—g at Thunder.

abt. Sept. 1783.

London Pub by W Holland N 50 Oxford Street

Sold by W Humphrey 227 Strand London

Two contemporary cartoons

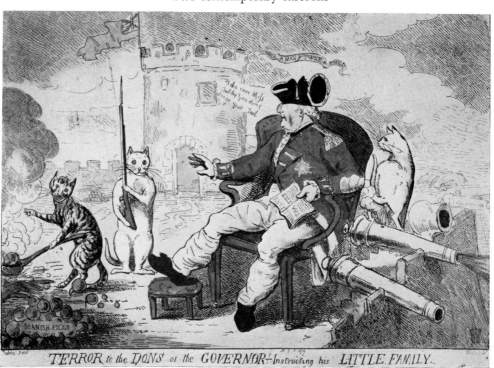

TERROR to the DONS or the GOVERNOR—Instructing his LITTLE FAMILY.

General Eliott with the Key to Gibraltar, by Sir Joshua Reynolds. (On the left, Koehler's cannon)

in the sides, and plating them with timber; and unloading stores for the Camp. There was little activity in their advanced batteries, and their firing had almost ceased. On the 25th the garrison received a surprise reinforcement. At 6 a.m. a small privateer, the *St George*, slipped round Europa Point, bringing from Leghorn twelve Corsican privates and an officer who had volunteered to serve with the garrison. The next day the enemy received their reinforcement. One hundred and fourteen ships from the east arrived and anchored between the Palmones and Algeciras. During the next few days, 7,000 troops were landed and joined the enemy's Camp, already some 12,000 strong.

Whilst General Eliott and a group of officers were watching the disembarkation two days later, one of his aides pointed out a boat approaching from the enemy under a flag of truce. 'Before the purport of the flag was known, the Governor, speaking to the officers near him, said "he supposed the Duke was arrived, and had sent to summon the Garrison; but he should give him a short answer. 'No—No' —and hoped the gentlemen (addressing himself to the Officers present) would all support him".' Captain Drinkwater added, when it was learned that the flag was only to bring over a message from a merchant who had been captured, 'He had not, however, an opportunity of being so spiritedly laconic.'

The month of May was remarkable for the beginning of Serjeant-Major Ince's Gallery, which, with the aid of twelve miners, he blasted through the rock above Willis's batteries towards a projecting tower on the face of the Rock. Using hand drills and soft powder, the Serjeant-Major, whose name is famous on Gibraltar and can be found scratched in the plaster on the magazine behind Willis's, presumably by himself in an idle moment, began a tunnel of exact dimensions, burrowing, as it were, under the skin of the Rock.

June came, and it was hotter than ever. Brigadier Stanton of the 97th Regiment, who had been promoted some weeks before, died of sunstroke. The rains had been poor the previous winter, and water was scarce. The provisions brought in by Admiral Darby were rotting, and the prices of food exorbitant. The enemy were working on battering-ships reported to be impregnable, and their Camp was estimated to contain 19,000 men. It was King George's birthday, and the garrison fired forty-four times, and were answered some four

hundred and forty times by the enemy, who had been politely waiting
for them to start the celebrations. Fifty more ships arrived at Algeciras. It was hotter still.

On 7 June the artillery at the King's Bastion practised firing red-
hot shot, using the grates recently issued to them. They were not unlike the ordinary grates found in fireplaces, and could only heat a few
shots at a time; these were then picked up in tongs and either carried
directly to the cannons, or taken in wheelbarrows with fireproof
bottoms; the shot was loaded, and the gunner who had this risky task
had to dodge out of the way before the wadding took fire and exploded the charge. The gunners on the King's Bastion were firing at
the wreck of the Irish brig on the Old Mole, when one had his head
blown off, and the practice was stopped. The preparations for the
assault, which the garrison could see being advanced daily in Algeciras (where six of the battering-ships were apparently almost completed) and in the Camp, made the garrison's efforts seem feeble by
comparison. The casks of earth collected behind the Line Wall to fill
the breaches, the small grates, even the guns—could they defend the
Rock against the encircling enemy?

Garrison Orders, 10th June 1782.

Upon all occasions it is recommended that the men walk slow, and it is
positively ordered that all employed in the King's works drawing carts
or any other heavy work, do not only walk slow, but also rest at stated
Intervals, and upon no account run so as to overheat themselves during
the warm weather except when the service may require haste.

The Governor was not going to have his garrison rushed. There were
outbreaks of temperament, and on the same day one Corsican stabbed
another, and Captain Witham fought a duel with Lieutenant Burleigh. (What they fought over is not apparent; Ensign Sterne, Tristram
Shandy's father, fought a duel at Gibraltar over a goose in 1727;
Captain Witham doubtless had an equally good reason. On the
10th orders were given that no water was to be carried from the
Fountain by mule, and either gentleman meeting the other on the
Grand Parade could have got a repartee out of this. Boyd's Log
Book, which reported the duel, also mentioned that there was a small
boat out in the Bay taking soundings at cannon shot from the shore,
and so had M. d'Arçon on the page as well.) The day after, there was

a real tragedy. One of the few shells that the enemy threw over in the morning landed at the door of the magazine of the Princess Ann's Battery, and blew it up with a huge explosion, and a column of smoke. Unluckily there was a working party nearby, and fourteen men were killed, and fifteen wounded. Debris was hurled high in the air, and down into the lines, and for the moment there was consternation in the garrison. The enemy were heard cheering, and promptly increased their barrage. There was a second magazine near the first, but though two more shells landed before it, it was strong enough to resist the explosions and remained intact. These magazines were of remarkably strong construction, and in the rainiest weather remained perfectly dry, and it was only by chance that the one at Princess Ann's, which had withstood the heavy bombardment, was destroyed at this time. When the rubble had been cleared, the engineers found the damage to have been largely superficial, and the battery fired a few defiant shots that same night.

Earlier in the month all twelve of the garrison's gun-boats had been launched, and armed. Three carried 24-pounders and the remainder 18-pounders, and each had a crew of twenty-one sailors from the *Brilliant*, the *Porcupine* and the *Speedwell*. On the 14th the garrison had the opportunity to see them in action, or almost in action. Every day some enemy ships came in, and on this afternoon a Spanish xebeck coming from the east stood in so close to the Rock that she lost the wind, and lay helpless a short way out. The guns at the south opened up on her, and she fired a signal for assistance, whereupon two boats from Cabrita started out towards her. The gun-boats were manned and rowed out, but the Spaniards reached her first, and turned her into the wind, so that she escaped, much to the annoyance of the onlookers.

The 97th Regiment, which had been of no assistance to the garrison since it had arrived and had almost literally been quartered in the Naval Hospital, at last provided a picket of forty men on 17 June. This small help was made to appear ridiculous when, on the same day, a fleet of sixty transports, escorted by three frigates flying French colours, anchored off the mouth of the Guadaranque. Previously, three large ships and eight others had arrived at Algeciras, and there was a regular shuttle service of all sizes of craft in and out of the Bay, but these carried troops, French troops, and there were estimated to

be 5,000 of them. On the 18th the carpenters at Algeciras were seen
to be busy with the ninth junk ship, whilst a party of Spanish and
French senior officers visited the Lines. One general was bold enough
to walk forward to the advanced works and stood in front of the St
Martin's Battery, by the shore. The garrison were in no mind for
civilities and fired a shot, whereupon he took off his hat and retreated.
The Governor had other concerns. He was a cat-lover. 'Garrison
Orders 18th June. The order respecting the Dogs to be more strictly
observed by all the guards and every person in the Garrison.' On
22 June the guns on the isthmus ceased fire. Apart from one day,
4 May 1782, they had fired regularly at Gibraltar since 12 April
1781. Though at times there were no more than three shots in
twenty-four hours, the thunder of the enemy's guns had become as
much a part of the garrison's life as the foul salt meat, the sun, the
Rock itself. Over 150,000 shot and shells had been fired against
Gibraltar, and their monument was the ruined town and nothing
else. The cease fire marked the succession of the Duc de Crillon to
the command of the Armies of France and Spain. General Alvarez
left San Roque the next day.

The garrison continued to make the sort of preparations David
might have made when he went out to meet Goliath. The artillery
had discovered that by cutting large stones to fit a 13-inch mortar
and filling them with a charge of powder fired by a short fuse, they
could fire them so that they burst over the heads of the enemy's workmen, showering them with splinters. This was considered an important discovery, outranking the rock-mortar in its ingenuity, and
considerably more successful. (The rock-mortar was little more than
a hole cut into the rock near Green's Lodge of the calibre of a mortar, which burst on firing the first time. The unlucky gunner who
fired it died in October 1781 of a burst blood vessel.) The stone shells
were used until it was noticed, by Captain Spilsbury among others,
that they 'have a colly-flower head coming out of the mortar', whereupon they were quickly forgotten by the artillery. At this time the
garrison's musicians were issued with fire-locks and shovels, and
joined in the practice of parapet firing at targets placed in the Bay.
It was perhaps inevitable that more men would attempt to desert as
the position of the garrison became, apparently, increasingly hopeless. Three men were captured, and the body of another, broken in a

fall from the scarped cliffs behind the Signal House, was exposed on the Grand Parade as a warning to the faint-hearted of the penalty the Rock could impose without the need of the hangman. The latter became so unpopular in the garrison that it became necessary to issue a Garrison Order on 8 July forbidding anyone to obstruct or insult him.

Early in July the enemy started to build roofs over the decks of the battering-ships. General Eliott, who sent off his dispatches by whatever vessels left the Rock whether they were returning to Leghorn or to Lisbon, wrote that they resembled 'the most of anything an oblong floating Hay-rick'; he added, 'the Enemy's Preparations for an attack on the side of the Bay are uncommonly vast', and asked hopefully for a squadron of the King's ships to assist in his defence. He had heard nothing from the Government for a considerable time, and when the dispatches at last arrived, probably on 25 July, they gave him little comfort.

> The skill Perseverance and Courage which you have shown in this very long and fatiguing Siege give His Majesty's Ministers the strongest hopes that while they are stretching every Nerve to send you Relief, you will adopt the wisest measures and make the most vigorous efforts to conclude with Glory a Defence which has attracted the attention and has been honoured with the applause of all Europe ... The King has entrusted to your care the important Fortress of Gibraltar, one of the most valuable Possessions of his Crown.

The true worth of this pompous flim-flam will be seen when the actions of the King and his ministers are examined later. The Governor, having had a bookful of 'stretched Nerves' copied out by his secretary, Captain Rawleigh, must have realized that he could not depend on anything but his own generalship and the courage of his garrison. A fine example of this occurred on 8 July:

> An artillery-man (named Hartley) was employed in the laboratory, filling shells with Carcass composition, and driving fuses into five and a half and six inch shells: one of them, by some unaccountable accident, took fire in the operation; and although he was surrounded with unfixed fuses, loaded shells, composition &c. with the most astonishing coolness he carried out the lighted shell, and threw it where it could do little or no harm; and two seconds had scarcely elapsed before it disploded. If the shell had burst in the laboratory, it is almost certain the whole

would have been blown up; when the loss in fixed ammunition, fuses &c. &c. would have been irreparable, exclusive of the damage which the fortifications would have suffered from the explosion, and the lives that might have been lost. He was handsomely rewarded by the Governor.

Caleb Hartley received £3 10s. 0d. which, as Captain Drinkwater said, was handsome.

In this hot summer water was scarce, liquor was scarce, meat and vegetables were scarce. Yet Serjeant-Major Ince's gallery was now 82 feet long, 8 feet high and 8 feet wide, and progressing at the rate of almost a yard a day. It was considered so successful that the Governor ordered a second party of miners to blast a tunnel through the spur of rock that separated the King's from the Queen's Lines on the North Front. Working parties from the Navy were employed on the defences at Waterport, repairing the boom, and sinking anchors in the sand to tear out the bottoms of any craft attempting to land there. The Governor expressed his opinion that the attack would be directed on the Old Mole, and would be a combined assault from sea and land, but then he was a better general than the Duc de Crillon. He was having a house built for himself on Windmill Hill, as the Convent was open to any barrage from the Bay.

At the same time the enemy were busy roofing the battering-ships, and a deserter who came in to the garrison on 14 July reported that they would be ready at the end of August; the Combined Army before Gibraltar consisted of 37 battalions of Spanish infantry, 8 battalions of French infantry, 2 battalions of Spanish and 4 companies of French artillery, besides several companies of dragoons and cavalry; totalling some 28,000 men; but the informer reported that the men were discontented, and there were many desertions. Some French officers, doubtless to show their allies how easy it would be to take the Rock, walked up to Forbes and Bayside barriers, but were driven off by a few rounds of grape from Willis's. The enemy's ships were active in preventing any vessels coming to Gibraltar from the west, and on 7 July they took a brig flying the British flag.

The horrible example of the broken body left on the Grand Parade failed to stop others from attempting to desert from the garrison. Four sailors from one of the advanced guard-boats went over to the enemy on the 11th, and on the same day Serjeant Sorve of the 72nd, who had been missing for some days, was found halfway down the back of the Rock and, after being condemned by court-martial, was hanged a week later. On the 12th a prophet appeared in the garrison. He was a Scotsman of the 73rd, and publicly declared that in six weeks, six days and six hours from the previous Saturday, the garrison would be taken and the Governor killed. The Governor, in grim humour, ordered the man to be kept in the Provost ship until the fatal hour, and then, if he and the garrison were still alive, to be flogged for being a bad prophet. Captain Spilsbury had his own explanation for the outburst:

> The men have a number of stories among themselves, but their allowance of grog is drunk before night, and they are obliged to go to bed sober, so no wonder they have disagreeable dreams. Four gallons grog only to be sold by each wine-house per day.

A few days later the enemy soldiers watching the Rock might have thought there was a magician in the garrison when there was a sudden explosion, and a cloud of smoke poured out of a hole in the face of the cliff, where no man could possibly reach. Serjeant-Major Ince was opening the first embrasure in his gallery, primarily to give his miners air, but later, after the chamber had been widened to take the recoil, a 24-pounder was mounted there. It was hot, hazy and calm; 'sour crout' was served to the Hanoverians, but where it came from no one knew, and Captain Spilsbury's flour was 'so full of wevels that a plum pudding had the appearance of a currant one.'

On 25 July, on a strong east wind, two ships came in from Leghorn, the *St Philip's Castle* and the *General Murray*, with a batch of papers for the Governor; another sixty-eight Corsicans, two officers, twelve non-commissioned officers, a chaplain, and their leader, Signor Leonetti, a nephew of the famous Corsican patriot Pasquale de Paoli, who did his best to give his island to Great Britain; and news for the garrison of Rodney's victory at the Battle of the Saints.

> Garrison Orders, 25th July.
>
> Parole Rodney. A feu de joye to be fired this day to celebrate the victory gained by his Majety's fleet, under the command of Sir George Rodney, over the French fleet in the West Indies. All the ordnance from the rock gun to Princess Carolina's inclusive to be fire at one o'clock, beginning

at the rock gun shotted. At six in the evening the regiments will take
post on the line wall, in the following order, drawn up two deep:

The 72nd regiment right to the Prince Hesse's battery; 12th join the
left of 72nd; the two town companies of artillery on the King's Bastion;
the 39th on the left of the 12th; Lieutenant-General Reden's left of the
39th; Major-General La Motte's left of Reden's; 73rd right at Ragged
Staff; 56th on the left of the 73rd; the three south companies of royal
artillery in the New Mole fort—Two rockets will be thrown up on the
right as a signal to begin the first round—two from the left when the fire
returns from thence for the second round; and two more from the right
for the third round. Three cheers when the firing is finished, to begin on
the right, and pass along in the same manner as the firing did.

The Navy joined in, and the enemy watched the garrison they considered doomed firing and cheering as if the victory was theirs, and
they were returning home the next day.

General Eliott was in his study at the Convent shuffling through
the papers from Lord Shelburne in vain for the one piece of information he wanted—the date a relief convoy would sail with sufficient
line-of-battle ships to destroy the enemy in his harbours. The British
secret service was excellent and had provided Lord Shelburne with
reports describing the battering-ships, which Lord Shelburne had
sent to General Eliott, and which General Eliott, if he looked out of
his window, could confirm were substantially correct. The description of the landing-craft was new to him: 'There is to be a number of
large boats to lay at the outside of them [the battering-ships] and
gunshot from the Garrison, full of Troops, with a high parapet so as
to conceal the men; said parapet is to have hinges so as to be laid
down on the shore when the Troops land to prevent their being wet',
and this report might have hinted to him that all was not as it should
be in the Spanish Camp: 'At present they dispute who is to lead the
attack: Crillon says it should be the Spanish forces: the Spaniards say
it should be the French', but nowhere could he find a word from His
Lordship about the Nerves that were supposed to be being stretched.
If he looked out of his window, beyond the two red lines of soldiers,
in the west, from where the ships would come, he saw nothing.

CHAPTER XVII

Crise, contradiction, fâcherie, et jalousie

WHEN M. d'Arçon arrived at Cadiz in March 1782, he examined the ten ships which were to carry his aspirations, and declared that seven of them were too old and too light to be used. However, there was little time, and no inclination on the part of the Spanish authorities, to procure others, and he set about converting them into the incombustible and insubmersible machines of his plan. The first requirement was absolute secrecy, and this was met for several days, until Chicardo reached the garrison on 1 April. The second was the accumulation of huge quantities of wood. D'Arçon estimated 200,000 square feet of timber was needed and in addition quantities of old cables, junk and cork, and he left the task of collecting these materials to the Chief Marine Engineer at Algeciras. The third requirement was the move of the ships from Cadiz to Algeciras, some sixty miles away, and this took a month, the ships arriving at last on 9 May. When d'Arçon arrived at Algeciras himself in the same month, he found nothing ready. He expressed himself forcibly:

> It must be said that the old Commodore at Algeciras, Don Valcarel, was a half-witted man, uniformly inept, full of the most vile prejudices, seeking to re-awaken the ancient enmity of our Nations, who made ridiculous complaints against France, hearkened back to 1744 . . . and called the floating batteries treason.

The old Commodore wrote to the Chief Marine Engineer, 'Beware of this Frenchman, he'll ruin everything and make you responsible.' It was not an auspicious beginning. However, d'Arçon's enormous energy was communicated to the workmen at Algeciras and, as the garrison observed, the cutting down of the ship's rigging and the boarding up of their port sides went on at a great rate. D'Arçon, now a Colonel, was praised in the newspapers, and even the most sceptical began to be impressed:

Extract of a letter from a Mr Anderson at Tavira, 1st June 1782.

Great preparations are making in Spain to attack the Garrison: when at Algeciras we saw them hard at work at what you call Cork-ships; the sides of these ships are covered with large square green timber and junk, the whole to be about seven or eight feet thick; only one side is to be covered in this manner, the other to remain as before; the deck is to be made shot and shell proof, at least so they endeavoured to make us believe. These ships when ready are to be ranged along the Front of the Garrison in order to make breaches in the Wall, when the Troops are to be landed in Boats building at Carthagena for that purpose. While at Seville we saw them shipping off brass guns.

Whilst the credulous talked as if the victory had already been achieved.

M. d'Arçon, who everyone admitted was, in the words of the Duc de Crillon, 'homme de mérité en effet, de beaucoup d'esprit, et passionné en faveur de son projet, jusqu'au fanatisme', was supervising the installation of his fire-extinguishing systems in the floating batteries when he was called to Madrid by the Minister Floridablanca to meet the victor of Mahon, who was to command the Grand Attack. This meeting of the brilliant and bustling engineer and the elderly cautious self-opinionated general (d'Arçon was then forty-nine and Crillon sixty-four) is only recorded in the Mémoires of the latter, which are, to say the least, jaundiced, purblind and partial, but the balance will be redressed later. Crillon was busy at Port Mahon shipping off the British prisoners and supervising the destruction of Fort St Philip, when he received a letter from Floridablanca telling him to go to Madrid. He arrived in May, and was well received by King Charles III at his summer residence at Aranjuez, but when he saw Floridablanca, and was told that it was not his plan that was to be executed against Gibraltar, but a French plan, sponsored by the Court of Versailles and the French Ministry of War, he was upset. When he heard that the plan was already in progress, and that d'Arçon was busy at Cadiz and Algeciras, he was worried, and desired to meet him as soon as possible. They met at Minister Floridablanca's house at eight o'clock one morning, with Floridablanca present. D'Arçon put a map of Gibraltar on the table, with a plan of his floating batteries battering the place and a sketch of one of the batteries, which seemed gross and enormous to Crillon.

Crillon: Sir, do you believe that your floating batteries will be in a condition, by their measurements, to resist cannon placed in an amphitheatre, which will thunder at them without respite, and with the greatest violence?

D'Arçon: The batteries will be stouter than the size of the greatest ships, and I will make them more bomb-proof by the netting, the big cannons, and the thickness of their sides, so that a ball will only be able to enter through an embrasure, and if it did that, it would go straight through and out the other side.

Crillon: Then they will be too heavy; they will lie too deep in the water to approach near enough to the walls to make a breach.

D'Arçon: They will be able to approach within a distance of 250 toises [500 yards].

Crillon: I would say 600 toises [1,200 yards]. What if a red-hot ball pierces your floating battery?

D'Arçon: I have communicating pipes lying in the wood itself, which run all over my battery, and which pour water perpetually into every part, in sufficient quantity to prevent everything but a momentary blaze.

Crillon: What if a ball breaks the pipe?

D'Arçon: The pipes will be like the veins of an animal—blood will flow out . . .

Floridablanca: I don't understand at all.

Crillon: (With a shrug) Perhaps we can see a trial?

D'Arçon: Of course.

Crillon: Assuming that your batteries can make a breach, how will you transport the troops these 500 yards?

D'Arçon: (Excitedly) We will collect 2,000 vessels of every kind at Cadiz. The sea will be entirely covered in ships. All the batteries in the place will be destroyed. All the walls knocked down. It is certain that the Governor won't wait for the place to be taken by assault.

Crillon did not reply and, shortly afterwards, M. d'Arçon collected up his papers and left. Crillon turned to Floridablanca.

Crillon: The plan is impossible. You cannot oppose batteries made of wood, which will undoubtedly catch fire, to those on land. Everyone knows that cannonballs fired from a ship have less power than those

fired from a fixed position. These floating batteries will only be able
to approach to within 600 toises of the Garrison, and the balls, re-
bounding from the walls, will form another barrier to the small
landing-craft. A siege can only be made by columns of troops . . . .

Floridablanca: My dear General I agree with you, but the plan is so far
advanced, and it is the particular pleasure of the French Commander-
in-Chief, and the Ministry, and the King. It is too late to object. Too
much money has been spent.

Crillon: Certainly. Then proceed without me, Minister.

Floridablanca: Without the Victor of Mahon! It is absolutely essential
that you are there. The King desires it.

Crillon: The King is master of my life, but not my honour.

Floridablanca: Listen to me. We are in the course of making peace, and
it is the capture of Gibraltar that will determine the conditions. All
Europe has its eyes on M. d'Arçon's project, and regards it as a certainty: France does not doubt it, and we know (from all the English
newspapers) that the English are so much in anticipation of the
success of this enterprise, that there is every chance that the Governor
of Gibraltar, a man of merit and as wise as he is brave, will not wish
to persist to the point of danger, or wait to be carried by assault.
When he sees his place open to assault, or at the least, when he sees
that there is a chance to surrender . . . and you will be in a position
to stop the attack at any moment.

Crillon was still reluctant to risk his reputation.

Floridablanca: The responsibility of seeing how near the batteries can
approach, and how they are to remain unburnt is not yours. You will
have the glory of capturing the two most impregnable places in the
world in one campaign, and you will achieve the greatest peace ever
for France and Spain.

Crillon hesitated.

Floridablanca: If we fail, I will publicly announce that you were against
the plan, and only obeyed the orders of the King.

Crillon was won. He insisted that he would be under the command
of M. d'Arçon, and that if the batteries caught fire he would immediately advise the King, when his declaration of disagreement
would be made public. So the meeting ended. This conversation, reconstructed from Crillon's Mémoires, which were written as his defence against d'Arçon's later attacks, goes some way to confirm

d'Arçon's opinion 'que le général, ayant été contradit sur ses projets particuliers, avoit eu l'intention de faire manquer l'opération des flottantes . . . qu'il étoit naturellement ennemi de tous succès qui n'étoient pas a lui'.

But Crillon went further. Before leaving Madrid for Gibraltar to take command of the Grand Attack, he deposited a letter with a certain Madame de Marco to be opened and published the moment a messenger arrived from San Roque with the news that the attack had started. Never before or after did a general advancing to the attack cover his own retreat with such care, or reveal his own dishonesty and hypocrisy in accepting a command in which he had no faith.

Je pars pour Gibraltar, et je déclare que c'est par pure obéissance aux ordres du Roi que j'ai accepté le commandement que Sa Majesté m'a fait l'honneur de me confier, pour aller exécuter contre cette place le plan des batteries flottantes, et m'enjoignant aussi d'aider M. d'Arçon de tous mes moyens, et d'avoir l'air d'approuver de bonne-foi son projet jusqu'au moment où les batteries auraient commencé leurs attaques. J'ai fait tous mes efforts auprès de Sa Majesté, pour m'opposer à l exécution de ce projet, qui me paraît contraire à l'avantage et à l'honneur des armes du Roi; ainsi je déclare ici, dans le cas (que contre mon attente la place serait prise par le réussite des batteries flottantes et de l'assaut qui s'en suivrait) que toute la gloire doit en appertenir à M. d'Arçon, Ingénieur français, qui est l'auteur de ce projet; je déclare aussi que dans le cas où les batteries flottantes n'auraient pas un heureux succès, en n'aura nul reproche, à me faire, comme n'y ayant aucune part et n'y étant entré pour rien.

Je prie M. et Mme de Marco (au nom de toute ma confiance en eux, de leur amité pour moi et de l'intérêt qu'ils prennent à mon honneur, que je dépose dans leurs mains) d'ouvrir ce paquet dans l'instant seulement qu'on connaîtra dans Madrid, par le courrier que j'enverrai au Roi, qui viendra vous apprendre que l'attaque des batteries flottantes était commencé à son départ du camp; ce qui, par ce moyen, sera connu du public à Madrid au moins vingt-quatre heures avant qu'on y apprenne le succès par le second courrier que je dépêcherai au Roi vingt-quatre heures après le départ de ce premier.

Certifiant en même-temps ici que la présente déclaration de ma part a été faite avec la permission expresse de M. de Comte de Florida-Blanca, Ministre d'État, et approuvée par Sa Majesté.

Signé   B.B. Duc de Crillon.

A Madrid, en partant pour Gibraltar, le 12 Juin 1781.

The careful General left twenty copies of the letter to be distributed in France and Spain.

The Duc de Crillon arrived at San Roque at the same time as the French force under the Baron de Falkenheim was disembarking and joining the Spanish Camp. He took command of an immense army, compared to the total strength of the garrison on Gibraltar of 6,700 soldiers and 900 sailors (the effective strength was about 7,000 men). The list of regiments appears in 'Histoire du Siège de Gibraltar. Par un Officier de l'Armée Françoise' (who was M. d'Arçon).

SPANISH REGIMENTS

	Officers	*Other Ranks*
Gardes Espagnols	121	2,912
Gardes Wallones	115	2,912
Saboya	31	689
Cordova	31	688
Burgos	63	1,377
Murcia	63	1,377
Ultonia	32	689
Volontaires d'Aragon	23	387
I Regt de Catalogne	45	1,805
La Princesse	31	688
Naples	63	1,377
Betchart	43	1,191
Compagnie de Grenadiers	66	1,338
Cavalerie Démontée	69	1,347
Dragons Démontée	66	
Grenadiers Provinciaux	201	4,509
Artilleria		1,341
Dragons et Cavalerie	141	2,440

FRENCH REGIMENTS

Regt de Lyonnais	61	1,024
Regt de Bouillon	48	1,025
Regt de Bretagne	61	1,016
Regt Royal Suedois (German)	61	1,000
	1,490	31,132

Allowing a large number of deserters and sick, the army which lay from the Queen of Spain's Chair to the hills above Carteia was one of the largest ever assembled for the siege of one fortress; and these figures did not include the workmen, or the sailors at Algeciras. There was also assembled a large number of guns of heavy calibre and, in

Algeciras, the floating batteries which Crillon saw for the first time. He both despised them, with all the contempt of the old guard for the new, and coveted the glory that they might bring their inventor. In the long councils of war held at Algeciras, he expressed both feelings. The reports are now d'Arçon's, and if in Crillon's Mémoires d'Arçon appears as the idiot he was not, in d'Arçon's pamphlets Crillon is revealed as the hypocrite he undoubtedly was. On one occasion Crillon said to him: 'When I asked them to send you to Spain, it was to carry out my project, because my project has always been to attack Gibraltar with floating batteries; now, Monsieur, your commission is fulfilled, the rest belongs to me.' And on another:

> *Crillon:* I know all your proceedings; I am here to oppose everything you do and everything you say; to do you justice, you are valuable, but you are also extremely obstinate.
>
> *D'Arçon:* (Continuing an argument that had been going on some time already) To attack everywhere is to attack nowhere; one would be weak all along the line, and the enemy would be stronger at each point than the batteries singly; they would be spread out, and abandoned, at the risk of falling into the enemy's hands . . .
>
> *Crillon:* You have the bowels of a father towards your batteries: you only think of preserving them: but I have other views, and if the enemy wants to take them, I'll burn them in his face.

Communication at these councils became even more difficult when Admiral Moreno, who was young, inexperienced, ambitious, and disliked by both Crillon and d'Arçon, was present with other Spanish officers, because d'Arçon spoke Spanish badly and could only express his opinions with plans and memos which no one bothered to look at. The main argument at this time was concerned with where the attack should be made. The original target had been the New Mole, but this was out of range of the land batteries, which could only effectively enfilade the bastions and the guns behind the Old Mole. D'Arçon, who had been out in a boat to make soundings off the New Mole, said that he thought it was possible to range the floating batteries off the Old Mole, but that the laying of anchors, on which they could be warped back in order to retreat, would be more difficult. At the word retreat, the rest of the council burst out laughing, and Moreno announced that Gibraltar would fall in twenty-four hours, in fact he had only to appear before Gibraltar and the Governor would surrender. Eventually, the claim that the army should share in the enterprise and the glory prevailed, and the Old Mole was decided on as the target. D'Arçon immediately drew up a plan for the floating batteries to lie in two ranks, 500 yards off the Old Mole, whilst thirty gun-boats fired from between them, and two divisions of fifteen gun-boats each lay on the flanks, out of range of the British guns. When the breach was opened, eight or ten ships from the fleet would make a diversionary attack on the south. The barrage was to be supported by an immense fire from the land . . . and so on scribbling his memos late into the night.

Whilst the councils of those commanding the attack proceeded in this extraordinary manner, the relations between the armies of France and Spain on the field before Gibraltar were hardly less hostile. Perhaps they can best be illustrated by some verses addressed by a French officer to his Spanish colleagues:

> Gentlemen of St Roque, between us let's say
> This is a joke that passes belief.
> Are your here for life? Will you finish one day?
> I know you are brave—why aren't you brief?
> Doesn't your patience permit a foray,
> To end the affair, in laughter or grief?
>
> Gentlemen of the Camp, of the big blockade,
> Stop! You don't hold them any more.
> I keep hearing your cannonade,
> But alas, dear Sirs, what is it for?
> The sleepy English are not afraid
> Of your mortar's mouth, your cannon's roar.
>
> And if, now and then, they answer you clear,
> Out of respect for your cautious spleen,
> I wager it's only to say—'We can hear',
> Before they return to a rest serene.
> You should learn, after four years in the rear,
> If you want to besiege, you must be seen.
>
> So leave your old works, your old trenches quit,
> Retire old besiegers, before you are done,
> This famous siege, if God thinks fit,

> Will by your children be fought and won.
> Unless, my friends, like you they sit
> Behind the sandbanks, under the sun.
>
> Your bombs, your ships, your mortars, your mines,
> Have captured the readers of the Gazette,
> But not a man in the English lines,
> Nor taken an English ship—But yet
> Perhaps you are feeding them stores and wines
> To make them grow fat, and die in a sweat!

This is a loose translation, but in the spirit of the piece. So throughout July the huge combined army lay in Camp, and the generals and admirals jostled for glory, and the floating batteries took shape under the jealous eye of their inventor, in spite of the inefficiency, the delays, the intrigues, and the opposition, that caused d'Arçon to cry out: 'Crise, contradiction, fâcherie et jalousie!'

The same four words might well be applied to the political situation in England following the resignation of Lord North on 20 March. For twelve years Lord North had been titular head of an Administration which, to quote Horace Walpole,

> had given the most fatal stab to the glory and interests of England, by (I believe) planning (certainly by taking no step to prevent), pushing on, and persisting in the American war, and who had, by the countenance of the Crown, and by the arts of the Scotch, and the intoxication of the nation, maintained themselves under the greatest disgraces and losses that ever this country had sustained—disgraces in a great measure the consequences of impolicy, early neglect, and rash perseverance in a hopeless project.

Which ignored the fact that North's Ministry was the first stable one of the reign, and expressed the typically English annoyance at having lost something which they were quite prepared to give away. But if Walpole, or anyone else, had anticipated that the new Whig Cabinet would reject the jobbery, venality and nepotism of the old Tory one, they were disappointed. George III went as far as to draft his abdication, but soon discovered that what his new ministers craved was no different to what had sated and dazzled his old: the sweets of office, the honey of pensions and reversions, and the glitter of decorations.

There were two exceptions: Lord Shelburne wanted to be First Lord of the Treasury; and Charles James Fox wanted to negotiate a peace, as quickly and as honourably as possible.

Fox first approached the Courts of Prussia and Russia with the proposal for an alliance to bring pressure to bear on the Bourbon Courts to agree to reasonable terms. When this failed, he sent Thomas Grenville to Paris in May 1782, to open negotiations directly with the American commissioners, and the Courts of France and Spain. Lord Shelburne, not to be outdone, sent his own agent, Richard Oswald, to Paris, to carry on separate talks with the Americans. So the confused situation arose that, whilst Grenville was telling d'Aranda, the Spanish Ambassador, that there was little or no likelihood of Britain ever agreeing to the cession of Gibraltar, Oswald was jockeyed by Benjamin Franklin into admitting that the Government might consider exchanging Gibraltar for a territory elsewhere, and suggested Puerto Rico. The negotiations were suspended by the death of Lord Rockingham on 1 July, though before then Floridablanca and Vergennes had agreed to delay them until the outcome of the Grand Attack was known. With Rockingham gone, by his cultivation of the King, Shelburne reaped the post he desired, and in his Cabinet Lord Grantham took over the Foreign Secretaryship from Fox, who had resigned in disgust. We know something of Lord Grantham's diplomatic talents already. In this Cabinet, the young William Pitt, then twenty-three, became Chancellor of the Exchequer.,

It was no secret that Gibraltar was to be the object of the Grand Attack in September. On 9 June George III wrote: 'I hope Lord Shelburne will get the relief of Gibraltar discussed by the Admirals whilst at Portsmouth: if the Navy do not clearly declare that it cannot be succoured I am certain that great blame will be due if that Fortress should fall.' Shelburne knew on 17 June 'that the object of the Campaign was to be Gibraltar and that both the Count d'Artois and Count of Bourbon were setting out for the Siege'. Which was more than they knew in Gibraltar or San Roque at that time. Yet no preparations were made to send a relief; at the very moment when the dispatch was written to General Eliott that His Majesty's ministers were 'stretching every Nerve', they were indeed doing that, not to assist the beleaguered fortress, but to pick up the strings of government dropped from the palsied hand of the expiring Marquis of

Rockingham. The First Lord of the Admiralty under Rockingham and Shelburne was Lord Keppel, and the first distinguished exertion of his authority had been to send the indifferent Admiral Pigot to replace the brilliant Admiral Rodney after the news of Rodney's great victory of the Saints. Lord Howe was appointed Admiral of the Fleet. Nothing was done in July, and on the 31st the King wrote to Lord Shelburne again:

I also think the Relief of Gibraltar ought not to be delayed till September, the way to keep up the spirits of the men is to shew they are not neglected, the Enemy avow that is the time they mean to make their attack, therefore our succours ought to be there before that time.

Shelburne replied:

As to the Relief of Gibraltar I find the Comptroller against waiting till September, and inclines much to detaching ten ships. This depends so much upon local as well as naval knowledge of the entrance of the Bay and other circumstances, that I dare not offer to decide and I am apprehensive the Cabinet not being naval men will find a good deal of difficulty in doing so. It appears to me that a great deal should depend upon the experience and convictions of the officer who commands.

This shelved the matter for two more weeks. As a relief would probably be sent, providing it was not too late, some time in the future, the Secretary for War, Thomas Townshend, was instructed to write to the Governor to this effect, which he did on 10 August: 'I send this to acquaint you that measures are taking to give you as early a Support as possible, in Men, Provisions, and Stores: They may reach you a little sooner or later, but you may be assured that the Relief is intended to be effectual.' Which must stand unrivalled in the ranks of letters from governments to the governors of besieged fortresses. The next day Lord Shelburne wrote to the King, giving some indication of the public outcry against the abandonment of the Rock in the face of the impending attack:

I have been oblig'd to have a very grave conversation with Lord Kepple upon the Relief of Gibraltar and upon the damp thrown by the Admiralty upon the Spirit shewn by the County of Suffolk, the City of London and other places. Lord Kepple alledges the Indispensible necessity of seeing the Baltick Fleet home in the first instance, and the futility of any exertions beyond the very moment.

There seems little doubt that it was the pressure of public opinion, rather than the considered policy of the admirals or the Government, to save Gibraltar at any risk, that induced the Cabinet to include in the minutes of 14 August: 'The Fleet . . . to proceed at latest in the first week in September with the Necessaries and Supplies for the relief of the Garrison of Gibraltar.' Of course, it arrived too late to reinforce the garrison before the Grand Attack.

Whilst stately messengers padded between Whitehall and the Palace with these papers, so vital to the old Governor and garrison of the Rock, tucked in their hats, the monumental task of reconciling the various demands of the belligerents was again taken up in Paris. In August Lord Shelburne's new representative, Alleyne Fitzherbert, arrived in Paris. He discovered that, whilst Vergennes was anxious to conclude a peace providing that Great Britain recognized American independence and restored the islands of St Lucia and Dominique, the Count d'Aranda was eager to continue the war for another year, when Spain would not only have taken Gibraltar, but would have had an opportunity to mount an assault on Jamaica. Not for the first time, the British and French interests coincided to the exclusion of those of Spain, in spite of the Family Compact. The negotiations were stimulated by the arrival of the Comte de Grasse, captured by Rodney at the Battle of the Saints, and returned to France with some unofficial proposals which the English and French hoped might provide the basis for a treaty. De Grasse's opinion of how much the British Government would sacrifice for a treaty was informed by his desire to be a better peacemaker than he was an admiral, and he speculated that they would be prepared to exchange either Port Mahon or Gibraltar for some other port in the Mediterranean. This excited Floridablanca to empower d'Aranda to complete the negotiation under these conditions:

The three points which can be looked upon as conditions sine qua non are: the clearing of the Gulfs of Honduras and Campeche, freeing those establishments for the cutting of log-wood (from England), or reducing them to a status of supervised permission; the exclusion from the Gulf of Mexico of all foreigners as far as the exit of the Bahama channel at Cape Carnaveral; the cession of Gibraltar and Minorca, although Oran and Mazalquivir may be given for them if Gibraltar has not been conquered (at the time of the negotiation. If Gibraltar is conquered) the

king does not wish those places exchanged, and will only give the
English the use of the free port of Mahon for their commerce, without
jurisdiction or authority.

Vergennes considered that the English might well accept these conditions, and sent his secretary, Gerard de Rayneval, to London. In
the meantime the negotiations in Paris were suspended. De Rayneval
arrived on 12 September, and saw Lord Shelburne immediately. He
knew the Grand Attack would be launched at any moment, and was
anxious to reach an agreement before the event was determined one
way or the other, which would either stiffen the attitude of Spain, or
Great Britain. Lord Shelburne was equally anxious for a settlement,
but a more profitable one than Floridablanca allowed. He wrote to
the King after his meeting with de Rayneval: 'I upheld the im-
possibility of ever ceding it so strongly, that I could form no guess
about their disposition regarding Porto Rico.' On 14 August the King
answered: 'That Oran is a good port is quite new to me, and I certainly doubt it, as it is offered as an equivalent for Gibraltar; Porto
Rico is the object we must get for that Fortress.' Lord Shelburne replied to the King: 'I have held the point of Gibraltar so high that the
alternative of Porto Rico may be catched at, I flatter myself, whenever the time comes for it to be hinted by way of compensation or
exchange on the part of Your Majesty.' And King George III, who
had already lost the greatest part of his empire, and was still prepared
to sacrifice a possession dear to his nation and to the men who had
defended it for more than three years, who had been driven to the
extremity of hunger, had endured constant bombardment, and had
faced the greatest combination of forces ever brought against one
place, concluded: 'The holding Gibraltar very high is quite judicious, and if not taken I should hope Porto Rico may be got for it.'
This was three days after the Grand Attack.

CHAPTER XVIII

Spain's ensigns spread

THE Dons were burning their hills. The August sun, no bigger or brighter than an orange, glimmered through the gauze of smoke rising from the Sierra de Carbonera, tingeing the Rock yellow and grey with an unreal, theatrical light. The heat was intolerable, and the air stagnant and hard to breathe. Small moving hedges of flames crossed the brown slopes behind the Bay, leaving them black and smoking, and the crackle of dead trees, brittle ferns and thorns and dusty grass, was like distant musket-fire. The men of the garrison, their jackets faded pink, the regimental facings hardly discernible, their shirts and breeches grimy with sweat and dirt, their legs and feet bound with strips of blankets, dragged themselves slowly up and down the Rock. Their faces showed the marks of three years of siege, drawn and hollowed, living only in the excitement of their eyes. Yet, like wood, they had hardened in the heat, and knowing that the Rock was their strength, they scraped it and burrowed in it, carved their defences out of it and piled its stones into new batteries and walls. Their discipline was hard, and their pleasures short. A gunner's daughter, who had been too free with too many, was found drowned in a well; yet they reared chicks and wept when they died, kept tame lizards, and jealously guarded their dogs against the Governor's ordinances to destroy them. The officers tried to maintain some sort of social existence, their etiquette was inviolable, but in the face of the enemy's huge preparations across the Bay it was increasingly difficult to maintain a cool, well-bred indifference. When the men went too far, and bathed naked off the New Mole, or fished indiscriminately in the Inundation, orders were soon issued to stop these enormities. General Eliott, brooding over his garrison from the cloisters of the Convent, relaxed only in the young company of Roger Curtis. Lieutenant-General Boyd, pacing the King's Bastion composed letters in his head to the new Administration: 'I presume to flatter myself that my Royal Master does not intend to make me quite so insignificant as my present Commander seems to wish', and even sent one of them. The garrison was feverish.

If the tiny figure of this last elderly gentleman was visible from the Spanish Camp, nobody remarked it. In Buena Vista, a house below San Roque which had once served as a cavalry barracks but was now the Duc de Crillon's headquarters, the Councils of War were still meeting and still arguing. The incentive to shine was greater now that it was known that His Royal Highness the Comte d'Artois, Louis XVI's brother and Charles III's nephew, intended to honour the Grand Attack with his presence, accompanied by his cousin the Duc de Bourbon. Like the French nobles before the Battle of Agincourt, these, their successors, and the grandees of Spain, indulged in the same contempt for their small, ragged enemy. Two men only refrained from this sport, but for very different reasons; the wary Crillon, who hankered for glory without the courage to seize it; and the impulsive d'Arçon, who did not underrate anyone, least of all himself. Crillon knew how many reputations lay buried under the sand of the isthmus. D'Arçon knew that it took exactly sixty-four minutes for a red-hot ball to lose sufficient heat to make it harmless, and was anxious for one of his floating batteries to be tested to prove his calculations correct, and his invention foolproof. The others were brave men, who did not care to know too much about anything.

Unfortunately, the divisions amongst the enemy were not communicated to the garrison, and from across the Bay, the enemy Camp, from Algeciras to the Spanish Lines, had an appearance of bustling confidence. When a deserter came in on 5 August the Governor, according to Boyd's Log Book, 'locks him up in Cook's empty pantry and nails up the window'. The man told General Eliott that the enemy numbered 34,000; that there were so many mortars in the Lines, they expected the British guns to be immediately silenced and the batteries beaten to powder; and that the attack was planned for 25 August. But though he might nail up the pantry window, the Governor could not stop his men from looking across to Algeciras—where three of the floating batteries had been fitted with jury masts and appeared to be complete—or at the lines of tents covering the hills above the Bay. On the 4th the Corsicans were formed into a corps under Captain Leonetti and sent to guard Windmill Hill—no one was quite certain from what; the next day all the miners in the garrison were ordered to assist with the opening between the King's and Queen's Lines; on the 11th, feeling perhaps that they were not busy enough, the 72nd Regiment volunteered to build a covered way from the Grand Parade to Orange's Bastion. The Governor was so delighted that he awarded the men engaged on the work 9d. extra and a pint of grog a day. This was the time that the garrison was distressed by a sudden epidemic of influenza. It affected almost everyone with 'a weakness and soreness in all their limbs, hoarseness and sore throats: with a stuffing and lightness in the head', (Boyd's Log Book). The cure was simple: bleeding, and a night's rest, the latter being a luxury that few of the men enjoyed more than once or twice a week, but for several days the weakness had them hamstrung. The influenza disappeared as quickly as it had come, and the general hope was that it had gone over to the enemy.

The Royal Prince arrived in the Spanish Camp on 15 August. The fires in the hills had burned themselves out, and the curtain had been lifted from the scene. Looking from the Orange Grove at The Place, it seemed to float upon the sea, its rambling length making it appear deceivingly low. From three miles away, it looked deserted, until a tiny puff of smoke and the echo of a shot captured the Royal attention, and there was a willing aide to point out the battery, no bigger than a child's brick in a garden. Then the straight unnatural lines of the defences became apparent, and the white tents on the slopes at the south; the two Moles, the masts of the ships, and, in a drift of wind, the garrison flag opened above the Grand Battery. When His Royal Highness turned, there was the old Duc de Crillon bowing low behind him, and between the splendid figures of the admirals and generals, the agitated figure of a French Colonel of Engineers, dodging about, waving a large rolled-up plan.

D'Arçon's plan (Crillon said 'd'Arçon had sketched something ridiculous' and claimed the credit himself) was carried out that night. As soon as it was dark, 10,000 soldiers moved quietly out of Camp, passed the Spanish Lines, and took up defensive positions in advance of the St Carlos Battery, the parallel, and the Mahon Battery, continuing their lines to the eastern shore. They were followed by 15,000 workmen, carrying casks and sandbags. There were 25,000 men within 1,000 yards of the Rock, and no alarm was given in the British garrison. Working with barely credible speed and efficiency, and so quietly that the batteries on the Rock only fired a few light balls, which were immediately extinguished, this force erected in five hours an epaulement 500 yards along, 9 feet high and 10 feet thick, continuing the parallel from the Mahon Battery to the Mediterranean shore. The work was entirely composed of sandbags, and it was reported that over a million and a half were used. Not only that, but a communication was made from the centre of the Lines to the eastern end of the work, with two traverses, composed of casks filled and covered with sand, 1,300 yards long, and 6 feet high. Having completed this tremendous work, the whole force retired before dawn. To have built this flying sap, as d'Arçon called it, in one night, under the guns of the garrison, without a single casualty, was a magnificent achievement, and one which boosted the spirits in the enemy Camp, and was a fitting welcome to the Comte d'Artois, and the Duc de Bourbon, who joined the Camp the next day.

By first light on the morning of the 16th the garrison guards on night watch could not believe what they saw. On hearing their report, the Governor and General Green went hurrying up to Willis's to see for themselves. When Captain Witham suggested that the batteries should open on the new work, the Governor answered him shortly that they fired too much when there was little to fire at, and not at all when the enemy were swarming below them. He decided to wait, as he had done before, until the Work was nearer completion before attempting to destroy it. General Eliott had a good understanding of his enemy, who, when opposed, was both cautious and brave, but when ignored, became careless and over-confident. Not every man in the garrison had his sang-froid, and Captain Spilsbury noted that the most worried appeared to be the parsons, who kept stopping the men and exhorting them to do their duty. The following day the enemy hauled out one of the floating batteries and anchored it off Barcello's Battery, north of Algeciras; with its sloping roof, and list to the port side, dragged down by the protective wooden buttress, it looked to the garrison like an ungainly house that had fallen into the water, and was sinking.

On the 18th the floating battery was visited by the Royal Princes. At eleven o'clock in the morning seven barges with crimson awnings were rowed to the Orange Grove from Algeciras, accompanied by a squadron of twelve gun-boats. Whilst they waited there for the Royal party to board, the Admiral's 50-gun ship, the frigates, cutters and all the smaller craft were dressed over-all, with the Spanish ensign flying above the British, at the main-top-gallant mast-head of the flagship. Half an hour later the barges and gun-boats set off again towards Algeciras, with a great deal of firing and saluting. A frigate loosed her topsails and steered gently forward to meet the procession, firing a 21-gun salute and, as the barges reached the floating battery, the other 'flottantes' hoisted their ensigns, and there was general firing. Under the bulky armoured side of the battery, the barges almost disappeared. Had the garrison been able to look much closer, they would have been as impressed as the young Prince.

In the barge M. d'Arçon was next to the Comte d'Artois whilst the Duc de Crillon was sulking in the stern. Rough, square boards of wood were bolted to the side of the big merchantman above them, the only gaps being 21-gun ports in two banks lined with tin to protect the wood from the cannon's flash. The boarding covered the whole side from the water-line to the deck; both bow and stern of the ship had been cut down, giving it the appearance of an unwieldy, but strong, box. Along the deck, where a handrail might be, there was a pipe, and from holes at regular intervals along its length, water sprayed gently onto the wood below. D'Arçon was explaining his theories to a new, and interested, audience. Between the wooden armour and the side of the ship was a packing of wet sand, cork, cables and junk; the whole protecting wall was seven to eight feet thick, and the strongest known calibre gun could not fire a ball to pierce more than five feet of wood. The outside was kept wet, so that the passage made by a ball would close after it, depriving it of air; and inside, there would be a network of pipes, like the veins of an animal . . . regrettably not yet working, due to the negligence of the caulkers, who had not yet fixed the pump, and would His Highness like to come on board?

On board the floating battery the Prince found himself under the sloping roof, covered with nets and hides, with the deck tilting beneath his feet, and cleared for the workmanlike action of the gun crews. There were eight brass guns on the upper deck, which resembled a large cow-shed. The starboard side was open and unprotected, and through it he could see more sky than land or sea. Some of the wood was worm-eaten. He did not stay long. The battery fired eight guns as the barges pulled away towards the Admiral's ship, where the Princes were to dine with Admiral Don Bonaventura Moreno. There was still a trial to be watched, not of red-hot shot in spite of d'Arçon's constant requests, but of the floating battery's sailing power. At three o'clock the sails were shaken out, and the anchor weighed, and the lopsided vessel lumbered out into the Bay, making sluggish but steady going of it, past the Admiral, and then attempted to turn: this it failed to do, and was obliged to be rescued and towed back by ten gun-boats, to avoid ignominiously running ashore. At six o'clock three barges carried the Royal party back to the Orange Grove, accompanied by the gun-boats, firing and saluting as before.

That night the garrison kept up a brisk fire on the new works, which did not deter the enemy from raising the parapet of their communication with fascines, or strengthening the epaulement with the evident intention of erecting several mortar batteries along its length. The next morning a small magazine in the Spanish Camp blew up, and occasioned the remark of M. d'Arçon: 'Ce fut l'incurable habitude qu'ont les Espagnols de fumer par-tout.' At noon a barge, one of those with crimson awnings, came across from the Orange Grove under a flag of truce and rowed along the Line Wall to the wharf at Ragged Staff before it was stopped by a shot from the *Repulse*; then it was steered out into the Bay to wait for the Governor's commands. Captain Valloton returned the flag of truce, and brought in presents of ice, fruit and game for the Governor and Lieutenant-Governor, and letters for the Governor and garrison. The presents were from the Duc de Crillon, and General Boyd received 'five hampers, two containing ice and the other three were Melons, Callabash, Parsley, Greenbeats, Tomatisses, Berryhoness's, Onions, Pears, Apples, three sorts of Plums, Lemons, two sorts of Figgs, Kidney beans, Grapes, Peaches, two Rabbits and three brace of Partridges'. Or so it says in the Log Book. General Eliott received this letter from the Duke:

Camp of Buena-Vista, 19th August 1782.

Sir,

His Royal Highness Count d'Artois, who has received permission from the King his brother to assist at the siege, as a volunteer in the Combined Army, of which their Most Christian and Catholic Majesties have honoured me with the command, arriving in this camp the 15th instant. This young Prince has been pleased, in passing through Madrid, to take charge of some letters which had been sent to that capital from this place, and which are addressed to persons belonging to your Garrison: his Royal Highness has desired that I would transmit them to you and that to this mark of his goodness and attention I should add the strongest expressions of esteem for your person and character. I feel the greatest pleasure in giving this mark of condescension in this august Prince, as it furnishes me with a pretext, which I have been anxiously looking for these two months that I have been in camp, to assure you of the highest esteem I have conceived for your Excellency, of the sincerest desire I feel of deserving yours, and of the pleasure to which I look forward of becoming your friend, after I shall have learned to render myself worthy of the honour, by facing you as an enemy. His Highness the Duke de Bourbon, who arrived here twenty-four hours after the Count d'Artois, desires also that I should assure you of his particular esteem.

Permit me, Sir, to offer a few trifles for your table, of which I am sure you must stand in need, as I know you live entirely upon vegetables: I should be glad to know what kind you like best. I shall add a few game for the Gentlemen of your household, and some ice, which I presume will not be disagreeable in the excessive heat of this climate at this season of the year. I hope you will be obliging enough to accept the small portion which I send with this letter.

I have the honour to be &c. B.B. Duc de Crillon.

The General, whose opinion of presents was well known, grumbled that it was 'intended I presume to inform me of the arrival of the Princes in order that they might not particularly be singled out by our gunners or marksmen'. But he also noticed the veiled hint that it was more pleasant on the other side of the Bay, and to disillusion the Duke, in case he felt that ice and vegetables might be followed by a more tempting lure of the kind offered to General Murray, and perhaps to show him that the garrison was devoid neither of provisions nor courtesy, he sent him back a cask each of beef, pork and butter, a cheese, a puncheon of rum, a sheep, a goat, some poultry and a sack of potatoes, with this letter:

Gibraltar, August the 20th, 1782.

Sir,

I find myself highly honoured by your obliging letter of yesterday, in which your Excellency was so kind as to inform me of the arrival in your camp of his Royal Highness the Count d'Artois, and the Duke de Bourbon, to serve as volunteers at the siege. These Princes have shewn their judgement in making choice of a master in the art of war, whose abilities cannot fail to form great warriors. I am overpowered with the condescension of His Royal Highness in suffering some letters for persons in this town to be conveyed from Madrid in his carriages. I flatter myself that your Excellency will give my most profound respect to His Royal Highness, and to the Duke de Bourbon, for the expressions of esteem with which they have been pleased to honour so insignificant a person as I am.

I return a thousand thanks to your Excellency for your handsome present of fruits, vegetables, and game. You will excuse me however, I trust, when I assure you, that in accepting your present I have broken through a resolution to which I had faithfully adhered since the beginning of the war; and that was, never to receive or procure, by any means whatever, any provisions or other commodity for my own private use: so that, without any preference, every thing is sold publickly here; and the private soldier, if he has money, can become a purchaser, as well as the Governor. I confess, I make it a point of honour to partake both of plenty and scarcity in common with the lowest of my brave fellow soldiers. This furnishes me with an excuse for the liberty I now take, of entreating your Excellency not to heap any more favours on me of this kind, as in future I cannot convert your presents to my own private use. Indeed, to be plain with your Excellency, though vegetables at this season are scarce with us, every man has got a quantity proportioned to the labour which he has bestowed in raising them. The English are naturally fond of gardening and cultivation; and here we find our amusement in it, during the intervals of rest from public duty. The promise which the Duke de Crillon makes, of honouring me in proper time and place with his friendship, lays me under infinite obligations. The interest of our Sovereigns being once solidly settled, I shall with eagerness embrace the first opportunity to avail myself of so precious a treasure.

I have the honour to be &c.   G. A. Eliott.

In the meantime the armies on whose triumphs or defeats the solid settlement would rest increased their efforts, as the days before the Grand Attack could be counted. In the garrison Serjeant-Major Ince had driven his gallery 165 feet, and opened two more embrasures; the artillery increased their fire, though now its effect was dissipated amongst the targets that stretched from one side of the isthmus to the other; the working parties were busy opening new embrasures for guns to cover the eastern extremity of the parallel, and raising defences against the new angles from which the enemy's fire might come. The navy were erecting palisades and bedding anchors below the Line Wall. The Spaniards pushed on their works, and prepared four 14-gun batteries, and one 8-gun battery in the parallel east of Mahon, and a mortar battery behind St Carlos.

On the 21st thirteen large boats arrived in the Bay, the first of the landing-craft. During the daytime the enemy seemed to concentrate most of their attention on the floating batteries, and to leave the dumps of fascines and timbers, which they brought up in the night, lying around on the isthmus. They were a good target for the artillery, who could make little impression on the sandbags. On that afternoon an incendiary shell from Willis's started a fire in the eastern communication, which the enemy soldiers and workmen struggled bravely to extinguish under a rain of bursting shells. Eventually they were forced to pull down the works on either side of the blaze to stop it spreading. They did not return the fire immediately, as if their efforts were being conserved for a later day, but on the appearance of an officer in the Lines that evening, they opened up, but without their usual resolution, and the garrison were firing four to one. On the 22nd the St Martin's Battery was put on fire, though the guards there exposed themselves with determination, and soon had it out. These incidents did not deter them from increasing their dumps of wood every night.

August 25 was now approaching, the date mentioned by the deserter in the pantry secretly to the Governor but which everybody knew about, and the townspeople began to make another move from Hardy Town to Europa. This second unhappy exodus to the caves and clefts of rock left their second homes at the mercy of the troops in the south, and there seems little reason to suppose they were more merciful than before, except that now there was barely anything left to steal. The day passed, and some poor people came back, but many stayed, the outcasts of the Rock. On the night of the 24th the enemy opened the sixty-four embrasures in the parallel. The 25th was St Louis' Day, which suggests that it was chosen for the attack but that the preparations were not completed. The ships in the Bay and at Algeciras flew their flags and fired salutes. D'Arçon wrote to Madrid: 'A plan must be well founded in deed to resist such violent shocks.' He had just been told that the attack would be made on 7 September.

The 26th and 27th were occupied in securing the ships that remained at Gibraltar, three ordnance ships and the *St Philip's Castle*, behind the boom at the New Mole, and in withdrawing the *Repulse*, *Fortune* and *Vanguard*, the three guard-ships that had served so well against the gun-boats. The Governor had agreed with Captain Curtis that the sailors should be brought ashore and formed into a Marine Brigade to serve with the garrison. Tents were erected at Europa from spare sails and yard-arms, and the tars were issued with fire-locks, to the amusement of the soldiers, who watched their first attempts to rest, shoulder and poise. Two deserters came in, one an Irishman who had served under General Murray at Mahon, been captured, enlisted in a French regiment, and now returned to his first allegiance; he reported that a colonel and seventeen men of the regiment had been killed by the garrison's shots whilst fighting the fires in the enemy's works. During the last days of August the garrison paraded 1,700 workmen every day, the majority being employed in building flank walls, splinter-proofs, and new communications for Willis's batteries, which were enfiladed by the new enemy batteries on the east of the isthmus. Two 24-pounders were hauled up to Ince's gallery and mounted in the embrasures, and the small-calibre guns along the sea-wall were replaced with heavy guns, including the Spanish 26-pounders taken from Rodney's prizes; the purpose of this was to enable the garrison to use the enemy's shot fired from the land against their own ships, whilst the smaller British shot would be of no use to the enemy's land batteries. The gunners kept up a steady fire, night and day, but the enemy strengthened their new batteries, built five magazines and a large number of traverses to protect their gunners in action. Great piles of fascines were built up behind the parallel, carried up in the night by hundreds of mules, and these unlucky animals suffered greatly from the barrage. On the 28th six Spanish line-of-battle ships and a xebeck came in from the west, and joined the 50-gun ship, three frigates, three cutters, and the swarm of gun-boats, mortar-boats and smaller vessels in the Bay. Six floating batteries had been hauled out to anchor off Barcello's Battery, and boatloads of troops were ferried to the men-of-war daily to practise working the guns, in preparation for their duty aboard them. On the 30th a coach was seen being driven along the Spanish Lines, and the Governor ordered the batteries to cease firing. This inspection by the Royal Princes suggested that the enemy were almost in readiness. The same day the Marine Brigade was brought ashore, and Captain Curtis was given the rank of Brigadier. The General considered some reward due to his men for their efforts:

Garrison Orders, 30th August.

The restriction respecting the confinement of the Dogs is taken off, but no Puppy on any account to be reared under pain of Disobedience of Orders.

He wrote to Lord Shelburne:

A very considerable supply of Powder and Shells, especially Ten inch is so indispensibly necessary that if not timely thrown [in] the Consequences may be fatal, and the Fatigue of the Garrison will be so great that a Reinforcement must be sent out without loss of Time.

This dispatch was sent, hopefully, in a small boat that set out for Portugal on 1 September.

Gibraltar was famous. The long resistance of the defenders, the impending Grand Attack by the incombustible and insubmersible floating batteries and a vast army, the presence in the Camp of the Royal Princes and many other noblemen including the Prince of Nassau, and the certainty that at last the proud British were about to be reduced to a size fitting their insignificant island were immensely attractive to the courtiers of Versailles and Aranjuez, and also to the peoples of France and Spain, whose intense nationalism was turned against General Eliott and his garrison. It was the people as much as the kings who wanted Gibraltar, the people who would later turn against their kings and form the great patriotic revolutionary armies of France, and the patriotic guerrilla armies of Spain: Liberté, Egalité et Fraternité were strictly for one's compatriots. Their sentiments found expression in the theatrical presentation of *The Siege of Gibraltar by the Floating Batteries* in Paris, where the Rock, and the curtain, fell to thunderous applause; and in the Gibraltar fans, popular among the ladies of the Court, which fell to pieces when they were opened. A huge crowd assembled on the hills surrounding the Bay, filling the inns and taverns for miles around, and there were few enough in this sierra, sleeping in their carts and coaches. It was a living theatre. The giant semicircle of hills accommodated the audience; the Bay, the isthmus and the Rock were the stage; the sea and the mountains of Africa were the background; and the armies and navies were the actors. The plot was simple, the climax certain, the entertainment guaranteed. If the cannons fired real shot, the blood was real blood, and the dead really died, there was not a critic who would not applaud the more. Charles III, a sedate and phlegmatic monarch, was caught up by the general fervour, and inquired every morning when he awoke: 'Is it taken?' and when his gentlemen shook their heads, he always said, 'It will soon be ours.'

The Duc de Crillon was under pressure from all sides to open the Grand Attack at the earliest possible moment. The Minister was impatient to see the results of the huge outlay in men, money and materials; the King and Court were anxious for the glory of the restoration of the Key of Spain to Spain; the audience wanted their show; the Comte d'Artois and Duc de Bourbon were not prepared to endure the discomfort of life in Camp for very long; nor could the officers and gentlemen afford the continued expense of entertaining them; the longer the troops remained idle the more discontented they became, and the officers were straining to hurl themselves against the ramparts of the Rock and overwhelm the weak, ragged and outnumbered defenders. Crillon's own inclination, remembering his disclaimer tucked in Madame de Marco's bosom in Madrid, was to start the attack immediately. Only M. d'Arçon wanted to delay. His 'flottantes' were not ready. He was told to have them ready by 7 September.

H

Looking down from Rock Guard 1,400 feet to the isthmus, the Spanish works appeared no more formidable than a child's sand-castle; bright red, white and blue tin soldiers stood behind them; strings of toy mules with peasant drivers carried matchsticks to the tiny cannons mounted in the lines. The long, stumbling walk down the Rock was a descent into reality, though even at the bottom the men felt the drama of the occasion:

> But as we're actors—Europe the spectators,
> I trust we shall perform in this great cause,
> As men determined to maintain the right
> Of George our King, and Britain's fame and welfare.
> Although the foe have made a hect'ring boast,
> That each discharge from land and sea we'll find,
> Two thousand shot and shells from guns and mortars;
> Will constantly be show'ring on the garrison.

(Ancell)

On Sunday, 1 September, the garrison paused for breath. Some took the opportunity to collect their belongings, and to hide them up amongst the rocks on Windmill Hill; others worked in their patches of garden, for all the world as if it was an English Sunday; and others stood and stared across the Bay. Working parties delivered coal to the grates and furnaces behind the batteries, and the cooks and the orderlies, the clerks and the officers' servants practised with the weapons they had drawn from the Stores, to the peril of anyone in the vicinity.

On the 3rd the enemy squadron in the Bay was reinforced by two French ships-of-the-line. On the land side they had been occupied in bringing up powder and shot to the new magazines, and that day and the next they brought mortars from the batteries in the Lines forward to the new positions in the parallel. By the Governor's orders the gunners were conserving their fire, and this gave the Spanish and French an added confidence to hurry their preparations for the attack. On the afternoon of the 4th fifteen landing-craft, with high flat bows, appeared from the Palmones river and anchored off Point Mala. The same evening the seven floating batteries that had been lying off Barcello's Battery, apparently completed, sailed to he Orange Grove. Two grand salutes were fired by the warships in the Bay. As soon as they arrived, small boats began to ply between

them and the pier, shipping shot and powder on board by the dying
light of the sun. The 5th, and in the morning, a large body of men
marched from Algeciras to the Camp. Captain Drinkwater guessed
from the 'irregular manner' in which they marched that they were
the workmen who had been employed on the 'flottantes'. Later in
the day thirty more boats arrived, and were anchored in a line
off Rocadillo Point with some 120 more from Algeciras. The same
evening Drinkwater watched as 'about five hundred men, escorted
by a body of cavalry, embarked from the pier, on board the battering-ships: the singular mode of conducting them to the beach could
not fail to attract our notice, and to cause in us some degree of
surprise'. Apparently the men who were to sail in them had less
confidence in the floating batteries than their inventor. A deserter
came in that night and reported that the Grand Attack would be
launched on the 8th. He added that there were 110 guns ready to
open on the garrison in addition to a large number of mortars.

Captain Spilsbury wrote on 6 September, 'Our magazines and
works well finished in the Lines', and Mr Ancell, watching the tenth
floating battery being rigged to sail at Algeciras, remarked: 'A few
days more and then we shall fall to it ding dong.'

General Eliott issued his orders to meet the attack he expected
in two days' time. A field-officer was appointed to the lines as well
as the one in the town, and they were instructed to take such action
on their own responsibility as would be required in the course of the
assault: a subaltern and twenty men were posted on the New Mole
head: the pickets were to mount 'fully accoutred with ammunition
complete': the 39th Regiment were brought from the south to
encamp outside Southport, the flank companies to take post in the
bomb-proofs of the Picket Yard. Garrison Orders of the 7th completed the Governor's orders for the disposition of the garrison during
the attack:

The 39th flank companies, to take post on the North-bastion town:
three battalion companies of the same regiment, the South bastion; the
remaining five, at Ragged-staff; extending towards the eight-gun
bastion. The 72nd regiment: right, the North-bastion town; left,
Orange's bastion, extending as far further towards the King's bastion
as possible. The 73rd regiment [which was quartered at the southward]
to take post on the left of the 72nd towards the South bastion. Captain

Martin's company of artillery, the Grand battery and Waterport. Captain Lloyd's company, the King's and South bastions. Brigadier-General Picton to command the corps in town. The Hanoverian brigade, from the eight-gun bastion south, to Prince Edward's battery inclusive, under the command of Lieut. Colonel Dachenhausen. The 56th regiment, South parade. The 12th regiment New-Mole parade. The 97th regiment, Rosia parade. The 58th regiment, in front of their encampment, detaching a flank company through the hole in the wall upon Windmill-hill, to reinforce Europa-advance guard. [This regiment was to receive orders from Brigadier Curtis, whose Marine Brigade mounted at Europa]. The engineers and artificers in two divisions, one to assemble at the Esplanade town, the other at the Esplanade south.

Almost his whole defence faced the Bay. It was left to the artillery to meet any assault from the isthmus. Captain Drinkwater gives the strength of the garrison at this time as about 7,500 men, including the Marine Brigade, though nearly 400 of them were in hospital, and the 97th Regiment could barely muster 100 men. Guard and picket duties required 1,700 men day and night, and a further 1,725 men paraded daily for the working parties.

On 6 September there was a discernible repercussion in Gibraltar of the change of the Administration in England, when the Governor listened to a suggestion made by Lieutenant-General Boyd, and gave him command of an operation. (Whether the suggestion actually originated with General Boyd, as the Governor wrote in his report to Lord Shelburne, or whether the honour was tactfully conferred on him as a gesture of politic good will, is difficult to say. Captain Drinkwater confirms the Governor's statement, but the action itself was typical of General Eliott.) The enemy's hurried preparations of the advanced batteries, encouraged by the reduced fire from the garrison, had resulted in a situation where many of the guns and mortars in the Lines had been dismounted to be carried forward and replaced by new pieces, whilst the new batteries were either unarmed or were in such a state of confusion that piles of materials lay around them obstructing the use of the guns. The officers were not slow to remark the parallel between this scene and the one which had occasioned the sortie almost a year before. Be that as it may, it was officially General Boyd who, on the morning of Friday the 6th, wrote to the Governor suggesting a barrage of red-hot shot and incendiary bombs on the enemy works. The Governor immediately agreed, and ordered Major Lewis, who had succeeded Colonel Tovey in command of the Royal Artillery, to attend the Lieutenant-Governor for his orders. The barrage was to commence first thing on the morning of the 8th.

The enemy's Councils were as chaotic as their precautions. Having made an arbitrary decision to attack on the 7th the Duc de Crillon did nothing to ensure that his forces would be ready in time. The land batteries were evidently unprepared, whilst the floating batteries were being hurriedly finished. Seven were sailed over to the Orange Grove on the 4th, and loaded with powder and ammunition, and had their crews escorted on board, as the garrison had witnessed. M. d'Arçon was still insisting that they should be tested with red-hot shot before being sent against the British, but the answer he received was from one Don Cayeton Langara, who, in d'Arçon's words 'se chargeoit lui seul de recevoir dans l'estomac tous les boulets rouges de l'enemi'. More serious than the boasting of this buffoon was the refusal of the Spanish Court to allow the test. D'Arçon's original plan had been supported by the results of innumerable and lengthy tests he had already made; he wrote a treatise entitled 'Experience of the thirst of a red bullet'. To allow the 'flottantes' to be tested at this stage of the attack would not only cause delay but, if they proved neither incombustible nor insubmersible, Spain would be ruined, both in pride and pocket. Moreover everyone believed that they were incombustible and insubmersible as they believed that Gibraltar was part of Spain, because they wanted to. Crillon continued to insist on attacking on the 7th, though there was every appearance that neither the batteries nor the 'flottantes' would be ready. Admiral Moreno, who now commanded nine ships-of-the-line as well as five frigates, seven xebecks and a great number of small vessels (Admiral Barcello kept command of the gun-boats, and claimed he could take Gibraltar with them alone), was also in command of the ten floating batteries. According to d'Arçon, he 'sometimes thought the batteries good, sometimes bad—but he found them excellent when the Prince of Nassau stood on the deck', and apparently had no other criterion of their readiness or worth. There was now a new reason to push the attack as soon as possible. There were rumours that a British fleet had sailed under Lord Howe, consisting of 200 ships. However, it was at last impressed upon on the Duc de Crillon that if he was to maintain the role of a senior and vastly experienced general, forced by loyalty to serve with upstart engineers and admirals, he could not order the attack to start with only seven out of the ten 'flottantes' ready and with half his guns unmounted on the land; he had to give way, and made the most of it by writing later that the decisions were all in the hands of Admiral Moreno and M. d'Arçon. The latter claimed that only adverse winds prevented the attack from being prematurely launched on the 7th, and this may have some truth in it as the last three 'flottantes' sailed from Algeciras to the Orange Grove that morning, and took three hours to get there.

The Council of War fixed the next date for the Grand Attack— Friday, 13 September 1782.

CHAPTER XIX

Braver men were never seen

THE grates were lit before dawn on Sunday, 8 September, behind the batteries on the North Front. The cannonballs which took almost three hours to heat, were a dull red by seven o'clock, innocent enough to look at, but a terrible weapon which set fire to wood on contact and inflicted fierce, blistering wounds on any unfortunate enough to be in their path, or unwise enough to touch them within an hour of firing. The garrison called them 'roast potatoes' and treated them with great respect. The new guard was mounted, the morning gun fired, Lieutenant-General Boyd was helped to a chair in the Grand Battery, and the cannonade began. From the Old Mole head to the Rock gun, the garrison mounted some sixty pieces of ordnance of large calibre which could be brought to bear on the enemy's new works, and they made quite a clatter with them. In the nine hours the barrage lasted, 5,543 shots were fired, a little over 600 an hour, or ten a minute; by a similar calculation, each gun fired once every six minutes; but the figures can only be approximate, as the rate of fire depended on the availability of shot and powder, on the exertions of the gunners, and the condition of the guns. General Boyd and Major Lewis had decided to concentrate the fire on the Mahon redoubt and the batteries on the west of the parallel, and in the first few hours a rain of red-hot balls and burning carcasses beat down the parapets, crashed into the platforms and trenches behind and fell hissing and cracking amongst the fascines and timbers, setting them smouldering into flame.

The crash of the first salvo awoke the Spanish Camp, San Roque, Algeciras, and the hills beyond, and brought the spectators tumbling out of their beds, expecting to see the Grand Attack begun, and

Gibraltar sinking in a sea of flame. Instead they saw wreaths of
smoke drifting from the face of the Rock, the harbour empty, the
isthmus dotted with a few figures, some running back, some forward, and then the first smudges of fire on the yellow banks of the
batteries. Perhaps those nearer heard the screams of injured and
dying men. Crouching behind the parallel in the Mahon redoubt
and the St Carlos and St Martin's batteries, stunned by the sudden-
ness and violence of the attack, were soldiers of the French regiments,
who were by chance on duty. It was unlikely that they would have
met red-hot shot before: it was a sailor's trick though the Moors had
used it, and they cursed the devils on the Rock who had conceived
this form of torture for them. Under the sandbanks, or in the bomb-
proofs, they were safer, leaving the dead to scorch outside, until a
spluttering carcass, or dimly glowing ball, rolled against a timber
support, or set the fascines lining the ditch alight, then they had to
smother the fire with sand or, in the western batteries, run the
gauntlet to the sea for water. Soon the fires were too great for single
efforts; wood dried in the heat of summer flared up, and the flames
began to spread along the parallel like a train of powder. It was the
officers who first exposed themselves to drag down the burning
fascines that topped the parapets; in their shirt-sleeves, arms and
faces blackened by the smoke, smeared with blood and sweat and
sand, these men of gentle families (all of whom had satisfied the Court
genealogist they were possessed of sixteen quarters of nobility), tore
at the burning works with their bare hands, whilst the cannonballs
thudded and rolled amongst them, not without terrible effect. The
men followed their example, fighting, and dying. At the Mahon
redoubt they stood on the glacis, in full view of the gunners on the
Rock, shovelling baskets of sand over the blazing planks and platforms; at the 13-gun battery between St Carlos and the Bay they
formed a chain to carry buckets of water across twenty unprotected
yards, new men replacing those who fell. The same spirit was not
displayed in every part, and Boyd's Log Book noted: 'We saw the
officers and non-commissioned with drawn swords pricking and
driving up some of their men to quench the flames', but it is here
that was also written: 'For braver men were never seen then the
Enemy on the Batteries that was on fire.' They toiled for an hour,
running from fire to fire, without support from the Lines, or from

their guns. At eight, some mortars started firing from St Martin's and the new batteries east of the Mahon redoubt, and an hour later the the guns in the forts and one battery in the Lines opened against the British positions. As General Boyd, to give him the credit, expected, the enemy's fire was badly maintained until a feverish activity, following the arrival of a general officer, cleared the guns for action, when it became more effective. The garrison kept up the cannonade all morning, pausing only to heat their shot or cool their gun barrels. It was too much for the gallant Frenchmen in the Mahon redoubt, on which the hill batteries literally poured their shot. By 2 p.m. Mahon was one great fire, spreading along the communications towards the parallel. The men withdrew to stop the flames by pulling down the works between, and so exposing themselves again. A French officer wrote later:

> The eye is fatigued and the heart rent with the sight and groans of the dying and wounded, whom the soldiers are this moment carrying away; the number makes a man shudder; and I am told that in other parts of the lines, which are not within view of my post, the numbers are still greater. Fortunately for my feelings, I have not, at this instant, leisure to reflect much on the state and condition of mankind.

By four o'clock in the afternoon the fury of the barrage was spent. The gunners, as black and grimy as the French, were allowed to rest; the guns, swollen and hissing at the swabs, were drawn back to cool; the fires under the grates were kicked out. On the isthmus the Mahon redoubt, which had mounted eight guns, was a pyre, and the batteries near the Bay were much damaged and smouldering in places. The French guards trudged back towards the Camp with their dead and wounded (140 casualties were reported), past the horrified stares of their compatriots, and the sympathetic glances of the Spaniards, whom they no longer mocked. They had felt the garrison's teeth.

General Boyd was helped up from his chair and off the Grand Battery. As he walked across the Picket Yard and along Main Street through the ruins of the town, receiving the salutes of those he passed, he must have felt some consolation for his previous neglect. When the Governor called to congratulate him that evening, it crowned his day. In an attack that cost the enemy his main position

in the centre of his lines and many dead and wounded, the garrison
lost two or three dead and several wounded. Among the latter was
Lieutenant Boag of the Artillery, who was laying a gun in one of the
batteries when a shell entered the embrasure and burst, firing the
gun, under which he had thrown himself; he was deafened by the
explosion, though recovered partially later. His lucky escape was
equalled by that of Major Martin, also of the Artillery, the top of
whose hat was shot off by a cannonball; but, like Bombardier
Campbell, he suffered no more than the solicitous inquiries of his
colleagues for some time after. The cannonade was to have a much
greater effect on the fortunes of the garrison than General Boyd, or
Major Lewis, or the Governor could possibly have conceived.

The plan for the Grand Attack, for what it was worth after the
secret defection of the Commander-in-Chief, required that the
bombardment up to the moment the breach was made was to be
shared by the floating batteries, the land batteries, and the warships.
Even in a plan attributed to Crillon this was envisaged:

> The vanguard of the combined squadron will be commanded by Senor
> Cordova, and among the divisions that compose it will be included the
> 3rd of 12 fire-proof ships, which will anchor in Algeciras until Senor
> Alvarez completes the 60 paces of intrenchment opposite the fortress.
> Our ships will then attack; four by the Europa Point, two by the New
> Mole, their fire being supported by that of the gun and mortar-boats
> and bomb-ketches, which will hold themselves in readiness to support
> where it may be required. At a given signal, the fire from our whole line
> will open with that of the intrenchment, which will not cease until a
> breach shall have been made at the Europa Point.

(This plan, which appears in a Spanish manuscript, is a concoction
of Crillon's original plan to attack the south of Gibraltar and
d'Arçon's plan of the fireproof ships. D'Arçon referred to it once
with derision, when he had taken the trouble to discover that the
cliffs at Europa Point were scarped and thirty feet high.) Any commander of land and sea forces might have been expected to realize
that to combine their fire-power was more effective than to dissipate
it. In spite of two delays and the cannonade of the 8th, Crillon could
still deploy the 'flottantes', the army and artillery on the isthmus,
and Moreno's nine line-of-battle ships and a host of gun-boats.
Moreover he had agreed a date for the Grand Attack to start.

However, the British cannonade piqued him. He, Crillon, had seen his batteries burnt under his nose, and under the noses of two Royal Princes and a large audience. On the night of the 8th, out of what d'Arçon called 'a futile desire to astonish the English', he ordered the five new batteries in the parallel to open fire at daybreak. Admiral Moreno, not to be outdone, announced that he would lead his warships and bombard the Rock the next day as well. If there was Spanish dancing in the Camp that night, the strait-laced abandon of its performers, their peacock posturing and strutting, their stamping and clicking, their strained contortions and agonized expressions, mimed the military fandangos in the minds of the commanders in the audience.

The day had not yet decided to dawn, it was five o'clock in the morning, when the enemy anticipated it with a tremendous salvo from sixty mortars, that sent the apes leaping, the birds flying and the salamanders scuttling for shelter. And whilst the shells were still in the air, 100 cannons in the parallel and the Lines flashed and thundered, and almost in the same instant, 160 shot and shells crashed into the Rock batteries, against the bastions at the north, or fell over the ridge into the town to roll against the reverse of the Line Wall parapet. As the thunder rolled off the Rock, splitting the sky and the sleep of the spectators in the hills, who hurried into their clothes determined not to miss what they had come hundreds of miles to see, a few men in the lines lost arms or legs. No one in the garrison had thought that, after the damage inflicted by the cannonade the day before, the enemy would be able to open his new batteries so soon. The Mahon redoubt was still burning, and the Spanish gunners in the western emplacements worked their cannons amongst the debris scattered around them; but it was the 64-gun battery that mauled the garrison in the early discharges; its guns enfiladed the lines, hit the flanks of Willis's, shot into the corners of Montague's and Orange's Bastions, and the North Bastion. After eighteen months' bombardment the garrison knew where to expect the shots from the forts, the lines and batteries round the Mill Tower, but it was only after several salvoes from the sixty-four guns in the parallel that they learned to avoid this new danger. Those who stood in the cool grey dawn watching from the hills, looked in vain for the floating batteries, which were huddled darkly off Rocadillo

Point, and some, no doubt, went back to bed. After the first volley, the enemy did not manage to co-ordinate their fire, so that General Eliott could later write: 'The impression on our works is scarcely perceptible.' However, a steady fire was maintained throughout the day, 5,403 rounds were counted, and it was exceedingly warm, in Captain Drinkwater's opinion, on the North Front and the walls, batteries and bastions north of the Grand Parade.

There was a Levant wind and it was cloudy, but the garrison could see great activity on the enemy's ships in the Bay. The first visitor to the Rock was a small boat from Algiers that rounded Europa and slipped in under the guns in the face of the Spanish squadron. The next was less welcome. Slowly the seven Spanish ships-of-the-line, and the two French, followed by a large frigate and a xebeck, stretched over in a line from the Orange Grove and, coming opposite the garrison at the Ragged Staff, they fired several broadsides. As the wind took them south, they tried to sink the Algiers boat, without success, and then passed Europa, firing at the positions there, which were manned by the Marine Brigade and a company of Artillery. South of the Rock, they wore round and returned to open up again on the southern defences. They received some smart fire from the garrison and stood off to the east. This operation, which was of small consequence, occupied several hours, and it was near sunset when the attack was taken up by fifteen gun- and mortar-boats, which approached the town opposite the King's Bastion. The gun-boats had previously attacked in the dark and, now the gunners on the Bastion could sight their guns, they made good use of the opportunity to score several hits, and forced the enemy craft to retire in precipitation.

So the Duc de Crillon exposed two of the three cards in his hand. The effect of the 64-gun battery was not as devastating as the garrison had feared and by opening fire prematurely, Crillon gave them time to raise new traverses, communications and barricades, unhindered from the sea. Meanwhile Admiral Moreno's flourish against Europa was no more than an unco-ordinated gesture, which allowed the garrison to prepare and practice for the eventual trial of the floating batteries. The Governor's immediate reaction was to order the grates and furnaces along the Line Wall and at the New Mole to be lit, so that the warships would get a hot reception next time they called, and the gunners there would become acquainted with the handling of the 'roast potatoes'.

At dusk on 9 September the barrage slackened and the enemy started firing short-fused shells to explode over the heads of the working parties which were employed clearing the batteries and lines of the rubble brought down by the bombardment, and refilling the magazines the garrison gunners had emptied during the day. Evening Garrison Orders called for 600 men to work all night, and a detachment of all the officers and 100 men of the 97th Regiment to help relieve their comrades. The 26-pound shot that lay about in profusion was collected and carried to the grates to be heated up for the benefit of the enemy ships the next day.

The bombardment continued from the north all that night but, in spite of the bursting shells, the work parties toiled up and down the hill with their wheelbarrow loads of ammunition and barrels of powder. They cleared the lines, using the stones to restore broken walls and damaged emplacements. Meanwhile the rest of the garrison snatched a few hours' sleep. At 2 a.m. there was the sound of firing from the south, and out of the night the nine warships returned from the east to cannonade Europa, and then, the broadsides and the answer of the British guns coming nearer, Rosia, the New Mole, the South Bastion, Ragged Staff, the Line Wall and King's Bastion. Perhaps fearing to negotiate the rocky shore, the ships kept far out, but not far enough, as they stood over to the Orange Grove and next morning one was seen at Algeciras with her bowsprit unshipped. The Spanish batteries resumed their attack the next morning, and kept it up throughout the day. The Governor ordered the hill batteries to withdraw their guns behind the merlons and, apart from some shooting at enemy workmen at the Mahon redoubt, which was still burning, the garrison ignored the barrage. The enemy fired 4,160 times, with no more effect than the day before, to the 194 shots from the garrison. The troops took the opportunity to crowd along the Line Wall to watch the manœuvres of Admiral Moreno's ships, so little did they respect their broadsides, when they steered for the Rock again in the morning. The line, as before, came within range opposite the South Bastion, and were met by a volley of red-hot shot. They sailed south, their passage marked as each battery took its turn to fire at them, to Europa, and wore about as before. The garrison expected them to return, and cheered derisively as they suddenly tacked and headed back for the Orange Grove, where a sudden activity on board one of them suggested that a red-hot ball had lodged in her, which was later confirmed. Two men were killed and three wounded in this attack, but the line-of-battle ships did not approach Gibraltar again. On the 10th the two frigates, *Brilliant* and *Porcupine*, were scuttled by the Navy in the shelter of the New Mole: there was no question of their being employed, and they were safer half under the water than on it. Every attempt of the enemy that fell short of the garrison's expectations put the men into the best of spirits, except one party mentioned by Captain Spilsbury: 'The workmen of the 39th had carried one load of wood to the Rock Gun, desired to carry another, but they refused saying they ought to have grog.' They deserved it. That night the workmen again paraded to clear the debris of the day's bombardment, whilst the enemy again and with as little effect, fired shells in the air.

The 11th, Wednesday morning, and the garrison felt that the threatened attack of the floating batteries could not be delayed much longer. They had been lying in the Bay for four days, armed and partly manned, with a flotilla of small craft behind them. The wind had blown steadily from the east since they had been there, and the general expectation was that the attack would start when it changed. There were other indications: the enemy's fire that day was concentrated on Landport and its approaches; some detachments of soldiers were embarked in the landing-craft; the hills were dotted and fringed with thousands of spectators, more than had ever appeared before. When, in the evening, a light breeze was felt from the north-west, they believed that the next day would witness their greatest trial. General Eliott ordered the fires to be lit under the grates and the guards at Waterport and Landport to be increased. When the word spread to the poor inhabitants at Hardy Town, they hurriedly collected their belongings and made for the rocks on Windmill Hill. Only the most hardened or the most phlegmatic could sleep without a care that night. The firing from the isthmus seemed far off as they gazed out at the Bay, straining to see the dim shapes of the battering-ships, which they believed would advance during the night. But the alarm when it did come was from the isthmus. It was between nine and ten o'clock when the guards in the Queen's Lines heard movements below them at Forbes Barrier. Their challenge was answered by a tinder spark and suddenly the palisades and the wooden hut at the barrier were alight: at the same moment, the enemy fired the palisades at Bayside. The flames lit up the Inundation and part of the Governor's Meadow, where several bodies of troops were seen. The guards discharged their muskets but, nothing else transpiring, were ordered back to the shelter of their bomb- and splinter-proofs. The enemy barrage, which had been intensified during the burning of the palisades, was supported after midnight by the gun-boats, which lay off the Old Mole and directed their shot at Waterport. Whilst they were firing, music was heard across the Bay. After two hours they retired, and the garrison had a few cold hours of sleep before dawn.

The Spaniards had built a grandstand decorated with scarlet bunting, and some booths, on the shore in front of the Camp. The garrison saw them the next morning. The palisades were charred, and what was left of them could easily be flung aside by the attackers. The enemy bombardment was as brisk as ever. But all this was as nothing when at 7 a.m. the report was circulated that the Europa Guard had seen the sails of a large fleet approaching from the west: 'We hope it is the British coming to our relief—every one seems impatient to discover their colours: A gentleman who has been taking a view says they are French and Spanish men of war; if so our fate is inevitable,' so wrote Mr Ancell, and neither he nor the garrison were long in suspense. On a brisk west wind that blew some of Gibraltar's high hopes away with it, the Combined Fleets of France and Spain came into the Bay, under the broad pennant of the Commodore, Admiral Don Luis de Cordova, and the flags of ten admirals; seven three-deckers, thirty-one two-deckers, three frigates, and several xebecs, bomb-ketches and hospital ships. This huge fleet which, with the ships already in the Bay, numbered forty-seven ships-of-the-line, eight frigates, and a large number of smaller vessels including over 100 gun-boats and 300 troop carriers, was now added to the ten floating batteries, reputed invincible and carrying 142 large cannon, the army of nearly 40,000 men, and the massive concentration of some 200 pieces of heavy artillery on the land. This great force, unequalled in any siege in the world, was commanded by men of high reputation and achievement, Crillon, Cordova, Moreno, supported by the engineering genius of d'Arçon, and officered by the nobility of Spain and France. In the Camp were two Royal Princes of France, with their trains of nobles, and many others of high rank, who wished to be associated with the enterprise. On the hills behind were 80,000 spectators from all Europe, eager to see the humiliation of Great Britain, and her expulsion from the continent, and the gate of the Mediterranean.

On the Rock of Gibraltar stood General Eliott and the garrison of 7,000 men; and, for a few moments, high above all on the flagpole of the Signal House, an ancient omen recalling all the past glories of this Pillar of Hercules, golden in the morning sunlight, an eagle.

CHAPTER XX

The sacrifice of folly

THE arrival of the Combined Fleet before Gibraltar was the ultimate pledge of the Spanish King of his determination to restore the Rock Fortress to his crown. The presence of this overwhelming force in the Bay was expected not only to assist the Grand Attack, but to deter the British Government from making any attempt to relieve the garrison in Gibraltar before the defeat, which now appeared inevitable. The French King too, by sending twelve line-of-battle ships under the Comte de Guichen, as well as his 4,000 troops, and the Royal Princes, linked arms with his uncle of Spain against the outpost of their common enemy. The honour of the two Crowns flew on the standards in the Bay.

Honour, with her tawdry sister Glory, presided over the councils of the commanders at Buena Vista. Much of the day was occupied in the exchange of courtesies between the Admirals, the Princes and the Duc de Crillon, and it was not until evening that an agitated French Colonel of Engineers was able to talk to the Commander-in-Chief about the Grand Attack, which, almost incidentally, was due to take place the next day. It seems probable that Admiral Moreno, who was to command the 'flottantes', was present, and these three jealous men who courted glory with Gallic ardour decided the fate of Gibraltar between them. The conversation is reconstructed from M. d'Arçon's various publications in 1782 and 1783:

D'Arçon: M. le Duc, it is impossible to mount the attack tomorrow.
Crillon: On the contrary, Sir, it is essential.
D'Arçon: There is still much to be done: for example, Admiral Cordova and the Combined Fleet are in the Bay, we must concert measures

with them, and agree signals, so that they may know their stations, and be ready to take them.

Crillon: Should the assistance of the Fleet be required during the attack I am certain Senor Cordova will not hesitate.

D'Arçon: Then there are the batteries on the isthmus: they are not firing correctly, in order to enfilade the batteries that will be combating the 'flottantes' . . .

Crillon: M. d'Arçon, I had you sent here to construct these floating batteries; the rest concerns me alone; we will start as planned.

D'Arçon: But no markers have been placed in the Bay to guide the 'flottantes' to their positions: no soundings have been taken of the sandbanks off the Old Mole: no anchors have been sunk on which they can be warped back in case they are obliged to retreat.

Crillon: You mean that they are not incombustible and insubmersible?

D'Arçon: There has been some difficulty with the system of pipes. It will take several days.

Crillon: If you have been remiss . . . but there is no question of any further delay. We have postponed the attack twice because you were not ready. Everyone expects us to attack tomorrow, to postpone it again would only make us appear ridiculous. Besides, everything is ready, isn't that so, Senor Moreno?

Moreno, who had been sulking since the puerile performance of his battleships on the 9th and 10th, did not reply.

D'Arçon: Let me explain. Because I was not permitted to test the 'flottantes', they were no sooner completed than they were rigged, and the powder and balls were loaded. Today the captains ordered the water pumps to be started to fill the main tanks, and to circulate the water through the pipes, like the blood in the veins of an animal . . .

Crillon: We know your metaphor.

D'Arçon: Unfortunately, due to the negligence of the caulkers, water began to leak out, and the captains ordered the pumps to be stopped, in case the powder was dampened. I must have time to repair the caulkage.

Crillon: I regret, Sir, that it is out of the question. We are already in September, and can expect bad weather, even storms. More than that, the enemy are sending a fleet to the relief of Gibraltar . . .

Moreno: (Waking up) Am I to be expected to risk the lives of my sailors on these 'flottantes' when they are not properly armed? If it had not been for an unlucky hit by a red-hot ball the other day, I would have destroyed the defences in the south . . .

Crillon: Let us see what you will do tomorrow.

D'Arçon: But M. le Duc . . .

Crillon: (Standing up and shouting) The attack must proceed. The time is right. There will not be another opportunity like this. The enemy is waiting for reinforcements. These are my orders!

D'Arçon: (With a shrug) I will do what I can in the time . . . but I begin to despair already . . . M. le Duc, Admiral.

D'Arçon went out, leaving the victors of Port Mahon together.

Moreno: I protest . . .

Crillon: And I command. If you do not attack you will be dismissed! If you do not attack, you have no honour!

Moreno, white in the face, slammed out of the room. And so it was decided.

After he left the room d'Arçon went to his tent and wrote out a list of targets for every gun on the isthmus, which he gave to an orderly to deliver to the Lieutenant-General commanding the artillery. It suffered the same fate as all the other lists and memoranda he had painstakingly drawn up. It was dark when he finished, and he went down to the Orange Grove and climbed into a small rowing-boat, and went out to take soundings between 800 and 1,000 yards off the Old Mole. He was concerned to discover a sandbank shelving out into the Bay opposite Fort St Philip, allowing a depth of only 3½ fathoms, 1,000 yards from the Old Mole Head, though there was a deeper channel between it and the Old Mole. In order to reach a position from where they could bring their fire to bear on the defences facing north and the curtain wall between Orange's and the King's Bastions, where the breach was to be made, the floating batteries would have to head out into the Bay, before looping round in line to avoid the sandbank. D'Arçon rowed back hurriedly, and ran to his tent to prepare charts for the captains indicating the routes they must take to bring the batteries within range of the walls. At 2 a.m. on the morning of the 13th he was still working, when an orderly rushed in to tell him that Admiral Moreno was aboard the *Pastora*, the leading 'flottante' that carried the flag, and that two of the others were already under sail. D'Arçon hurried down to the shore, to find everything in confusion: troops of soldiers, joking and laughing, dozens of small boats bobbing in the Bay, and no one in

command. He could see eight of the hulks still at anchor, and then
two others, under their giant sails, drifting down from Rocadillo
Point to join them. It was a false alarm, but as the captains were all
aboard their vessels, and they might sail at any moment, he went on
to the *Talla Piedra*, the second largest, commanded by the Prince
of Nassau, from where he had decided to watch the attack.

When Moreno had stormed out of Buena Vista he went straight on
board the *Pastora* without talking to anyone. He would have started
the attack at that moment, but the troops who were to fire the guns
were still in the camp. He sent a short note to M. O'Conel, who was
to command the French detachment on the batteries, that the attack
was about to start, and then stayed, fuming, in his cabin. Each
regiment was to provide 100 men commanded by a captain and two
subalterns, and this party gathered by the quay. Moreno's urgency
somehow failed to communicate itself to M. O'Conel, as the men
had time to dine off a bullock and some sheep before eventually
embarking, when d'Arçon came down amongst them. The sailors
were already on board, and the Spanish detachment had embarked
earlier, some having been there since the 7th. The lists of the floating
batteries and the number of guns and men they carried all differ,
which is not surprising considering the confusion at the start of their
journey and the lack of evidence at the end of it. These figures are
compiled from French, Spanish and British sources.

Ship	Guns	Men	Captain
Pastora	24	700	Don Buenaventura Moreno, Admiral
Talla Piedra	23	700	Don Juan Mendoza, Prince of Nassau & M. d'Arçon
Paula Prima	23	700	Don Cayetan Langara
Rosario	21	700	Don Francisco Munos
St Cristoval	19	650	Don Frederico Gravino
Principe Carlos	11	350	Don Antonio Basurta
San Juan	9	340	Don Josef Angeler
Paula Secunda	9	340	Don Pablo de Cosa
Santa Anna	7	300	Don Josepf Goicochea
Los Dolores	6	250	Don Pedro Sanchez
	152	5,030	

The larger ships had ten to seventeen guns in reserve, and the
smaller three or four; all the cannon were brass and of heavy calibre.

From observations made later it is probable that on the main decks of the larger ships there were small altars, where priests held services before the attack, and whilst it was proceeding. D'Arçon wrote before he left: 'We go to throw ourselves at the centre of the Fortress, where the walls are strongest.' But they did not go for several hours.

When the garrison considered the forces on the other side of the Bay, the brief visit of the eagle could hardly have appeared more than a touch of dramatic irony. The gentlemen, who had had a classical education flogged into them, which might account for their preference for imposing this particular form of instruction on their men, would certainly have exchanged the feathered Victory for the flag signalling the approach of the British Fleet which, at first, everyone thought it was. The enemy barrage was maintained on the 12th as on preceding days, and there was a brief visit by the gunboats, but the garrison was now practically immune to these irritations, and was more concerned with the threat from the battering-ships and the fleet in the Bay. Fifteen new furnaces for the heating of shot were built along the Line Wall, and the pickets were increased, and stationed in the town. That evening General Eliott wrote: 'The Wind having come to the Westward there is all probability the Enemy will determine upon his final Attack by sea.' But neither the Governor nor the garrison knew when or where the attack would take place.

General Eliott spent the night, as he had done for some time now, in his new home on Windmill Hill, a place he was later to refer to as 'the hutt' in a letter to Roger Curtis. The Convent was too exposed to an attack from the Bay, and too obvious a target, and besides, the Captain-Brigadier was stationed at Windmill Hill.

Dawn, Friday, 13 September 1782, and there was a great stir in the Spanish Camp, as soldiers, visitors and spectators, hurried, not to arms, but to the best vantage points from which to watch the Grand Attack. One man alone had his back to Gibraltar, the Duc de Crillon's courier, riding north to inform the King, who was even at that moment asking 'Is it taken?', that the assault had begun. This gentleman, who was also the duke's messenger to Madame de Marco, was M. de Salinas, by one of Clio's quirks of the same name as the unlucky Governor who surrendered the fortress in 1704. But the floating batteries had not moved; in spite of Moreno's piqued pride, he was enough a sailor not to risk setting out at night, with the channel unmarked, and no landmarks, on a journey that might well have ended beached a few yards from the garrison's walls. However, shortly before 7 a.m., the *Pastora* weighed anchor, her sails were shaken out in the north-westerly breeze, and she steered slowly to the south, tilting slightly to port with the weight of the guns and men assembled on that side. The other captains made haste to follow, in whatever order they could, and, so eager were they to forestall the Admiral, they executed what appeared to be, to everyone watching, a perfect manœuvre, though they had only the vaguest idea where they were going. D'Arçon, who had been in a frenzy of agitation on board the *Talla Piedra* waiting to sail, began to hope that the prayers of the priests had succeeded where the command had failed.

The Governor of Gibraltar came off the morning parade when he heard that there was some movement among the enemy's ships. The naval gentlemen had so often given it as their opinion that the floating batteries would only move forward at night that, after a cursory glance at the Bay on getting out of bed, General Eliott believed his Rock and garrison to have another day's grace. Now, however, as he trotted his horse along the rampart of the Line Wall, it became apparent that if the attack was not to be made that day, half Europe had assembled in vain. Moreover, the floating batteries were wearing round towards Gibraltar, in the words of Boyd's Log Book, 'as so many invincible Aligators', though they looked more like a string of Noah's Arks. The Governor ordered the guns to be manned and the grates and furnaces lit.

It was splendid. The Comte d'Artois in the grandstand said so, and the 80,000 spectators undoubtedly agreed. Just after 9 a.m. the 'flottantes' had worn round to the north, and were heading in a line for Fort St Philip. Their brave banners and glistening sides (the exterior sprinklers were working though the inner pipes were shut off) were brilliant in the morning sunlight. That the fleet made no move, and the armada of small craft stuck near the shore, did not concern the onlookers. The slow stately progress of the 'flottantes' was sufficient evidence of their invincibility; they must be incombustible and insubmersible to proceed against the enemy alone. Admiral Moreno knew that eleven ships-of-the-line ought to be heading for Europea to make a diversion, and that sixty of Admiral Barcello's mortar- and gun-boats ought to be sailing to support him, but he was too concerned to prove his honour to pause, or send for help. M. d'Arçon knew that the 'flottantes' were headed straight for a sandbank. As the *Talla Piedra* came level with the King's Bastion, he persuaded the helmsman to turn her to the east, straight towards the Rock. They were still over 2,000 yards out and had they continued in file behind the new leader, would have missed the sandbank, but Moreno, believing that the Prince of Nassau was trying to steal his glory by being the first to open fire, had his helm put over, and steered the *Pastora* alongside the *Talla Piedra* for the walls. The move from file to line-of-battle was familiar to every ship's captain, and was followed without hesitation, the 'flottantes' spreading out on either side of the Admiral with beautiful precision, to the admiration of everyone who watched. *Los Dolores, St Christoval, Principe Carlos, Paula Secunda, Santa Anna, Pastora, Talla Piedra, San Juan, Rosario, Paula Prima:* the line stretched from the Old Mole to the Church Battery on the Line Wall between King's Bastion and the South Bastion, with the *Talla Piedra* opposite the King's Bastion. In this order, they sailed in, with the *Pastora* and *Talla Piedra* leading, so that when they came within 800 yards of the walls, furled their sails, dropped anchors, and lay broadside on: *Los Dolores, St Christoval, Principe Carlos* and *Paula Secunda* were bumping gently against the edge of the sandbank 1,200 yards from the Old Mole; *Santa Anna* was between them and the Admiral; *San Juan* was to the west of the *Talla Piedra*, and aiming at her unprotected side, and *Rosario* and *Paula Prima* were trailing away to the south. But they came to anchor at 9.45 a.m., and swung their armoured sides opposite the walls, as if they were exactly in the positions planned for them.

The garrison had watched this manœuvre with as much admiration as the crowds around the Bay. The very daring of the operation, bringing the floating batteries within cannon range of the walls, in broad daylight and unsupported, almost convinced them that the stories they had heard of their impregnability must have been true. They were entirely convinced when, as the first battering-ships dropped anchor, they opened fire on them. As the grates and furnaces had not been lit until 8 a.m., the red-hot shot were not ready, and the first attack was made with cold shot and shells which, to the

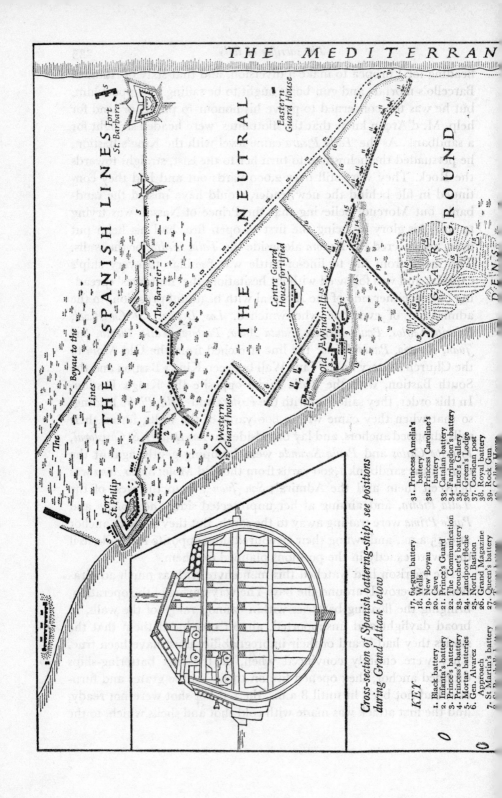

Cross-section of Spanish battering-ship: see positions during Grand Attack below

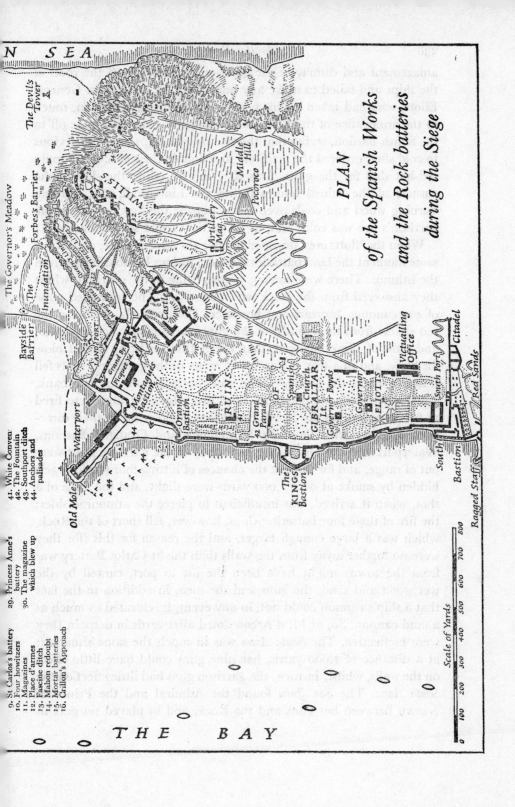

PLAN
of the Spanish Works
and the Rock batteries
during the Siege

N SEA

THE BAY

The Devil's Tower

The Governor's Meadow

The Forbes's Barrier

The Inundation

Bayside Barrier

WITHIS

Middle Hill

Pocoroco

Artillery Mag.

Castle

LAND PORT

Grand By

Piquet

Montague's Bastion

Waterport

Old Mole

Oranges Bastion

RUINS OF

New Town

41 Grand Parade

GIBRALTAR

Spanish Church

Lt. Governor Boyds

Governor

Governor Boyds

V ELIOTTS

The KINGS Bastion

Victualling Office

South Port

Citadel

Red Sands

South Bastion

Ragged Staff

9. St Carlos's battery
10. Four howitzers
11. Magazines
12. Place d'armes
13. Fascine ditch
14. Mahon redoubt
15. Mortar batteries
16. Crillon's Approach

29. Princess Anne's battery
30. The magazine which blew up

41. White Convent
42. The Fountain
43. Southport ditch
44. Anchors and palisades

Scale of Yards

0 100 200 300 400 500 600 700 800

amazement and dismay of the garrison, rebounded off the roofs of the ships and failed to make any impression on their sides. General Eliott, who had taken up his position on the King's Bastion, much to the annoyance of the Lieutenant-Governor, who had gone off to the South Bastion, seeing that the two nearest ships were impervious to cold shot, ordered the artificers to redouble their efforts to supply red-hot shot for the guns. This they did by piling the shot in the corners of the ruined houses facing the Line Wall, and heaping burning wood and coals over them, but for the first few hours the garrison's fire was cold, and, as far as they could see, ineffective.

When the 'flottantes' dropped anchor they opened fire, and at the same moment the land batteries started a furious bombardment from the isthmus. There were some 300 guns firing at the garrison, whilst they answered from the Rock with about 100. The combined noise of 400 cannons, mortars and howitzers, the umbrella of smoke, the red sparks from the mouths of the guns, convinced every spectator, and most of those engaged, that the battle was being fought blow for blow, and in a way it was, for as many of the garrison's shots fell into the sea as the enemy's. The four 'flottantes' on the sandbank, 1,200 yards from the garrison, fired away bravely, and were fired at by every gun on the North Front that could point in their direction, together with those on Montague's and Orange's Bastions, Waterport and the Old Mole; but many of the garrison guns were out of range, and for the rest the chances of hitting four small targets hidden by smoke at over 1,000 yards were slight, and the force of a shot, when it arrived, was insufficient to pierce the armoured sides: the fire of these four battering-ships, however, fell short of the Rock, which was a large enough target, and the reason for this (for they were no further away from the walls than the St Carlos Battery was from the town) might have been the list to port, caused by the wet wood and sand, the guns and the men, in addition to the fact that a ship's cannon could not, in any event, be elevated as much as a land cannon. So, as M. d'Arçon noted afterwards in despair, they were ineffective. The *Santa Anna* was in much the same situation; at a distance of 1,000 yards, her nine guns could have little effect on the walls, whilst, in turn, the garrison guns had little effect on the *Santa Anna*. The *San Juan* found the Admiral and the Prince of Nassau between her guns and the Rock, and so played no part in the battle whatever, whilst the *Rosario* and *Paula Prima* were too far to the south to do more than fire aimlessly at the Line Wall and the South Bastion, and to receive the garrison's fire from this quarter and, for the same reasons that applied to the 'flottantes' to the north, they were virtually not engaged in the battle. The burden of the attack was borne by the *Pastora* and the *Talla Piedra*, and the real battle was between these two floating batteries and the King's Bastion. The fire from the land batteries, and particularly the 64-gun battery, harassed the garrison's positions in the north and was the the main cause of the casualties suffered. The artillerymen operating the guns on the Line Wall between the King's Bastion and Orange's had little protection against the shot that came on them from the flank and from behind, and that was the hottest part of the Rock that morning. There is no reason to question that every man on the floating batteries was under the impression that he was fighting as hard as the men on the *Pastora* and the *Talla Piedra*, or that every man on Gibraltar felt as involved in the struggle as the men on the King's Bastion; they could not see the effect of their shot once the smoke thickened, only that the 'flottantes' and the walls were still there. They could see each other's shot however, and Captain Spilsbury on the British side noted: 'They fired a great deal into the water', but he had no intention of publishing his diary. The only reporter on the Spanish side was in the thick of the fight on board the *Talla Piedra*.

By twelve o'clock the shot on the grates were glowing red, and the pyramids in the furnaces had a flush of more modest heat, when the Governor signalled for the artillery to start firing them. He had watched over two hours steady cannonade and bombardment of the two big battering-ships opposite the bastion, with no more effect than to shoot away their masts and rigging. Boyd's Log Book recorded one unique shot that nobody else noticed:

> A shot from one of the Enemies Junk ships, came into one of our howitzers on the King's Bastion which fir'd her off and the Ball re-turn'd with the Howitzer shell to its own Ship again through one of the Portholes and the shell exploding between decks killed and wounded about 40 men.

The cannons were firing with only a slight elevation and did not require wadding, and the first batch of red-hot shot was discharged at a tremendous rate, and as fast as the balls could be brought from the furnaces to the guns by the working parties of the 39th and 72nd Regiments, who had this delicate and dangerous duty. General Eliott noted that shortly after they began to use red-hot shot the fire from the two battering-ships slackened slightly, but the garrison did not see the immediate results which they had hoped for from their 'roast potatoes'. Sometimes, through the cannon-smoke, they saw men pouring water on the roofs of the ships, and guessed that, even when their shot lodged in the protective armour, the enemy had little difficulty in extinguishing it.

On the *Talla Piedra* twenty-five men had been killed or wounded by 11.30 a.m., so perhaps Boyd's story had some truth in it, but the protective wall and roof were resisting well, and when some stones were knocked off the parapet of the King's Bastion the soldiers cheered and carried d'Arçon about triumphantly. The first red-hot shots that came aboard were tracked down and soaked until they were harmless. The Prince of Nassau wrote to the Comte d'Artois: 'The danger is great: we lose many men, but the ship resists well. The red balls are easily put out, and I hope soon to make at least one breach, and to open the gates of Gibraltar.' He asked for reinforcements of a captain and twenty-five men, but no ships approached the 'flottantes' to support the attack. The Combined Fleet lay at anchor as calmly as if the battle on the other side of the Bay was of no concern to them, whilst the gun-boats, mortar-boats and bomb-ketches made no move. There can be little doubt that Admiral Barcello was aware that the plan demanded thirty gun-boats and thirty mortar-boats to advance and fire from the flanks and in between the 'flottantes', and there is equally little doubt that their presence would have embarrassed the garrison considerably. They had already proved an effective weapon in much smaller numbers, and their failure to attack allowed the garrison to concentrate its fire exclusively on the 'flottantes'. D'Arçon wrote: 'The auxiliaries maintained a perfidious silence', and on board the *Talla Piedra* said to a French officer, 'Ne voyez-vous pas, mon ami, que nous sommes abandonnés de Dieu et des hommes?' He spoke more truth than he knew, for at that time one red-hot ball was lying in the timbers of the ship, unnoticed. The only excuse that can be found for Barcello, or Cordova, was made by Captain Drinkwater:

About noon, the mortar-boats and bomb-ketches attempted to second
the attack from the ships; but the wind having changed to the south-
west, and blowing a smart breeze, with a heavy swell, they were prevented taking a part in the action.

But the line-of-battle ships could have sailed on a south-west breeze,
and the smaller boats had rowed across the Bay on many a stormy
night before. The real reason lay in the minds of one admiral who
was superseded, and another who had already shown a marked
disinclination for battles.

The scene behind the wall and bastions of the Rock at noon was
like a leisurely inferno, with black-faced demons tending altars of
glowing balls under columns of dirty smoke, while puffing and
sweating acolytes carried the offerings in wheelbarrows lined with
sand to other blacker demons, who seized them in tongs, rolled them
into the mouths of their cannons, and blasted them off at the
unlucky souls in their wooden coffins under the cross of Spain. Proof
of the ineffectiveness of the cannonade from the floating batteries,
officers and men stood along the Line Wall south of the King's
Bastion watching the fray, but to the north, the Grand Parade was
a skittle-alley for the shot and shells from the isthmus. There, the
soldiers dodged the cannonballs, or flung themselves down for the
tense moments before the bursting of a shell. The wounded were
carried off on stretchers under the pall of smoke, and others took
their places. And all under a sulphurous cloud and a hot sun.

What with the heat of the day, the forges, furnaces, and piles of flaming
shot, amidst clouds of smoke and sulphur, accompanied with heavy toil,
you may judge we found ourselves very feeble and thirsty, and in this
situation a drink of water which was all the allowance could scarce be
procured. An officer (Lt Galpin of the 72nd) who commanded a
battery, observing the men at the guns almost exhausted with drought
he chearfully took a keg, which holds about a pail, went to the fountain,
filled it with water, and brought it through the enemy's fire to the men
on the battery. (Ancell).

Other gunners, whose officers were more discreet, drank the water
in which they soaked their sponges. It was the Royal Artillery's day,
and the regiments, apart from those working between the furnaces
and the guns, remained spectators. Eighty cannons, seven mortars
and nine howitzers were in action, each firing, on an average, once

every five minutes. Their reward came at 2 p.m., when it was confirmed, with a shout from the King's Bastion, that a steady stream of smoke was coming from the largest and nearest battering-ship.

Admiral Moreno, on board the *Pastora*, could see that after four hours battering against the walls he had made little impression on them, nor was he likely to, as behind the wall and rampart raised in the 1730s was the old Moorish wall and rampart. But he had no intention of retreating, even if it was possible without anchors on which to warp the ships back. His honour was in the balance, and though he knew he could no longer aspire to glory, that was inviolable. When he was told that the *Talla Piedra* was on fire, it did something to restore his spirits: if after all the 'flottantes' were not incombustible or insubmersible, he, Moreno, was not to blame. He ordered the guns to keep on firing, and made no signals, and sent no messages. On the *Talla Piedra* there was confusion. The first hint of catastrophe was a slow seeping of smoke through the boards of the upper deck. The gunners, as black as their enemy, still plied their cannons in the hot, dark, choking atmosphere under the roof: the dead were dragged back and piled into the empty spaces between the powder barrels, whilst the wounded were carried to a bloody table where surgeons performed crude operations, and the priest hovered to perform the last rites over those they declared hopeless, though most died, blessed or not. Between the blasts of their own guns, the cries and groans of the dying, the soldiers heard the British shot thudding against the side of the ship, tearing into the wood, cracking the timbers over their heads. Mixed with the stench of sweat, blood and gunpowder, they could smell burning wood, and in each others' red restless eyes, they could see their own fear. The officers shouted for men to find out the burning cannonballs, and they slithered across the blood-wet tilting decks, and climbed up onto the roof, slopping water from their buckets, cursing their commanders, and the hulk in which they were trapped. Most of the balls were discovered, prised out, or quenched, but one, somewhere in the ship, was smouldering, slowly blackening the wood around it, glowing, ready to burst into flame. In one hour twenty men were killed outside the ship, on the roof, or clambering between the embrasures, searching for the hole that would reveal the source of the smoke. Inside they prised up the boards, and hacked away the planks, in a desperate search. The smoke increased, the gunners slackened in their efforts, and in the longer pauses between their firing, the ship seemed to shudder under the pelting shot from the garrison.

From the moment that the fire from the floating battery opposite the King's Bastion began to lessen, the artillerymen, urged on by General Eliott, loaded, aimed, fired and swabbed with greater spirit than before. Smoke was now coming from several holes in her sides, from her deck, and through her roof, and the battery to the north was also seen to be smoking. As the sun appeared through the yellow haze on the edge of the battle-cloud, dully glowing like a roast potato, the garrison had another presentiment of victory. One by one the land batteries on the isthmus closed down, until there was only a scattered firing, and then silence. No silence from the garrison, who cheered, and continued to pound the battered ships as hard as they could.

At five o'clock they discovered the red hot ball on the *Talla Piedra*, or rather it discovered itself, when a bulk-head below the top deck began to smoke violently, and when the men broke through they looked into a glowing cavern in the side of the ship. M. d'Arçon was called, and hurried down past the stares of hate of the men, who had cheered him six hours before, but who now stood about, defeated and demoralized. D'Arçon saw that the ball had penetrated the outside layers of wood, cut through the lining of sand, and, ironically enough, one of the pipes that hung dry and useless, and had lodged three feet inside the timbers of the ship. In the four or five hours it had lain there, the heat had slowly eaten out a hole that smouldered and smoked, but, deprived of air, had not burst into fire. Now that it was opened, small ripples of flame were playing on the charred wood, and any moment the whole cavity might explode into a furnace. D'Arçon thought that there was still time to control the fire, which he estimated was some seventeen yards from the nearest powder, but on his way to the top deck to report to the Prince of Nassau, he saw men carrying buckets of water, not to the fire, but to the barrels by the guns and on the starboard side of the ship, which they were prising open. It was too late, the Prince had already ordered the powder to be damped. D'Arçon found him with Don Juan Mendoza, discussing the only possible course of action— retreat. Slowly the immensity of the disaster dawned on the three men. There was no anchor behind them, no signals for help that could be made and understood, no sails, for the rigging had been shot away. Mendoza proposed to row out a boat carrying an anchor to be dropped out in the Bay, on which they might warp the 'flottante' back, but there was only one boat, and the Prince had an alternative use for it. D'Arçon asked permission to return to find out what assistance could be sent from the Fleet and to suggest a diversion whilst the *Talla Piedra* was towed back, but the Prince insisted that he should remain on board, as the 'flottantes' were, after all, his responsibility. Shortly afterwards the Prince of Nassau himself left the *Talla Piedra* to its fate. On the deck, in the strange quiet broken by the continual battering outside, and the cries in Spanish and French of the wounded, the men waited.

There were several small smouldering fires on the *Pastora*. When the word spread amongst the soldiers that the *Talla Piedra* had stopped firing, their own efforts appeared more futile than ever, and they avoided their officers' eyes, and began to look about for some way to escape from their smoking hulk: there was none. At sunset, when a boat brought an officer from the Comte de Guichen to Admiral Moreno, offering the assistance of the French ships, the Admiral took a grim satisfaction in replying that as everything was proceeding as expected, he would not trouble the Comte. About seven o'clock, however, with the fires gaining ground, and the firing stopped, Moreno had to face the same decision that had barely troubled the Prince of Nassau and, sending his pride after his glory, he dispatched a messenger to the Duc de Crillon asking for help. Crillon sent the messenger on to Cordova, who sent him back to Moreno, saying that the wind was blowing the wrong way. In the meantime, the men on the *Pastora* waited.

On the 'flottantes' to the north, *Los Dolores, St Christoval, Principe Carlos, Paula Secunda* and *Santa Anna*, where the guns had fired for nearly nine hours to no purpose, the barrage became sporadic towards evening, as the uncertainty of the captains spread to the men. Stuck on the sandbank, they could not move, yet they were in no danger. They waited. On the *San Juan*, where they had waited throughout the battle, they continued to wait. On the *Rosario* and *Paula Prima*, whose captain Don Cayetan Langara had been wounded (this was the gentleman who had boasted he would take all the red-hot shot the garrison could throw on his stomach, and perhaps he tried), they waited.

On the isthmus, in the forts and batteries in the Lines, in the St Carlos Battery, and the 64-gun battery, where all the ammunition had been exhausted by four o'clock, and there were no orders, and no senior officers to give them, they waited. In the Spanish Camp, and on the ships of the Combined Fleet, they waited. On the stands, and the beaches, on the foothills and the hills from Cabrita to the Queen's Chair, in Algeciras and San Roque, in Cadiz, Seville, Cordova, Toledo and Madrid, they waited. Spain waited.

By six o'clock the garrison of Gibraltar knew that they had won, but not what they had won. Two of the larger battering-ships were burning, but the fires did not appear very serious, and the other eight were still undamaged. Most of them were still firing, though this did not continue for long. The Combined Fleet was still in the Bay, and the Combined Army in the Camp. They had perhaps won the day, but the floating batteries would be there to fight the next day, and then they might be supported by the fleet and the gun-boats. With this in mind, General Eliott ordered the artillery to be relieved by 100 sailors of the Marine Brigade under Lieutenant Trentham, who could manipulate the guns, and who had officers and N.C.O.s of the artillery to supervise them in the use of the red-hot shot. All the time, the firing was maintained on the silent hulks. For the rest, the garrison had little to do but to watch and wait.

In Buena Vista the Duc de Crillon, the Commander-in-Chief whose word had sent the 'flottantes' against Gibraltar, and whose silence had sent them unaided, hesitated to give the second word to save the 5,000 men aboard them. His was a delicate problem. The attack had failed, but the 'flottantes' had not: they had lain off the Rock since ten o'clock in the morning, and eight were undamaged, whilst two had fires aboard, but the powder had been damped, and there seemed little doubt that they could be saved if they could be withdrawn. Whilst the 'flottantes' remained unburned and unsunk, d'Arçon's reputation was secure, whilst his own was in jeopardy. He had dispatched M. de Salinas the night before, and could expect him to reach Madrid by next morning, when his letter would be published disowning the plan of the 'flottantes', and exculpating himself from its failure; if it failed. The longer the 'flottantes' lay

i

helpless under the garrison's guns, the more chance of failure. So he waited.

It grew dark. The Bay was ringed with eyes. 150,000 people, soldiers, sailors and spectators, stood in the growing dark of night watching the Bay. Along the sprawling length of The Dead Man, fierce pins of fire flashed from the guns, and the sound of their shots echoed distant and dull. Then, startlingly, a rocket was fired from the other side of the Bay, just below the Rock, leaving a trail of stars that died almost immediately. There was another rocket from the same place, then one beside it, and another from the other side. The 'flottantes' were still there, and they wanted Spain to know it.

The fire on the *Talla Piedra* had taken hold, but had not yet burst through the side or the deck. Shots still thudded against her, but not with the same insistence as before, and the men ignored them. They were only concerned to leave the ship as soon as possible, though they were safer in her than in a small boat within range of the batteries. The rockets were discovered and fired in the hope that someone might come to take them out of the vessel they now detested. The other ships followed suit. The soldiers who had set out gaily that morning stood about dejected by a defeat they could not understand: the ship that they had been promised was proof against fire, had taken fire; the walls that they had been told could be breached had not been breached; the red-hot shot that their officers had sworn could not be fired quickly or aimed correctly had been fired with the same aim and speed as cold shot; the support that they had believed would come from the fleet and gun-boats had not come; and now they were marooned, unable to move, their powder damped, their captains gone, a sitting target for the enemy, whilst the lights of forty of their own battleships, and the camp-fires of 40,000 of their comrades, were within sight. In the darkness under the roof the few wounded who had not yet bled to death lay groaning, and the priest knelt, praying. The boats did not come until midnight, and when they came they brought death.

CHAPTER XXI

Twixt fire and water who can live?

THE Duc de Crillon's ante-room began to fill with officers who had taken the few boats from the 'flottantes' to return to headquarters to demand assistance for their soldiers. Some wounded, M. O'Conel in three places, all weary and disillusioned, their stained and torn uniforms contrasting with the gilded elegance of the aides, they talked of nothing but retreat. They understood as little as their men the reasons for their defeat, and the common butt of their execrations was the unfortunate M. d'Arçon. When Crillon eventually came out to them, accompanied by the Prince of Nassau, he shared their concern, their contempt for the 'flottantes' and their inventor, and assured them that he would do everything in his power to salvage what he could from the wreck of the enterprise. Everyone talked as if the 'flottantes' were already doomed. Crillon wrote in his Mémoires: 'They had to send to ask Crillon to dispatch boats to rescue the troops, as there was no hope of putting out the fires or of withdrawing the batteries which were stranded.' Between ten and eleven o'clock he set out with the Prince to ask Don Luis de Cordova to send his frigates to the help of the floating batteries. The old Admiral, who had been careful not to involve himself in the attack when it had a chance of success, was determined not to be associated with its failure, and refused to allow His Catholic Majesty's ships to be exposed to the fire of the enemy in a doubtful attempt to save the 'flottantes'. There was only one remaining course of action. Crillon had once told d'Arçon that he would burn the floating batteries, and this is what he did. At a Council held on board the flagship, it was decided that if the 'flottantes' could not be withdrawn, there was no alternative but to set them on fire to prevent the enemy from taking them as prizes.

As Crillon and Cordova had already agreed that they could not be withdrawn, what followed was, in effect, their personal decision. Honour would be saved, the insufferable d'Arçon and his inventions would be eradicated, and the odium for the failure of the Grand Attack would be heaped on his head. Orders were issued for the boats of the fleet to sail to take off the soldiers and sailors on the ships. In the same boats were officers carrying an order to each captain of a floating battery to set it on fire before abandoning it. Crillon returned to Buena Vista and went to bed.

The boats arrived at the 'flottantes' at midnight. Several were hit as they came within range of the garrison's guns, and a piece of wreckage from one of them floated ashore with an officer and eleven men clinging to it. It was barely possible to see them as they bumped against the sides of the hulks, but the men started to scramble down into them, cursing, shoving, and struggling frantically to escape. The officers had to fight their ways through to the captains to deliver their final orders. The boats taking the men off the 'flottantes' on the sandbank were barely molested, but the panic to take to them was as great as on the *Pastora* and *Talla Piedra*. It was worse when the men realized that there were not enough boats to take them all off at once, and that many would have to wait until they returned again from the shore. In the dark confusion men who had spent the whole day in safety began to die. Some leaped into the water and were left to drown: others crowded into a boat until it sank: where the shells and bullets from the garrison were hissing and crashing into the sea, the turbulence was more terrible, as, caught in the black whirlpool of fear, men dragged each other down, as if they were enemies. Many boats took on their complement of men and pulled for the shore; others left half-empty; whilst others never left at all, sunk, or smashed by shot, their wreckage drifting among the invisible faces below the surface of the Bay. That was the ordeal by water, and about half the Spaniards and Frenchmen who had been aboard the 'flottantes' went through it. The ordeal by fire followed.

The orders to burn the batteries were received almost gratefully by most of the captains. It was an honourable retreat, and they hurriedly passed the order on, and retreated. One captain, of one of the ships that had hardly been touched, refused to accept the order, and stayed aboard until, an hour later, he received a second order; as by this time two of the ships were burning, he was obliged to accept it. On board the *Pastora* honour returned with wings of fire to Admiral Moreno: the 'flottantes' were not only combustible and submersible, but they would be seen to be so. He went ashore on the first boat from the *Pastora*. D'Arçon, who had been waiting for five hours on the *Talla Piedra* for some sign from the fleet or the gun-boats that they intended to rescue the 'flottantes', refused to believe the order given to Don Juan Mendoza. He tried to argue with the officer who had brought it, but who refused to talk to him. He hurried to the side of the ship, and with desperate authority commandeered a small boat, which he ordered to be rowed towards the fleet. In the mêlée and confusion about the battering-ships, the trains were being laid that led to the final disaster: whilst the men were crowding the sides and clambering into the boats, the officers instructed to set them on fire hurried down into the holds, and stuffed rags soaked with sulphur between the timbers, lit them, and made their quickest way to safety. In some of the ships the powder had been damped, in others not: in some the fire took hold quickly, in others not: in every ship, however, men were left on board, ignorant that the hulks on which they stood were doomed.

The small boat carrying d'Arçon reached the first ships of the fleet about the time the Duc de Crillon was retiring for what was left of the night. To his first cries for assistance the answers were sympathetic but unhelpful, if he told them his name he was met with silence; he went on to the flagship. Admiral Cordova would not see him, and sent out a curt message referring him to the Commander-in-Chief. He returned to his boat and headed for the Camp. When at last he reached Buena Vista, it was 1 a.m. There was no one there. He burst into Crillon's study. On the table was a copy of the order to burn the 'flottantes'. He looked out of the window. There were two globes of fire, their reflections in the water long tracks of flame pointing towards him. They were the *Pastora* and the *Talla Piedra*. He wrote: 'I have burnt the temple of Ephesus: everything is lost and through my fault. What comforts me under my misfortune is that the honour of the two kings remains untarnished.' Honour smiled.

In Gibraltar, the Line Wall and the heights were crowded with the British and Hanoverian soldiers, who stared out into the darkness

wondering what the next move of the enemy would be, and marvel-
ling at the structure of the wooden battering-ships that seemed to be
able to withstand all their shot, without even taking the trouble to
answer it. When the officer who had floated ashore on the piece of
wreckage was brought to General Eliott, who was still on the King's
Bastion, the General asked him what on earth the ships were made
of? Shortly afterwards, the one directly opposite the King's Bastion
burst into flames, and the question became superfluous. Neither the
Governor nor the garrison realized that the conflagration, and the
others that followed, were not the results of their red-hot shots, and
if they discovered it later, which seems likely as they took many
prisoners, they did not admit it. There was for some time a patriotic
conspiracy, which did as much to conceal the disgrace of Spain as to
aggrandize the glory of Great Britain.

When the first flotilla of boats came at midnight to take the crews
and soldiers off the battering-ships, the garrison could not see them,
though they could hear, in the intervals between firing, the clamour
and confusion in the Bay. When a boat was hit they heard the
screams and cries of drowning men, but could only imagine the scene
before them. The extent of the horror only became apparent at 1 a.m.
when the two ships exploded in flames, reddening the water around
them, and bringing the Bay startlingly alive. The boats that had
returned from shore were clustered about the burning hulks, whilst
others were lying near the battering-ships more dimly seen on either
side. These now became the targets for the guns. The sea was churned
up with men struggling like trawled fish to reach the boats which, as
the garrison watched, began to pull away out of the light and range
of the artillery. It was a long agony before the sea was calm again.

Brigadier Curtis and the Marine Brigade, apart from providing a
detachment of 100 men to relieve the gunners, had played as little
part in the defence so far, as the line regiments and the Hanoverians:
stationed at Europa, there was little that they could do but climb up
the rocks and watch. According to Captain Drinkwater, it was not
until a certain Lieutenant Erskine, of the 73rd, approached the
Brigadier and remonstrated with him, that he awoke to the possibili-
ties of mounting an attack with the British gun-boats, which had, as
yet, hardly seen action. The sea was calm, and the enemy appeared
unable to defend themselves against a flanking attack from the sea.

Curtis and the 250 sailors required to man the boats marched down to the New Mole. At about 3 a.m., they set out; the *Revenge, Defiance, Resolution, Spitfire, Dreadnought, Thunder, Europa, Terrible, Fury, Scourge, Terror* and *Vengeance*; fierce and famous names, contrasting with the saintly battering-ships. They came out of the dark onto the *Paula Prima*, and their first volley, surprising and panicking the enemy, sent the rescue boats rowing away as fast as they could go. By now the fires in six of the hulks had burst through the sides and the decks, apart from the *Pastora* and *Talla Piedra*, which burned brightly. The boats fled from them all. Eight blazing ships gave light enough to read by, and already the first tinge of dawn distinguished the Rock from the sky. Governor Eliott, still at his station, ordered the firing from the Line Wall and bastions to stop whilst the gun-boats were out, and watched, with his garrison, the dawning of a complete victory, as the Navy drove the enemy before them. The gun-boats captured two launches: one escaped, the other was hit, and brought in to Ragged Staff. The prisoners looked anxiously behind them at the burning wrecks, and told the Brigadier that there were still men aboard them. With a resolution and humanity that go a long way to counterbalance the less flattering opinions of him, Roger Curtis decided to lead his gun-boats back to rescue as many as he could.

Dawn, Saturday, 14 September 1782, and in the bitterness of it each Spaniard still watching tasted the acid draught of defeat. They stood in a grey line on the rim of the hills, on the ships of the fleet, on the rises above the Camp, where the royal flags of France and Spain hung heavy with dew: they saw the fires spread along the line of the 'flottantes', the Rock leap out in red relief, as if it was some hill in hell, peopled with devils tormenting the ten martyrs burning before it. They turned away, the cross of glory, ashes, and the ashes dry and choking in their mouths. The French made a joke of it: 'Ce n'est pas le cheval de bois qui, cette fois, a pris Troie; c'est Troie qui a brûlé le cheval de bois.' At 5 a.m. one of the 'flottantes' blew up with a dreadful noise and a column of flame and smoke, as the fire reached the dry powder in the magazine.

The gun-boats were among the battering-ships at the time of the explosion. When the sailors had first rowed alongside and clambered up the smoking sides of the hulks, they found that many of the men left behind were wounded, whilst others, crouching back, refused to be rescued, because they feared that they would be put to death as soon as they were taken ashore. They dragged out as many as they could, and pushed them down into the boats below. After the first battery blew up the men were more willing to be saved, and those on the ships they had not yet visited leaned over the sides, or climbed onto the roofs crying for help. Slowly the ships were being cleared of men, even the *Pastora*, the British sailors risking their lives on the cracking decks to carry off their enemies, and it was here that they found the Royal Ensign of Spain which was to have flown over the captured Rock, and brought it back with them. They were busy about the centre of the line when the second ship blew up so near them that they were caught in an avalanche of burning timbers, bullets, broken masts and scraps of flaming canvas. One gun-boat was sunk, though the crew managed to swim to another. A beam of wood crashed into Curtis's boat, killing the coxswain and wounding an oarsman, and splitting the bottom, so that the water gushed in. The sailors grabbed their jackets, which they had removed in the heat of the action, and stuffed them in the cracks, and so kept the boat afloat long enough for others to come alongside and take them, their prisoners, and their Captain off. The danger of the other hulks now blowing up and destroying both rescuers and rescued was so imminent that Curtis ordered the gun-boats to retire. However, they went to two more ships before returning to the garrison.

The enemy guns on the isthmus opened fire on the garrison at their usual time in the morning, though the only action the British were engaged in at that moment was rescuing Spaniards from the burning wrecks. This was, presumably, for lack of orders to the contrary and, not being expected, caused several casualties. When the gun-boats came in to Ragged Staff with their load of prisoners, this fire was kept up, and several shells exploded above them. It was between eight and nine in the morning, and the scene was easily visible from the Spanish shore, where some officer, realizing the stupidity of the barrage, which was likely to kill their own men who had just been saved by the British, sent orders for it to stop. There were 357 prisoners, including the twelve who had come in on the wreck, and amongst them three priests who had stayed to the last. Many were terribly wounded, and Mr Ancell added to his list of horrors:

One in particular I cannot help mentioning who was carried by four men on a hand barrow. He had received a wound in his face, so that his nose and eyes were separated from his head, hanging by a piece of skin, and the motion of the men that carried him, occasioned its flapping backwards and forwards much resembling a mask, though he must have felt the most sensible agony, yet he looked round him with great complacency, as he passed the numerous crowds of people.

The wounded were carried to the hospital, the rest to a camp at Windmill Hill. The captured officers were entertained by those of the garrison and when they passed one of the furnaces piled with red-hot balls they turned to each other with hopeless shrugs, and then looked back on the blazing ruins of their hopes.

The worst came last, in the full light of morning, in full view of both camps. There were still men on the floating batteries. Two had blown up, and two, the *Talla Piedra* and the *Pastora*, were burning down to the water's edge, the Admiral's flag on the *Pastora* flying to the end: of the six others, two in the north showed no signs of fire, whilst the other four were in varying stages of distress. It was on these that men appeared, clambering onto the roofs and in the rigging, seen in brief glimpses through the flames and smoke, gesticulating wildly and crying for help. Between nine and eleven o'clock, three of the four blew up, whilst the fourth, the powder damped, burned down to the level of the Bay. The luckiest men were those who died first. Few could swim, and none who tried reached the shore. They could only wait their turn to be blown to pieces, or to feel the deck drop beneath their feet and fall into the furnace below. When a felucca came out from the Orange Grove, towards one of the ships that was apparently undamaged, the garrison guns drove her off, fearing that she intended to set it on fire and deprive them of a possible prize. There were few men on one of these last two vessels and none visible on the other; being in the north they had had longer to escape in the boats before the British gun-boats came up to them; the men who were left had seen the fate of their companions, and alone knew that their own could not be long delayed. It was their cries that came the loudest, and their desperate activity that was only explained when, about midday, the ship suddenly took fire, and shortly afterwards exploded. The last floating battery lay, tilted on the sandbank, amidst a scum of bodies, heads, legs, arms, wood, wool, cork, oakum, casks, boxes and timbers: when Captain Gibson of the

Navy went out in a boat to see if she could be salvaged, he found her
stuck fast, her inside gutted, but the fires out: under his direction, the
hulk was rekindled, and burned down that afternoon. There were
two Royal Standards on the Rock: that of Great Britain, flying above
the Grand Battery, where it had flown on victorious occasions during
the three years and three months of the siege; and that of Spain,
reversed and tied to a gun barrel.

Garrison Orders, 14th September 1782.
Password, King George. Countersign, Victory.

Was it a victory? Certainly, from the point of view of the garrison.
Reading General Eliott's public dispatch, which every Englishman
who could undoubtedly did, it is not surprising that Gibraltar emerged as a sort of extension of the white cliffs of Dover, and a syno-
nym for strength and invincibility.

The Enemy having collected his whole Force by Sea and Land: 44 Sail
of the Line besides 3 inferior two-deckers; 10 Battering Ships, 5 Bomb
ketches, several Frigates and Xebeques, a great number of gun and
mortar boats, a large floating Battery, many armed vessels and near
300 boats purposely constructed for carrying Troops.

The Land Batteries mounted with above an hundred pieces of
cannon and an equal number of mortars and howitzers.

An Army near 40,000 men.

On the 13th instant at eight in the morning all the Battering Ships—
commanded by Don Buenventura de Moreno Rear-Admiral, were put
in motion and came forward to the several stations previously determined they should take up, the Admiral being placed upon the Capital
of the King's Bastion the other ships extending three to the Southward
of the Flag, as far as the Church Battery, Five to the Northward about
the height of the Old Mole, and one a very little to the Westward of the
Admiral. By a quarter before ten they were anchored in Line, at the
distance of a thousand to twelve hundred yards; immediately a heavy
Cannonade began from all the Ships, supported by the Cannon and
Mortars in the Enemy's Lines and Approaches; at the same instant our
Batteries opened with hot and cold shot from the guns and shells from
the Howitzers and Mortars; this firing continued without intermission
on both sides until noon, when that of the Enemy from their Ships
seemed to slacken altho' but little; about 2 o'clock the Admiral's Ship
was observed to smoke, as if on fire, and a few men busy upon the Roof,

searching for the cause: our Batteries never discontinued: the Enemy's
fire from the Ships gradually decreased; about seven in the evening
they fired from a few guns and that only at intervals: at midnight the
Admiral's Ship was plainly discovered beginning to burn; an hour after
it was compleatly in Flames: eight more of the Ships took fire in succession: Signals of distress being now made, the Launches, Faluchos and
Boats of the whole Fleet began to take out the men from on board the
burning Ships: many shot were still fired from those in which the Flames
had yet made no considerable progress: and the Fire from the Enemy's
Batteries on shore did not in the least diminish: Brigadier Curtis, who
with his squadron of gun boats lay ready to take advantage of any
favourable circumstance left the New Mole at two o'clock and about
three formed a line upon the Enemy's Flank advancing and firing with
great order and expedition: which so astonished and disconcerted the
Enemy they fled precipitately with all their boats, abandoning the Ships
in which some Officers and numbers of their Men, including many
wounded, were left to perish: this unavoidably must have been their
wretched fate had they not been dragged from amidst the flames by the
personal intrepidity of Brigadier Curtis at the utmost hazard of his own
life: a Life invaluable to His Majesty's service: for sometime I felt the
utmost anguish seeing his Pinnace close to one of the largest ships, at the
instant she blew up, and spread her wreck to a vast extent all round: the
black cloud of smoke being dispersed I was again revived by the sight of
the Pinnace, little apprehending the Brigadier was in the utmost danger
of sinking, some pieces of timber having fallen into and pierced the
boat (killing the Coxswain and wounding others of the men) scarce any
hope left of reaching the shore: providentially he was saved by stopping
the hole with the seamen's jackets until boats arrived to their relief: one
of our gun boats was sunk at the same moment.

In the course of the day the remaining 8 ships severally blew up with
violent explosions: one only escaped the effect of our fire: which it was
thought proper to burn, there being no possibility of preserving her.

The Admiral's flag remained flying on board His Ship till She was
totally consumed.

Your Lordship will be pleased to inform His Majesty that the Royal
Artillery, Additional Gunners, and Marine Brigade only could be employed on this Service which they executed with the deliberate coolness
and precision of school practice: but their exertion was infinitely
superior: the fire was incessant and the Batteries abundantly supplied
with ammunition, every Soldier of the Garrison not on duty eagerly
pressing to share in the honourable labour of the Day. The Enemy's

daring attempt by sea was effectually defeated by the constant and well supported fire from our Batteries.

But the well timed judicious and spirited attack made by Brigadier Curtis rendered this success a compleat victory.

The garrison lost 1 officer, 2 serjeants, and 13 men killed, and 5 officers and 63 men wounded: half the casualties were from the Royal Artillery. They fired some 8,300 times, one half red-hot shot, and used 716 barrels of powder. The enemy had 1,473 men killed, wounded or missing, and 357 prisoners taken by the garrison. They expended a vast amount of powder and shot, and lost 10 floating batteries of an estimated value of £500,000 and some 200 cannons.

Was it a victory? The 'flottantes' were certainly defeated. M. d'Arçon, who began by blaming himself, ended by blaming everyone else. In a series of publications he attacked Crillon, Moreno and Cordova, and attempted to vindicate his 'flottantes', which, he wrote with pride, not only resisted the red-hot shot fired at them from the garrison, but also withstood the efforts of the incendiaries for several hours. He then embarked on a train of ifs, which led him to the conquest of Gibraltar. The Duc de Crillon, in answer, produced the long and tedious story of his life, and uncovered some of the intrigues and jealousies that d'Arçon had missed, managing, in his attempt to extricate himself from the debris of the Grand Attack, to crawl right out of his reputation and to appear as a shabby and old hypocrite. This shabby old hypocrite wrote to General Eliott on 15 September:

> Les armes sont journalieres, on ma' donné de mauvais machines pour combattre un General contre lequel on ne peut en employer de trop bonnes. Je m'en suis servi parce qu'il *faut obeir* comme vous le scavez mieux que personne et commandeur.

Was it a victory? 1,500 men had been killed or maimed by the incompetence of their officers and the incapacity or worse of their commanders. The garrison had fired and the battering-ships had blown up. The French prisoners who had been taken off the doomed ships by the seamen swore that they would sell their shirts at any time to release an Englishman who might be captured. General Boyd wrote: 'Braver soldiers and better practice from any Batteries in the Universe was never made than what has crown'd this day.' Spain had lost. Great Britain had won. As victories go, it was a victory.

CHAPTER XXII

I should have liked Minorca . . .

ON the day of the Grand Attack, George III wrote to Lord Grantham, referring to a prematurely optimistic report in the *Gazette de France:* 'Though not sanguine on the subject of Gibraltar I owne I do not give more credit to the account of the surrender of Gibraltar than Lord Grantham does.' Whilst his Secretary of State was writing to General Eliott: 'The security of that very important Post which His Majesty has entrusted to you is of a consequence hardly to be Equalled,' His Majesty was hoping to be able to exchange Gibraltar for a territory in the West Indies, and particularly Puerto Rico. The negotiations, which had been postponed until the result of the Grand Attack was known (they knew in Madrid twenty-four hours after the burning of the 'flottantes'), were again delayed until the Rock had been relieved by Lord Howe. This extraordinary process took a month, and it was not until 20 October, when the Spanish Court finally abandoned the hope of capturing Gibraltar, that Florida-blanca gave the first indication that Spain was prepared to exchange a territory in the west for the Rock. He began by offering the poorest possession, Spanish Santo Domingo. The conferences were now taking place in Paris between Fitzherbert and d'Aranda, under the eye of Vergennes; they were conducted with all the best principles of horse-trading, and the honesty of Barnet Fair. The Dutch and the Americans were negotiating separately with Great Britain, and the main impediment to a settlement between the latter and France and Spain was Gibraltar. Spain insisted that no peace was possible without the restitution of Gibraltar; France was anxious for peace, and content to allow the British to keep Gibraltar, as a block to any future Anglo-Spanish rapprochement; Britain was divided—the King and Cabinet anxious to exchange Gibraltar—the people and Parliament unwilling to part with it. The trading began:

1. 20 October 1782. Spain offered Santo Domingo. This was unacceptable to France, who occupied the other half of the island, and had no wish for a British neighbour.
2. Spain offered Santo Domingo to France, on condition France would give Corsica, or a West Indian Island to Britain, who would cede Gibraltar to Spain. France had no desire for Santo Domingo, or to part with Corsica, or an island. This proposal, however, allowed Vergennes to move more effectively into the negotiations.
3. 20 November. Vergennes sent de Rayneval to London. Lord Shelburne stressed the opposition in the country to the cession of Gibraltar, but eventually mentioned three possible equivalents, all to include the return of territories conquered by Spain during the war—Minorca and Florida.
   (i) Puerto Rico.
   (ii) Martinique and St Lucia.
   (iii) Guadeloupe and Dominica.
   In (ii) and (iii), France would have to be compensated with Santo Domingo. George III wrote: 'I am ready to avow that I think the exchange of Gibraltar for either of the three valuable Possessions as now proposed as highly advantageous to this Kingdom.' Parliament was due for recall, and the decision, war or peace, had to be made before it met, so France and Spain were obliged to find a solution in haste.
4. 1 December. The British Government decided on peace but postponed the opening of Parliament. De Rayneval presented a new Spanish offer: Gibraltar to be exchanged for Guadeloupe and Dominica (Spain to compensate France); Minorca to be restored to Britain; West Florida to be kept by Spain; Britain to give up her log-wood establishments in return for concessions. The King commented: 'I therefore hope Mons. Reyneval has power to give St Lucia and Martinique instead of Guadeloupe and Dominica, and that Spain will restore West Florida, but if he has not . . . I think peace so desirable that so far as relates to Myself, I should not be for another Year's War . . . It would be madness not to conclude Peace on the best possible terms we can obtain.'

3 December. The British Cabinet formally agreed to the cession of Gibraltar, but returned to the three equivalents demanded before, adding St Lucia or Trinidad to Guadeloupe and Dominica.

5. Parliament opened on 5 December with the expected opposition to the cession of Gibraltar voiced by Charles Fox. However, the protests were factious. The preliminaries of the treaty with America had been signed, and it was thought that Britain was in a better position to demand more for Gibraltar. (When it is considered that Gibraltar cost some £200,000 a year, produced nothing, prevented friendship with Spain, and was of small strategic value, it becomes hard to understand how it was not exchanged.)

6. Vergennes heard that Spain was preparing to negotiate directly with Britain. He wrote to Lord Grantham suggesting that Britain should make an offer to Spain to give up her insistence on the return of Gibraltar.

11 December. The Cabinet agreed to offer East and West Florida and Minorca. King George objected, to Lord Grantham: 'I am ready to avow that Peace is not compleat unless Gibraltar be exchang'd with Spain', to Lord Shelburne: 'I would wish, if possible, to be rid of Gibraltar, and to have as much possession in the West Indies as possible.'

7. 18 December. D'Aranda accepted, on his own responsibility, the British terms.

19 December. The Cabinet ratified the terms. King George III wrote to Lord Grantham: 'I sincerely rejoice at Spain's acquiescing to our retaining Gibraltar, as it now I hope makes Peace certain, which the Want of Public Zeal and the deficiency of Army and Navy makes me think indispensible. I should have liked Minorca, and the two Floridas and Guadeloupe better than this proud fortress, and in my opinion source of another War, or at least of a constant lurking enmity.'

The preliminary articles of the peace were signed on 20 January 1783.

It was a poor peace for Britain, which gave up Minorca, the two Floridas, her conquests in India and the West Indies, and America, and kept Gibraltar; a successful peace for Spain, though she had been forced to give up her claim to Gibraltar; it was a diplomatic triumph for Vergennes, who managed to defy the conditions of the Convention of Aranjuez, whilst gaining good terms for his ally, and ensuring the continuation of Spanish reliance on France, driven in harness with her by the spur of Gibraltar.

There are two questions which arise from this outline of the peace negotiations of the winter of 1782. Why did King Charles III of Spain agree to the terms accepted by d'Aranda when they did not include the cession of Gibraltar, which he had always insisted was a *sine qua non* of any peace? Why did the British Government not exchange the barren Rock for a fertile island, when this was the express desire of King George III?

By the end of December 1782 the Americans and the French had settled their terms with Great Britain (except for the return to Britain of Dominica, and this was eventually exchanged for Tobago), and Spain was in no position to support the war alone for another year. Though ships were collected at Cadiz for a proposed attack on Jamaica, there seems little doubt that this move, like the continuation of hostilities against the Rock, was made to bring pressure to bear on the British Cabinet to agree to the Spanish demands. The Spanish navy was in a poor condition; the Combined Fleet in Gibraltar Bay after the Grand Attack was desperately short of provisions and water, though they were a few hundred yards from the Spanish shore; and part of Admiral Cordova's hesitation to engage his ships must be attributed to their slowness, and the continual sickness of their crews. Moreover the initiative in the peace negotiations had been allowed to pass to Vergennes and d'Aranda, who was an ardent supporter of the alliance with France, and they presented Madrid with a *fait accompli;* not only that, but a *fait accompli* which gave Spain Minorca, and the huge stretch of territory then called the two Floridas, which comprised parts of Alabama, Louisiana and Mississippi. Added to this was the reluctance, even of a Spanish King, to exchange a flourishing and valuable West Indian island for a barren rock, and a special determination not to part with Puerto Rico, which was to the windward of the smaller islands, and therefore was a strong position from which to launch an attack on them in a future war. So Spain accepted the negation of her great efforts to regain the Rock.

How King George III failed to be rid of Gibraltar is harder to explain. Every argument of economy or diplomacy was overwhelmingly on the side of exchanging the Rock. In December 1782 the Cabinet

finally agreed in principle to the cession, Lord Keppel and the Duke
of Richmond alone dissenting. It is even possible that if the peace was
made to appear conditional on the cession, Parliament would have
agreed, and if the equivalent was valuable enough, the merchants
would have added their voices in favour. But again there were two
dissentients, though unusual ones: Vergennes, and the people of
Britain. Vergennes was following the same policy towards Spain as
Louis XIV, when in 1713 he had concluded the Treaty of Utrecht,
which gave Gibraltar to England. The British nation, or that voci-
ferous part of it that was capable of turning its politicians upside
down and shaking them, did not want to part with Gibraltar on any
terms at all. They had the same delight in it as their ancestors had in
Calais, and a pride in its stubborn resistance. Gibraltar was the symbol of victory, at a time when British victories were few and far
between. Gibraltar was a foothold in Europe, and a pass to the Mediterranean. Gibraltar was naval supremacy, the snook everlastingly
cocked against an old enemy. It was perhaps fortunate for King
George that Vergennes did not allow him to give away the Rock, as
he might have lost his crown with it. For it was Vergennes who
switched the negotiations from what Spain would give England for
Gibraltar to what England would give Spain. So Gibraltar stayed
British, and was, as, of all people, Captain Curtis called it, 'The
Golden Image of English Idolatry.'

CHAPTER XXIII

The British Salamanders

PEACE was not the word in Gibraltar on 14 September 1782. Beyond the wreckage of the floating batteries lay the enemy fleet, and across the Neutral Ground the enemy army: that afternoon they were both showing signs of activity. Several regiments marched up to the Spanish Lines, and the men-of-war loosed their topsails, but the soldiers stayed in the Lines, and the next day the sails were furled again, and the garrison was put to no more trouble than a night spent lying under arms by the light of the ovens and roast potatoes. During the next few days there were similar alarms, as if the Duc de Crillon intended to launch an assault on the Rock, but never got beyond the intention. In the meantime flags of truce were passing between the camps, the officers who had been taken prisoner were returned, and the enemy resumed their routine bombardment from the isthmus. In spite of this, and the heavy autumn rains, many of the men spent their free time at the water's edge, hooking out boxes, bits of wood, candles, and bodies, the debris of the battering-ships, and their legitimate prize; though one, Dennis Murray, was hanged for burglary on 25 September; accused of stealing from his comrades, he protested his innocence to the last. The Navy were busy trying to raise the *Brilliant* and the *Porcupine* in the New Mole, as they had learned from the prisoners that Lord Howe and the British Fleet had already sailed, and might be expected to arrive whilst the Combined Fleets of France and Spain were still in the Bay. Before the end of the month the gun-boats attacked the garrison at night, and it became apparent that whilst the Grand Attack was not to be resumed, the enemy had by no means given up the hope of preventing the

the Rock. It was an anxious night, for nobody believed that the Spanish Admiral would hesitate to attack the British Fleet, for which he had evidently been waiting, and now it was within his power to capture the troop transports and ordnance ships as well. Captain Curtis sailed with the frigate *Latona* to advise Lord Howe of the number and condition of the enemy ships. The next morning the convoy was seen to the east off Marbella, with some frigates, like worried sheepdogs, trying to herd the transports to the windward, to reach the Bay. The enemy were busy embarking troops on board their battleships, and kept up a steady fire from the isthmus in an attempt to hit the *St Michael*, which was still lying by Ragged Staff. During the night the *Panther* man-of-war and a few transports had crept round Europa, and were anchored in Rosia Bay. Garrison Orders of the 12th included two messages from the Government: one dated 10 July from Lord Shelburne encouraging the brave Officers and Soldiers, and the other from General Conway, Commander-in-Chief, dated 30 August, signifying that His Majesty had graciously allowed the Officers bat and forage money, a considerable award, which amounted, in Captain Spilsbury's case, to £40, with which he could afford to buy a cow, had there been one for sale.

Daybreak on the 13th found the British Fleet still lying off Marbella, and at 9 a.m. the Combined Fleet, having repaired the damage done by the storm, weighed anchor, and sailed slowly out of the Bay. It was an impressive sight, 44 line-of-battle ships, 5 frigates, 29 xebecks, cutters and other armed vessels, and 2 fire-ships: the Spanish prisoners from the *St Michael*, who had been sent to the camp on Windmill Hill, annoyed the garrison by cheering, and were pushed back into their tents with little ceremony. Even as the enemy were sailing out into the Mediterranean, Captain Curtis returned in a launch, with three boxes containing £20,000, and was lucky to escape being captured. In the south, those transports and ordnance ships that had come in were rapidly unloaded, though most of the garrison climbed up to vantage points where they could watch the two fleets, and the battle that everyone thought inevitable. The Combined Fleet were clear of the Rock by 3 p.m., and stood to the south: Lord Howe formed a line of battle, and the transports that had been tacking towards the Rock fell back to the leeward of the warships. So they stood when night prevented any further observation. The next morning, to everyone's surprise, the enemy occupied the position where they had last seen the British, who were now several miles off in the south-east: as the wind still blew from the west, giving Admiral Cordova the weather-gauge, it was his decision not to press the action.

Meanwhile General Eliott and Captain Curtis had important business in 'the hutt'. Both the change of Ministry and the prospect of peace were damaging to the Governor. The Eliotts were King's men, who had gained office under Lord North; Sir Gilbert had been Keeper of the Signet, and the General himself owed his position to the patronage of the Court. He had little influence with the new Ministry, and little doubt that a government that could deprive the victorious Admiral Rodney of his command, would not hesitate to do the same to a victorious General Eliott. Moreover, it was not only a question of command: there were also bounty and prize money, rewards, honours and titles. The old Cock of the Rock knew he would have little distinction in Lord Shelburne's anteroom, and groomed his young friend and protégé, already known to Lord Howe (who had trimmed his sails back into favour), as the hero of the moment. If Eliott went further in his eulogies of Roger Curtis than seemed to be required under these circumstances, there are nothing but surmises to explain it. On 15 October he wrote to Lord Howe:

> Unknown to Brigadier Curtis, I must entreat your Lordship to reflect upon the unspeakable assistance he has been in the defence of this place by his advice, and the lead he has taken in every hazardous enterprise. You know him well, my Lord, therefore such conduct on his part is no more than you expect; but let me beg of you not to leave him unrewarded for such signal services. You alone can influence His Majesty to consider such an officer for what he has, and what he will in future deserve wherever employed. If Gibraltar is of the value intimated to me from office, and to be presumed by the steps adventured to relieve it, Brigadier Curtis is the man to whom the King will be chiefly indebted for its security. Believe me, there is nothing affected in this declaration on my part.

General Eliott was going to do more than write letters for Roger Curtis.

On the morning of the 15th the Combined Fleet did not appear to have moved, though the British were out of sight in the east. The *Panther* weighed anchor to join them. At about 8 a.m. the wind veered about and began to blow from the east, and by noon the British Fleet appeared, standing off the African shore. During the night ten ordnance ships came in escorted by the *Latona*, and reported that the remaining twelve had separated from the Fleet, and that there was some fear that they had fallen in with the enemy. The next day, the *Latona* rejoined the Fleet.

There was little to do on Gibraltar but watch and wait, until the remaining ordnance ships came in, and the troops aboard the men-of-war landed. The enemy fleet had disappeared, some thought to refit in Malaga, and Lord Howe cruised about off Ceuta. On the 18th eleven of the missing ships came in, one the *Minerva* having been captured near Malaga, on board which were the wives and baggage of the two regiments coming to join the garrison. At noon the regiments arrived on five warships and immediately disembarked, and that afternoon the *Latona* returned to the New Mole with a fire-ship she had captured. By ten o'clock at night the regiments, the 25th and 59th, were in camps in the south, the men discharged and invalids were embarked, and the warships rejoined the Fleet. The fire-ship, being considered of no value, was burned, and the *Latona* sailed: on board were Captain Vallotton, the Governor's senior aide-de-camp, who was to have the honour of carrying the public dispatch announcing the victory over the floating batteries to the Court, and Captain Curtis, who carried a message from the Governor to Lord Howe, but who also carried a copy of the famous dispatch. The service that General Eliott rendered Captain Curtis, with the connivance of Captain Conway of the *Latona*, was to ensure that he sailed with Admiral Howe; ostensibly leaving his command at Gibraltar to take a message to the Admiral and then being unable to return because of the movement of the Fleet. Captain Curtis in Gibraltar was of little importance—but Captain Curtis with Lord Howe, returning to England and London might be of considerable influence when it came to sharing out the honour and the prize money.

The garrison, who expected to see neither fleet, were surprised to see both the next morning. Lord Howe started to move westward through the Straits under an easy sail, and the Combined Fleet, having allowed him a good start, pressed after him with determination. Unluckily, the wind changed again, and the van of the enemy could not prevent brushing the rear of the British Fleet, and there was an exchange of shots that both sides claimed as a victory, before the British sailed on to the Channel and the Spaniards returned to Cadiz. Both admirals had shown remarkable seamanship in avoiding a battle in the crowded Straits.

With the fleets out of sight to the west, the garrison returned to their old occupations of dodging the shells on the North Front, drinking in the wine-cellars, and added a new one, impressing the men of the 25th and 59th Regiments with their stories of the battering-ships and the Grand Attack; the newcomers, who had already lost their clothes and wives to the enemy, considered the old salamanders better off than they were. There was a lot of talk of bounty and prize money (the *St Michael* had been floated and was lying at the New Mole) and of the chances of peace. The latter were considered to have improved when, on the 21st, the French camp was struck: before the end of the month, twenty-six battalions marched out of the Spanish Camp. However, the guns in the enemy batteries continued to fire between five and six hundred rounds a day, and, out of apparent vindictiveness, the mortar- and gun-boats resumed their night attacks, aiming their fire at the *St Michael*. On the last day of October the *Tisiphone* fire-ship, that had been sent in from the Fleet with powder for the garrison, sailed, escorting six ordnance ships and 160 Jewish inhabitants who took passage to England. The relief brought by Lord Howe had not provided food, nor had there been any shipments in 1782 from Minorca or Africa: the soldiers lived on the provisions left by Admiral Darby, but the unlucky townspeople were facing their third trial by starvation. Though several of the masters of the transports and ordnance ships had been attracted by the exorbitant prices they had heard that the meanest articles commanded in Gibraltar, and had brought private stocks of food to sell, the inhabitants were in no position to buy them. Even the officers attempted to limit the profits of these speculators by agreeing not to allow them more than a mere hundred per cent. profit at the auctions: unfortunately the masters refused to sell their goods, preferring to take no profit than anything less than three hundred per cent.; the ring collapsed when some gentlemen started to buy by proxy, and then everyone was worse off than before, except the ships' masters who charged more than ever.

November—the Bay was almost empty, and the Spanish Camp

decreased daily. There was little to remind the garrison that two weeks before the hills had been ringed with people watching the spectacle of the Grand Attack, and that they had stood alone against the combined forces of France and Spain. The Rock of Gibraltar was as narrow and as steep as ever, though their duties were lightened by the pickets from the new regiments, and the relief had brought them some new clothes and boots: the equipment of the 25th and 59th had been captured, and they were soon the ragged regiments of the Rock. The daily bombardment, which barely served to annoy the guards in the lines and the artillery in the batteries, slackened to some 250 shots, and the gun- and mortar-boats appeared occasionally to fire at the *St Michael*, and nothing of importance occurred until someone discovered that amongst the ordnance stores landed by Lord Howe were 300 bibles, which the garrison had been sent as a present. During the month the Spanish prisoners from the *St Michael* were returned to Spain. The advance boyau continued to attract the attentions of the enemy's workmen and the garrison gunners and, early in December, a deserter brought news that surprised the garrison even more. The man, a German from the Walloon Guards, of which the garrison could now boast nearly a company, reported that every night a guard of 300 soldiers advanced to the Devil's Tower on the east of the isthmus under the Rock, where a party of miners was digging a hole with the intention of blowing up the North Front of the Rock. This odd scheme, which d'Arçon later averred was the idea of the Duc de Crillon's barber, amused the garrison, until it was observed that every evening a party did march forward in that direction. General Eliott wrote about it to Secretary Townshend, but showed more concern for the report from the master of a boat from Lisbon that the Spaniards were massing men and ships at Cadiz for a proposed expedition to Jamaica. Both this expedition, which never sailed, and the renewed activity in front of Gibraltar were part of Floridablanca's scheme to force the British to accept his proposals in the peace negotiations: they were both equally ridiculous, as the Spanish Navy was in the final stages of neglect, and there was as little chance of their reaching Jamaica as there was of blowing up the 1,400-foot-high vertical cliff from a small hole at the bottom. However, the Governor was in no mood to be trifled with, and ordered the enemy parties to be harassed and dislodged whenever they attempted to undermine his Rock. On 15 December the miners were met with a volley of grape shot from the batteries, and when they reached the apparent security of the base of the Rock, Mr Ince blew off some protruding chunks of stone above their heads: nevertheless they persisted until the end of hostilities, and two days later were observed laying three guns for Mr Ince. There was some activity in the Bay in December, and on the 12th seven seamen mutinied, knocked out two officers, and deserted to the enemy in the guard-boat of the *St Michael*. The *St Michael* continued to be the target of gun-boat attacks, one on the 18th being particularly spirited. The day before there had been an exchange of flags of truce, and the Duc de Crillon's aide had informed the officers that a peace was almost concluded. Whilst this news was passing round the garrison, the boats approached and started to fire at the *St Michael*. There were twenty-nine gun- and mortar-boats in three divisions, and their fire was so hot and accurate that Sir Charles Knowles, who had purchased and commissioned the *St Michael*, ordered the powder to be unshipped from her and eighty barrels for which there was no room in the launch were dropped into the sea. This was the occasion when Captain Gibson took out eight of the garrison's gun-boats and attacked the enemy, though General Eliott's account of the action (see Appendix) is not borne out by Captain Drinkwater, who writes: 'When the Enemy had expended their ammunition the mortar-boats retired, and the gun-boats covered their retreat in a most beautiful manner.' One soldier took advantage of the general interest in the action to steal General Green's cabbages from his garden in the south. On the next day the garrison's hopes for a peace that year were again raised when all the Spanish large ships loaded with stores left the Bay. The *St Michael*, which was valued at £14,000 and so was worth the saving, was almost lost on the 21st, when a sudden storm tore her from her moorings, and drove her half across the Bay. Fortunately there were no battleships to challenge her, and it was too rough for the gun-boats to venture out, and she was brought about to the New Mole again. On the 22nd the Duc de Crillon sent over the wives of the soldiers of the 25th and 59th Regiments, 150 women, who were sent straight to the Naval Hospital, where seventeen were detained with what was politely called 'the disorder'. The appearance of these fresh faces awoke the garrison to the privations they had endured for over three years, and not unnaturally caused trouble. The Governor, who had concerns of his own, wrote to Mr Townshend for 'a small supply of Tobacco and an ample quantity of Stationary'. He wrote again the next day: 'They have covered one of the new Lodgements under the North Face of the Rock with sloping Timbers which are much disordered by our throwing down large stones from the Top.' At this time the Corsicans were moved from Windmill Hill, where they were bored and squabbled with each other, and sent into the lines to fire at the enemy, of which they did a great deal without effect. The fourth Christmas Day of the siege was marked by a brisk attack in the afternoon from the land batteries and the gun-boats, which took the troops off guard and caused several casualties. Captain Gibson went out again, but the enemy held their stations for two hours, and bombarded the hospital and the camps in the south.

The year ended with a flurry of flags of truce between the Governor and the Duc de Crillon, which infuriated the garrison as the old General was as close as ever. They suspected that peace was soon to be concluded, and yet were obliged to suffer the irregular and vindictive attacks of the gun-boats, and the sporadic barrage from the isthmus, whilst their commander was in close correspondence with the enemy. There was nothing more sinister in this exchange of letters than well-worn courtesies and professions of friendship, but the Governor persisted in his delight in mystifying his officers whenever possible. Lieutenant Koehler had replaced Captain Curtis as the most regular attendant at the residence.

There was a colourful little ceremony to mark New Year's Day, when a gun which the Navy had salvaged from one of the battering-ships was drawn from Ragged Staff into the town with the Spanish flag draped over it, whilst a band played 'God Save the King': the gun was called 'El Bellicoso', which belied its activities on 13 September. On 4 January thirty-three gun-boats came over from Algeciras and were met by eleven of the British boats, and a strong fire from the King's Bastion. The Governor at last considered that these attacks, though petty, must be answered, and the same evening red-hot shot and shells were fired from the Old Mole into the Spanish Camp. The celebrations, however, were continued:

6th January. Some officers have been engaged in a riot among some Serjeants of the 73rd at a dance and some others in breaking open a ward

in the Hospital and attacking the women there ill of the disorder.
(Captain Spilsbury).

There was another gun-boat attack on the 10th, and an exchange of
fire whenever the enemy approached the foot of the Rock from the
isthmus. Serjeant-Major Ince's gallery was now 370 feet long, with
six embrasures, and was used for dropping rocks onto the enemy,
who, apart from the mine they were digging, had found a cave in the
Rock. The garrison refused to be dismayed. The Governor wrote
home: 'The Enemy still busily employed blasting under the North
East Cliff of the Rock: for what purpose I don't know: but am not
very apprehensive of bad Consequences to the Garrison.' He was
more worried by the officers. Captain Spilsbury was in the audience
when 'the Officers have acted a play "Cross Purposes" and "True
Blue" . . .' and they were certainly at cross-purposes with true-blue,
because a few days after the performance on 19 January, General
Boyd's clerk recorded:

This day the Governor has forbid the continuation of the Dramatic
Theatre, or plays performed on the Stage by a few Young Officers . . .
so austere and strict the Governor is in this place that he will not allow
the Gentlemen any amusement that he can prevent them of: and since
the above on the publick parades at Guard mounting, any of the Gentlemen that do not march to please, is rebuked with a theatrical carriage
or their legs muffled in petticoats, alluding to the Characters they represented, or the dress that the Gentlemen appeared in on the Stage.

The General's idea of public entertainment was a competition between the drummers of the various regiments, which he judged with
a pendulum, and which was won by the 39th. The enemy were apparently also rejoicing, as on the nights of the 18th and 19th they
let off fireworks in Algeciras, and fired salutes at the garrison, who
would have thought that the peace had at last been announced had
the guns not been shotted. There was a strange incident on the 25th
which harked back to 25 September 1782, when a soldier was hanged
for robbery, 'the noted Denis Murray':

This day was executed on the Gallows for robery one McDonald a
Soldier of the 97th Regiment at this time is discovered the disagreeable
circumstance of the last execution, when the Prisoner protested innocence to the last, which the guilty person has since confest to the crime.

Mr Ancell watched the hanging, as well as General Boyd's clerk, and noted that McDonald 'died with little emotion', unlike the unfortunate Denis Murray. The gun-boats attacked once more before the end of the month, and the garrison fired back, and nothing appeared as if it was going to change until 2 February. A boat flying a flag of truce came from the Orange Grove in the morning, and was approached by a launch from the Garrison. As the two boats met, the Spaniards jumped up and shouted: 'Todos amigos! We are all friends!'

Old Gib's relieved, with care away,
And safe return'd the fleet is,
And truly may each Briton say,
In Elliot no deceit is:
And since the fall of ancient Troy,
The pride of Greece to mention,
No siege like this did e'er employ
The wondering world's attention.
Duke Crillon to the Crown of Spain
His services who tender'd,
Presum'd the day to mention when
The fort would be surrendered.
But this impenetrable rock
For three long years and more,
Unhurt has stood the Bourbon shock
And still defies their power.
No scene could more attention draw,
Fond hope did all inspire,
And many thousands went and saw
The atmosphere on fire.
The Grandees, who the host survey'd
Were struck with melancholy,
And weeping stood to see them made
The sacrifice of folly.
When all in flames their Batteries
Were floating on the waters,
Mount Etna never pour'd a blaze
More dreadful to Spectators.
What mortal can such usage brook?
The Dons and all around them,

The Garrison for Devils took,
But Salamanders found them.
The Walloon Guards, when red hot balls
From Elliot's guns were pour'd,
Look'd wistful at his stubborn walls,
And mercy thus implor'd:
'Twixt fire and water who can live?
I fear we all shall lost be:
Your help we crave assistance give,
Or burn'd or drown'd we must be.'
Humanity attends the brave
By Britons ever cherish'd:
And many lives did Curtis save
Which otherwise had perish'd.
The Count d'Artois, till now cock-sure,
His tone began to alter,
And vow'd he'd never visit more
The siege of old Gibraltar.
From Cadiz Bay Cordova rode
The waves in fury smiting,
The British fleet he dodged but show'd
No appetite for fighting.
'Gainst powerful odds, for bloody scenes
Our tars were all in motion:
A proof that Britain still maintain'd
Her Empire o'er the ocean.
At Elliot's name (which none conceal)
Each Briton is delighted,
And foreigners a pleasure feel
To hear his deeds recited.
Then honour pay, with glass in hand,
The bravest of commanders,
Forgetting not his veteran band,
The British Salamanders.

"The British Salamanders" by a Soldier. 1782.

CHAPTER XXIV

My grateful acknowledgements

WHEN Lord Howe and the Fleet sailed home in October 1782 Captain Curtis was aboard the *Victory*, His Lordship's flagship, and when Captain Duncan was sent ahead in the *Latona* frigate with Howe's dispatches, and incidentally Curtis's letters describing the defeat of the Grand Attack, Curtis was appointed Captain of the *Victory*. Captain Duncan arrived at the Admiralty on 7 November and the next day, in an extraordinary edition of the *London Gazette*, Lord Howe's and Curtis's letters were published, and the triumphant defence of Gibraltar was revealed to the people of Great Britain. General Eliott's public dispatch appeared in the *Gazette* on 12 November and with it his letter recommending Major Valloton to the notice of the Commander-in-Chief and the Court. Captain Drinkwater, writing much later, suggested that Valloton was deliberately put on board a ship that went cruising in the Bay of Biscay, so that Curtis reached the Court first, but Curtis stayed on board the *Victory* until 15 November, and the most that was done was to contrive that the great news was broken to the public in his letters. However, it was Roger Curtis who was knighted and given a pension of £500 a year. The country was delighted, but the Government persisted in its efforts to dispose of the Rock. But they could not ignore the giant wave of public opinion in favour of the heroes of the siege that found expression in a Wedgwood plaque of Eliott, several cheap journals of the siege, some large and heroic paintings, and many indifferent verses, like this by Robert Burns:

> I lastly was with Curtis, among the floating batteries,
> And there I left for witness an arm and a limb;

Yet, let my country need me, with Elliot to head me,
I'd clatter on my stumps at the sound of the drum.

In the King's Speech at the opening of Parliament on 5 December, His Majesty was gracious enough to have said: 'You must have seen with Pride and Satisfaction the gallant Defence of the Governor and the Garrison of Gibraltar', and the Houses of Parliament added their voices to the general praise on 12 and 13 December. The Lords were unanimous in their thanks, but when General Conway proposed the thanks of the House of Commons to Lieutenant-General Boyd, Major-General La Motte, Major-General Green, Sir Roger Curtis, and to the officers, soldiers and sailors lately employed in the defence of Gibraltar, up stood a familiar figure to protest about the inclusion of General Boyd: it was none other than General Ross. His amendment to exclude General Boyd from the thanks of Parliament was opposed by Burke and Pitt, amongst others, and when it was known that General Eliott, whose coolness towards Boyd was common knowledge, had added his testimonial, it was defeated, and Ross walked out. There was another difficulty when General Conway moved the thanks of the House to General Eliott for his brave and gallant defence of Gibraltar. One member rose to suggest that to heighten the compliment, after the word Gibraltar should be added 'the most valuable and important fortress of all the foreign territories belonging to Great Britain', whereupon another protested that 'he always thought, and should ever think, that Gibraltar always hung like a dead weight round the neck of Great Britain'. The suggestion was withdrawn. On 8 January General Eliott's reward was decided upon. He was given the Order of the Bath and £1,500 a year. It was the least a Ministry could have awarded a victorious general; red ribbands were almost as abundant as red tape in Whitehall. On 14 February there was a motion to increase his reward, which Horace Walpole called 'an indecent motion' and which was rejected. Eliott had to wait until 1787, when he was eventually created Lord Heathfield, Baron of Gibraltar. So much for the glory, small enough in Great Britain, but, as is to be seen, great in Gibraltar. The more substantial rewards of prize and head money for the battering-ships and the *St Michael* were not decided until June 1784, and are given in a chart on page 286.

Jealousy, intrigue, faction and fortune-seeking were far from Gibraltar on 2 February 1783, when the garrison heard the first cry of 'Todos amigos'. In spite of the letters the Governor received that day from the Duc de Crillon, the artillery on the Rock continued firing until evening. The next day the Spaniards came forward from their works to talk to the guards in the lines, but the Governor ordered this friendly communication to stop, and the artillery officer on duty to fire a shot over the heads of any party advancing across the Neutral Ground. On the 5th he received a notification from Crillon that the blockade was over, and a placard was posted in the town announcing to the ruins that the port of Gibraltar was once more open. At noon someone fired a gun at Spain, whether maliciously or accidentally is not known, but it was the last shot of the siege.

The joy of the garrison was tempered with weariness, and that of the townspeople with the consciousness of their losses. There was also the uncertainty about the future of the Rock, which they had protected for nearly four years, and the pleasure of peace was redoubled when it was learnt that Gibraltar was to remain British, and that their efforts and sacrifices had not been betrayed. General Eliott had, as yet, received no communication from England regarding the cessation of hostilities, and was obliged to keep his garrison locked up until this should arrive; though when a Spanish deputation of three officers and a drummer came to Landport gate with a request for two bottles of Stroughton's Elixir drops, these were gravely handed over with the garrison's compliments. Instead of a general relaxation, he ordered the regiments on review. Each regiment took its turn, whilst the others looked on. The 73rd paraded in kilts, the Corsicans in disorder, and the 97th not at all, because they were not ready, and they were nicknamed the second battalion of the Corsicans. Peace brought some compensations, and the beginnings of a return to order. On 11 February, Captain Spilsbury remarked: 'Everything fallen to half price except wearing apparel—no more wood to be burnt by the soldiers coal being in plenty, and the inhabitants houses not to be inhabited but by their permission.' Gibraltar was still a garrison fortress, and whenever the guards mounted, there was General Eliott, as described in Boyd's Log Book: 'The Governor still continues on these movements to receive the Compliments and Honours of War near the gallows with his Posteriors to it to them that come in town

K

and his face to it to them going out.' It was also time to count the cost to the garrison of their long endurance.

Regiment	Killed & dead of wounds				Disabled				Dead of sickness				Deserted
				R. & F.				R. & F.				R. & F.	R. & F.
	O.	S.	D.	F.	O.	S.	D.	F.	O.	S.	D.	F.	F.
R.A.	2	1	0	28	0	2	0	11	1	1	0	34	1
12th Regt	1	3	1	23	1	0	0	10	0	3	0	32	3
25th	0	0	0	2	0	0	0	0	1	0	0	13	1
39th	2	4	1	22	0	0	0	10	0	1	0	37	5
56th	0	1	0	26	1	0	0	6	1	4	1	34	3
58th	1	2	0	16	0	0	1	8	0	1	1	53	11
59th	0	0	0	8	0	0	0	2	0	0	0	33	0
72nd	0	4	0	52	0	1	1	21	0	1	0	47	9
73rd	0	1	0	43	1	5	0	31	0	0	0	58	2
97th	0	0	1	12	0	1	0	4	1	6	0	106	1
Redens	0	2	1	12	0	1	0	4	1	1	0	16	1
De la Mottes	0	3	0	22	0	1	0	0	2	2	0	10	1
Hardenbergs	0	2	0	24	0	2	0	6	0	2	0	7	5
Artificers	0	1	0	6	0	0	0	7	0	0	0	23	0
Marine Brigade	0	1	0	2	0	0	0	0	0	0	0	0	0
Corsicans	0	0	0	0	0	0	0	0	0	0	0	0	0
	6	25	4	298	3	13	2	120	7	22	2	503	43

Total losses:

Killed and dead of wounds	333
Disabled by wounds	138
Dead of sickness (exclusive of scurvy)	534
Deserted	43
Discharged from sickness	181
Estimated deaths from scurvy	500
	1,729

It is more pleasant to be able to add that 870 men were wounded but recovered from their wounds. There is no record of the numbers of soldiers' wives and children who died during the siege, but Mrs Green estimated that 500 people died in the smallpox epidemic of 1780, and it would be too much to hope that none were killed by enemy action or by the scurvy. The townspeople who had fled from Gibraltar began to return from Morocco, Minorca, Portugal, Italy and England in the summer of 1783. Again, there are no figures of how many died during the siege, and the only comparison that can be made is between the census figures of 1777 and 1787.

	1777	*1787*
British	519	512
Roman Catholics	1,819	2,098
Jews	863	776
	3,201	3,386

From this it appears that the main sufferers were the Jews, and there is other evidence to this effect in the memorials submitted by those who were taken to England to various Secretaries of State begging for a free passage back to their homes: Judah Benates aged seventy-three, Kahna Botibol who lost her husband, Abraham Merous who was captured by the Spaniards, Jacob Levy his wife and five helpless children, Abraham Benady and five children, Jacob Henriquez Cardozo in a starving condition, David Nabarro with an old mother and two sisters, and many others, these suffered almost as much in England as those left behind on the Rock.

February ended without any word from England, and with little for the garrison to do but watch the Spaniards withdrawing their guns from the advanced works. On 5 March a Moroccan schooner came in with a present of bullocks for General Eliott, and a letter from the Emperor congratulating his old ally on his victory against the common enemy, assuring him that prayers had been said in the mosques for the defeat of the Grand Attack, and suggesting a return to the friendly relations that had unfortunately been disturbed. He returned twenty-six Corsicans, who had mistakenly been taken prisoner on his coast, as a proof of his goodwill. Later this crafty monarch promised to allow supplies to be sent to Gibraltar free of duty for a year, 'an action so irreconcilable to one ruling principle of his character we can only impute to the other passion which we are told sometimes gains the ascendant—his apprehensions', as Eliott wrote to London.

It was now a month since the Duc de Crillon had advised the Governor of the peace, and there was still no confirmation of it from England. The Spanish aides who passed between the Duke and the General were beginning to be exasperated, and the garrison no less so, when at last, on 10 March, the *Thetis* frigate arrived, carrying Sir

Roger Curtis, and dispatches for which everyone was waiting: peace, the King's speech, the thanks of Parliament, and the Order of the Bath. Characteristically, General Eliott's first thought was for his garrison, and he wrote to Mr Townshend, then Secretary of State in Lord Shelburne's administration: 'Great part of the Soldiers in this Fortress were as I apprehend inlisted only for three years or to the end of the War: some Expedient therefore will be necessary to keep up the strength of this Garrison', and the second for himself: 'But Sir your letter contains what I seize with avidity—My Sovereign's Approbation—that Sir, Oh that Sir, is all the World to me.' He also received a letter from Frederick the Great, to which he answered: 'No soldier can be insensible to the Commendations of His Prussian Majesty', and, with a remark that gains in significance when it is remembered that M. d'Arçon was publishing his accounts of the Grand Attack at this time: 'Chance is too often uncontrollable but must never be allowed a right to share in the success of any digested project.' General Boyd was sent the King's Commission to invest the Governor with the Order of the Bath, and promptly wrote to Mr Townshend: 'While hostilities continued I endeavoured to hide my Infirmities from myself but I have been long in a very feeble tottering state. My sight is so much weakened that I apprehend another Gibraltar summer might be fatal to it. My memory is what I dare not think of, but my spirits, thanks to all gracious Providence, have never failed me,' suggesting that he might put the precious red ribband away and forget where, or mistakenly hang it round the wrong person's neck. However, he did his duty, outlived General Eliott, and in 1790 was appointed Governor of Gibraltar himself, and was awarded his own K.B. He died in 1794, and was buried in his special niche in the King's Bastion.

On 12 March came the first meeting of the commanders of the opposing camps. In the morning the Duc de Crillon and his suite rode forward to the end of the boyau near the Bay, and shortly after General Eliott rode out through Forbes barrier, attended by his A.D.C., Lieutenant Koehler. They met on the beach halfway between the Spanish works and the British Rock and, dismounting, embraced each other, and talked for half an hour before riding back. On the 18th the Duke sent the Governor a white horse, and on the 23rd, accompanied by General Green and their aides, General Eliott paid a formal visit to the Spanish Lines and dined with Crillon at San Roque. The next day seven musicians from the garrison deserted in a boat, taking their instruments with them, which, as it was not the silly season in Gibraltar, is inexplicable. On the last day of the month the Duc de Crillon and several officers returned the Governor's visit. It was a memorable occasion for the garrison. They wore their best uniforms and the streets between the ruins were swept and sprinkled with water. At 10.30 a.m., the Spanish party arrived at Forbes where they were met by the Governor and conducted to Landport tunnel. As they entered the fortress, a 17-gun salute was fired from the Grand Battery, and when they appeared the other side the troops assembled gave a cheer, which disconcerted the old General, and someone had to explain that it was an English custom. As they passed through the ruins of the town Crillon regained his composure, and by the time the garrison officers were being presented to him at the Convent, he was on his best form. To the Artillery he said, 'Gentlemen, I would rather see you here as friends than on your batteries as enemies, where you never spared me', and at dinner that 'he had exerted himself to the utmost of his abilities; and though he had not been successful, yet he was happy in having his Sovereign's approbation of his conduct'. During a tour of the garrison, he pointed at the Old Mole and re-marked 'that had not his opinion been over-ruled he should have directed all his efforts against that part of the Garrison', and of Mr Ince's gallery: 'These works are worthy of the Romans.' He rode to Europa and each regiment turned out without arms as he passed; he commented on their youth and fine appearance to General Eliott, which did not pass unnoticed in that quarter either. At 8 p.m. he left Gibraltar and, as he emerged from Landport, there was another 17-gun salute which startled his horse and almost unseated the old soldier. He left for Madrid on 2 April and apparently succeeded in avoiding the blame for the failure of the Grand Attack, as he was honoured for the capture of Minorca, and ended his life in 1796 as the Duc de Crillon-Mahon.

M. d'Arçon went from siege to siege: Geneva, Breda, Gertruyden-berg, Toulon, and, retiring in 1795, he died in 1800. His philosophy, crystallized before Gibraltar, he summed up in one sentence: 'Le génie n'est qu'une longue patience.'

General Boyd had charge of the arrangements for the ceremonial investiture of General Eliott with the Order of the Bath. St George's Day, 23 April, was chosen for the occasion, and preparations were in hand to make it memorable. The garrison watched a wooden colonnade being erected along the rampart of the King's Bastion, and then painted in martial colours: there was little else to watch, the *St Michael* had sailed to England, and Sir Roger had taken the *Brilliant* frigate to Morocco on an embassy to the Emperor. One of General Boyd's supporters took time off to console his chief:

> Illustrious Boyd, a laurel Crown receive,
> A victor's meed, a wreath your friends did weave,
> The gift is truly Roman, so are you,
> Better than ribbons, green, or red, or blue.

The great day dawned, and of course it rained. Captain Drinkwater described the first part of the ceremony:

Detachments from all the regiments and corps with all the Officers not on duty, were assembled in three lines on the Red Sands at eight o'clock in the morning; and the Governor taking post in the centre of the second line, and the usual compliments being paid, his Excellency addressed himself to the Garrison as follows:

'GENTLEMEN,

I have assembled you this day, in order that the Officers and Soldiers may receive, in the most public manner, an authentic declaration transmitted to me by the Secretary of State, expressing the high sense His Majesty entertains of your meritorious conduct in the defence of this Garrison. The King's satisfaction upon this event was soon divulged to all the world, by His most gracious Speech to both Houses of Parliament. The House of Lords and the House of Commons not only made the suitable professions in their Address to the Throne, but have severally enjoined me to communicate their unanimous thanks by the following resolutions:

'*Die Veneris, 13 Decembris*, 1782.

RESOLVED, *nemine dissentiente*, by the Lords Spiritual and Temporal, in Parliment assembled, that this House doth highly approve and acknowledge the services of the Officers, Soldiers, and Sailors, lately employed in the defence of Gibraltar; and that General Eliott do signify the same to them.

'*Die Jovis, 12 Decembris*, 1782.

RESOLVED, *nemine contradicente*, that the thanks of this House (Commons) be given to Lieut. General Boyd, Major General De la Motte, Major General Green Chief Engineer, to Sir Roger Curtis Knt. and to the Officers, Soldiers and Sailors, lately employed in the defence of Gibraltar.'

The Governor then proceeded: 'No army has ever been rewarded by higher national honours; and it is well known how great, universal, and spontaneous were the rejoicings throughout the kingdom, upon the news of your success. These must not only give you inexpressible pleasure, but afford matter of triumph to your dearest friends and latest posterity. As a farther proof how just your title is to such flattering distinctions at home, rest assured, from undoubted authority, that the Nations in Europe, and other parts, are struck with admiration of your gallant behaviour: even our late resolute and determined Antagonists do not scruple to bestow the commendations due to such valour and perseverance.

I now most warmly congratulate you on these united and brilliant testimonies of approbation, amidst such numerous, such exalted tokens of applause: and FORGIVE ME, FAITHFUL COMPANIONS, IF I HUMBLY CRAVE YOUR ACCEPTANCE OF MY GRATEFUL ACKNOW-LEDGEMENTS. I ONLY PRESUME TO ASK THIS FAVOUR, AS HAVING BEEN A CONSTANT WITNESS OF YOUR CHEERFUL SUBMISSION TO THE GREATEST HARDSHIPS, YOUR MATCHLESS SPIRIT AND EXERTIONS, AND ON ALL OCCASIONS, YOUR HEROIC CONTEMPT OF EVERY DANGER.'

A GRAND *feu-de-joie* was then fired by the line, each discharge commencing with a royal salute of twenty-one guns. Three cheers closed the ceremony. The Commander in Chief, General and Field Officers, afterwards withdrew; and the detachments (formed two deep) marched into town, and lined the streets leading from the Convent, by the Spanish Church and Grand parade, to the King's bastion. About half past eleven o'clock, the procession began in the following order: ALL uncovered, and two deep, except the troops under arms.

MARSHAL.

Music, 12th Regiment,
Playing, '*See the conquering Hero comes.*'

ARTILLERY

Quarter-Master-General, and Adjutant-General,
Town Major and Deputy;

With other STAFF OF THE GARRISON.

First Division of FIELD OFFICERS, youngest first.

Music, 58th Regiment.

THE COMMISSIONER'S SECRETARY,
Bearing on a crimson velvet cushion the Commission.

THE COMMISSIONER'S AIDE-DE-CAMPS.

LIEUT. GENERAL BOYD, THE KING'S COMMISSIONER.

THE GOVERNOR'S SECRETARY,
Bearing, on a crimson velvet cushion, the Insignia of the
Order of the Bath.

THE GOVERNOR'S AIDE-DE-CAMPS,
AS ESQUIRES.

GENERAL ELIOTT,
THE KNIGHT ELECT;
Supported by Generals DE LA MOTTE and GREEN
Aide-de-camps to the Major Generals.

MAJOR GENERAL PICTON
His Aide-de-camp.

THE BRIGADIER GENERALS, eldest first.
Their Brigade Majors.
Music, De la Motte's.

Second Division of FIELD OFFICERS, eldest first.
Music, 56th Regiment.

The GRENADIERS of the Garrison.

NO COMPLIMENT was paid to the Knight Elect; but as the Commissioner passed, each Regiment, with the Officers, saluted. When the procession arrived at the Colonnade, the General and Field Officers placed themselves on each side of the Throne; the Artillery formed under the Colonnade, and the Grenadiers, fronting the bastion, along the line-wall. The proper reverences being made to the vacant Throne, the Commissioner desired his Secretary to read the Commission: which being done, he addressed the Knight Elect in a short complimentary speech, taking the ribband at the conclusion, and placing it over the Governor's shoulder, who inclined a little for that purpose: three reverences were then a second time made, and each took his seat on a crimson velvet chair on each side of the Throne, the Commissioner sitting on the right hand. The Governor was no sooner invested, than the music struck up, *God Save the King*. The Grenadiers fired a volley, and a grand discharge of a hundred and sixty pieces of cannon was fired from the Sea-line. The procession then passed forwards through the colonnade, and returned in the same order. The detachments were afterwards dismissed, and each Non-commissioned Officer and Private received a pound of *fresh* beef and a quart of wine. The Generals with their suites, and the Field Officers, dined at the Convent. In the evening, the Colonnade was illuminated with different-coloured lamps, and

transparent paintings in the back scene: and Sir George Augustus
Eliott, with the Lieutenant Governor, and principal Officers of the
Garrison, assembling at the King's bastion about nine o'clock, there
was a display of fire-works from the north and south bastions, and the
Spanish church; the principal of which were fired from the latter, being
opposite the Company.

Private Gordon of the 73rd Regiment gave this description of the
fireworks and paintings:

> The Union Arms, Star and Garter etc. were represented by fire with the
> Governor's name in the star, upon the centre arch (of the Colonnade).
> A Star burnt at South Port, but what was represented on top of the
> Spanish Church I cannot give any authentic account of, as I could not
> get into town

and Captain Spilsbury summed up the day's events (his usual good
nature perhaps a little soured by the fact that, whilst the Field and
Staff officers dined at the Convent, and the men had their beef and
wine, the Captains and subalterns were entirely neglected) by com-
menting that he had never experienced 'a worse feu de joye fired by
troops, worse weather, worse musick, worse fireworks, or worse entertainment'.

But it would not be fair to the Governor or garrison of Gibraltar
to end the story of the Great Siege on this sharp note. The celebrations continued, unofficially, for a day or two:

Garrison Orders, 24th April.

> No person whatever to presume, on any pretext, to maltreat a Moor by
> words or actions.

26th April.

> It having been reported to the Governor, from Spain, that some
> Officers from the Garrison, who attempted lately to land on the Spanish
> shore, made use of very indecent and improper assertions on the
> occasion, 'tis the Governor's positive order that no Officer shall for the
> future presume to approach the Spanish shore in Boats or otherwise.

Spain, in fact, refused to open communications with the Rock, and
tried to maintain her frontier at the advanced works; it was several
months before General Eliott succeeded in persuading the local commander to withdraw behind the Spanish Lines. Summer came to
Gibraltar, and the three years' men began to be unruly: 'Two or

three men of the 73rd are hurt by teazing a bullock: and a corporal and three men 97th and one 59th are stabbed by a Corsican, teazing him.' Captain Spilsbury added that the Corsican was punished with 800 lashes. The officers found another way of amusing themselves, and played cricket on Windmill Hill; a rougher pitch is hard to imagine. On 26 May the Governor received orders to disband the 73rd and 97th Regiments and send them home, and advice that all of the garrison, except the 25th and 59th would shortly be relieved. The garrison was slowly breaking up, with the old regiments recruiting from those disbanded, 'with', as the Governor wrote, 'as much frolic and mirth as at a country fair'. But he remembered some of them. When the Royal Artillery sailed for England, he wrote: 'This distinguished body of men during their service here have constantly behaved with such skill, exertion and courage as never has, and I believe will not be exceded by any Nation whatever.' He kept his prejudices however, and when, much later, he had a silver medal struck to commemorate the siege, he presented copies only to the officers of the Hanoverian regiments. Reden's, Hardenberg's (later Sydow's) and De la Motte's took Gibraltar as a battle honour, and emblazoned on their colours 'Mit Eliott Ruhm und Sieg'. The 12th, 39th, 56th, 58th and 73rd regiments included Gibraltar among their honours and, not to be outdone, General Picton had his own medal designed, but only seventy were struck off as the die failed twice, and there must have been some who did not want their medal, as Captain Drinkwater got several.

The more substantial rewards were not made until 10 June 1784, when the Report of the Board of General Officers respecting the distribution of the Bounty Money to the Garrison of Gibraltar appeared. The first distribution was of £16,000 to the credit of the battering-ships, and £14,000 to that of the *St Michael*. After a deduction of £3,187 10s. 0d. for the Navy, the money was proportioned:

	£	s.	d.		£	s.	d
The Governor	1,875	0	0	Captain	43	10	1
Lt-Governor	937	10	0	Lieutenant	25	5	6
Major-General	468	15	0	2nd Lieut & Ensign	22	0	6½
Brigadier-General	267	10	0	Serjeant	3	6	9
Colonel	156	1	0	Corporal	2	0	11¼
Lt-Colonel	80	16	0	Private	1	9	1
Major	57	15	6				

An Act of Parliament was later passed granting the garrison the value of any articles salvaged from the battering-ships, and, as many of the cannons were fished out of the Bay, these amounts were almost doubled, so that the Governor finally received £3,375 and a private soldier £2 12s. 4d.

As the townspeople began to return to Gibraltar, to rebuild on the ruins of their houses, and to litigate with the Governor for compensation for the losses they had suffered during the siege, the town slowly came back to life. New soldiers replaced the old Salamanders, but the Rock remained a fortress, and the town a garrison town, nor was there any significant change in the role of Gibraltar until, in the next century, the harbour was improved, and it became a coaling station on the route to the East. Sir Roger Curtis returned to England, appearing again as Lord Howe's flag-captain on the Glorious First of June 1794, and then disappearing into the Admiralty, until his death in 1816. General Eliott, or Sir George as he was now, or Lord Heathfield as he was to become, fell into old age without the good grace that mankind prefers to associate with that declension; like most successful British generals, he was soon forgotten on the return of peace and, if he was again brought to public notice, it was to criticize his service and deplore his reward. He stayed in Gibraltar, and fought several private campaigns against the inhabitants, and one against the naval commodore of the Mediterranean over which should salute the other, which he lost. In 1787 he went to England to receive his barony, and to be described as a toothless, chattering old septuagenarian. He was afflicted, very unfairly in view of his spartan habits, with gout, and succumbed to the palsy in Aix-la-Chappelle on 6 July 1790, two days before he planned to return to his Rock. Perhaps it is fairest to remember him, not as Heathfield, or even as Sir George, but as bluff General Eliott, the Cock of the Rock, standing triumphant on the King's Bastion on 14 September 1782, viewing the wreckage of the Grand Attack with the morning sunlight streaming over the Rock of Gibraltar behind him.

Four years after the Great Siege of Gibraltar was over this account of the defence and the destruction of the forces sent against the Rock appeared:

> During the late siege of Gibraltar, I went, with a provision fleet under Lord Rodney's command, to see my old friend General Elliot, who has,

by his distinguished defence of that place, acquired laurels that can never fade. After the usual joy which generally attends the meeting of old friends had subsided, I went to examine the state of the garrison and view the operations of the enemy, for which purpose the General accompanied me. I had brought a most excellent refracting telescope with me from London, purchased of Dollond, by the help of which I found the enemy were going to discharge a thirty-six pounder at the spot where we stood. I told the General what they were about; he looked through the glass also, and found my conjectures right. I immediately, by his permission, ordered a forty-eight pounder to be brought from a neighbouring battery, which I placed with so much exactness (having long studied the art of gunnery) that I was sure of my mark.

I continued watching the enemy till I saw the match placed at the touch-hole of their piece; at that very instant I gave the signal for our gun to be fired also. About midway between the two pieces of cannon the balls struck each other with amazing force, and the effect was astonishing! The enemy's ball recoiled back with such violence as to kill the man who had discharged it, by carrying his head fairly off, with sixteen others which it met with in its progress to the Barbary Coast; where its force, after passing through three masts of vessels that then lay in a line behind each other in the harbour, was so much spent that it only broke its way through the roof of a poor labourer's hut, about two hundred yards inland, and destroyed the few teeth an old woman had left, who lay asleep upon her back with her mouth open. The ball lodged in her throat. Her husband soon after came home, and endeavoured to extract it; but finding that impracticable, by the assistance of a rammer he forced it into her stomach, from whence it was discharged downwards in a natural way. Our ball did excellent service, for it not only repelled the other in the manner just described; but, proceeding as I intended it should, it dismounted the very piece of cannon that had been just employed against us, and forced it into the hold of the ship, where it fell with so much force as to break its way through the bottom. The ship immediately filled and sunk, with above a thousand Spanish sailors on board, besides a considerable number of soldiers. This, to be sure, was a most extraordinary exploit. I will not, however, take the whole merit to myself; my judgement was the principal engine but chance assisted me a little; for I afterwards found that the man who charged our forty-eight pounder put in, by mistake, a double quantity of powder, else we could never have succeeded so much beyond all expectation, especially in repelling the enemy's ball.

General Elliot would have given me a commission for this singular piece of service, but I declined everything except his thanks, which I received at a crowded table of officers at supper on the evening of that very day.

As I am very partial to the English, who are beyond all doubt a brave people, I determined not to take my leave of the garrison till I had rendered them another piece of service, and in about three weeks an opportunity presented itself. I dressed myself in the habit of a Popish priest, and at about one o'clock in the morning stole out of the garrison, passed the enemy's lines, and arrived in the middle of their camp, where I entered the tent in which the Prince d'Artois was, with the Commander-in-Chief and several other officers, in deep council, concerting a plan to storm the garrison next morning. My disguise was my protection; they suffered me to continue there, hearing everything that passed till they went to their several beds. When I found the whole camp—and even the sentinels—were wrapped up in the arms of Morpheus I began my work, which was that of dismounting all their cannon (above three hundred pieces), from forty-eight to twenty-four pounders, and throwing them three leagues into the sea. Having no assistance, I found this the hardest task I ever undertook, except swimming to the opposite shore with the famous Turkish piece of ordnance described by Baron de Tott in his Memoirs which I shall hereafter mention. I then piled all the carriages together in the centre of the camp, which to prevent the noise of the wheels being heard I carried in pairs under my arms: and a noble appearance they made, as high at least as the Rock of Gibraltar. I then lighted a match by striking a flint stone situated twenty feet from the ground (in an old wall, built by the Moors when they invaded Spain) with the breach of an iron eight-and-forty pounder, and so set fire to the whole pile. I forgot to inform you that I threw all their ammunition wagons upon the top.

Before I applied the lighted match I had laid the combustibles at the bottom so judiciously that the whole was in a blaze in a moment. To prevent suspicion, I was one of the first to express my surprise. The whole camp was, as you may imagine, petrified with astonishment; the general conclusion was that their sentinels had been bribed, and that seven or eight regiments of the garrison had been employed in this horrid destruction of their artillery. Mr Drinkwater, in his account of this famous siege, mentions the enemy sustaining a great loss by a fire which happened in their camp, but never knew the cause: how should he, as I never divulged it before (though I alone saved Gibraltar by this night's business), not even to General Elliot? The Count d'Artois and all his attendants ran away in their fright, and never stopped till they reached Paris, which they did in about a fortnight: this dreadful conflagration had such an effect upon them that they were incapable of taking the least refreshment for three months after, but, chameleon-like, lived upon the air.

(If any gentleman will say he doubts the truth of this story, I will fine him a gallon of brandy, and make him drink it at one draught.)

The strange thing is that the story of the siege told in the words of the British Salamanders, their General, and their enemy, is a good deal odder than Baron Munchausen's story, and if any gentleman doubts the truth of it, perhaps he should pay the same fine.

Appendix

LETTERS FROM GENERAL ELIOTT TO CAPTAIN CURTIS

Gibraltar
Oct 26th 1782

Dear Curtis,

I write in a greater hurry than if you was here, I'm rather more wanted since it has fallen out we are deprived of you, no remedy, perhaps 'tis right, you know how to do great services. I wish you to be consulted and have said so; you know everything and may say to *proper* people what you think *proper*: we shall and must hobble on. Sir Chas. (Knowles) purchases and commissions the St Miguel himself on board as a King's Ship. I have consented as I know the utility and I suppose it official. All happiness and Prosperity.

Dear Curtis
Ever yours
G. A. Eliott.

P.S. What a glorious manœuvre thro' the streights. Col. Gibson and I have appointed Simpson and Dere Agents here for the Prize. G. A. E.

My respects to Lord Howe.

Gibraltar
Nov 6th 1782

Dear Curtis,

I wrote by the Tissiphone, you will suppose I will continue to do so by way of opportunity, this goes by that good little man Capt. Elliston, he has observation enough to tell you how everything afloat goes here: remember the conversation between Capt. Conway you and I, Little Gibson is our mainstay but the Bow-sprit is carried away; *am I right*—let what will happen you won't neglect the main object if you have the opportunity. I have desired your opinion might be ask'd as the only man who knows things to the bottom—all that is is best. Do offer my respects to Lord

Howe, but I believe you can't venture to tell him that I and the rest of us half Sea Officers are in admiration and astonishment at what past under our eyes—'tis believed by many, I amongst others, that he gaind some advantage over the Combin'd fleet, but we are in the dark—

I only wish you as much happiness as you have deserved,

Dear friend,

Yours ever and truly,

G. A. Eliott.

I send a letter of Attorney for J & R Fuller Clements Lane & Robinson, to receive head-money—'tis signed by Capt. Gibson and me in your absence, this for the St Michael. Will you be so good to call in Clements Lane I wish my son may be in town.

Gibraltar

18 Dec 1782

Dear Brigadier,

In the first place remember the conversation that pass'd between Captain Conway you and I *the publick is much concern'd in the event.*

Sir Chas Knowes and all your friends here are well he is a very good natur'd man and almost ev'ry day at the Hutt which is very pleasant.

Now I can only tell you that my constant wishes that our Sovereign and his ministers may know you as well as I do, and then they will not love you less I hope.

Ever yours

G. A. Eliott.

My respects to Lord Howe

Gibraltar

Dec 19th 1782

Dear Curtis,

I write this by a Faro boat only a how d'ye—remember the conversation between Capt. Conway you and I near the New Mole—Capt Gibson led a Squadron of eight Gun-boats against the Enemy's thirty in all, he went out at least a mile with the wind at East and fairly drove the Spaniards in, kicking 'em all the way: they lay at a vast distance just for the shells to reach the St Michael's length all this before noon—you may mention this again if you please. My respects to Lord Howe.

Dear friend

Yours most truly,

G. A. Eliott.

Gibraltar
Dec 26th 1782

Dear Curtis,

Duc de Crillon return'd a Lieutenant and Midshipman carried away by the Crew of the St Michael's Guard boat, by whom I learn the high reputation Ld Howe has establish'd amongst the Spaniards for his great abilities: nothing more has reach'd us except that you are his Captain.

in lieu of the one who carry'd the dispatch—all this is very natural, and I rejoice [at] it. I hope however you will have some communication with ministry and tell them *your mind* and in return that they will not be wanting in acknowledgement for the very very great services you have render'd the State: if this is an object I am happy notwithstanding *my loss* that you are high in a more general line.

Don't forget the conversation at Cockcraft's hutt *you well know the importance.*

Gun and Mortar boats now come in the day, lie at a great distance and little Gibson leads his squadron to meet them.

All success and happiness attend you. My respects to My Lord Howe.

Dear Curtis
Yours ever
G. A. Eliott.

Sir Roger Curtis.

Gibraltar

Dear Sir

If Capt Phipps gets back in time all's well we were glad of his company: St George's day went off well—my Cook fail'd dreadfully on his part in every thing but his attack on the *flotantes* upon the King's bastion, which help'd to make us forget a damn'd bad dinner but with the assistance of your *Dates.*

I send copy of extract to office inclosed.

Col. Cochran without hesitation sends you his band: you know they must be governed; Capt Phipps I have injoined to look after 'em.

One thousand 3 pd Shot are aboard the Speedwell.

I send you a Tent better we suppose than what you have.

It is to be feared your stay in Barbary may be longer than we wish.

Three travellers arriv'd here from Lisbon the 22nd. Mr Russell, Mr Callaghan, and Mr Mason: the last is the King's Botanist and has visited the Tropical and other southern latitudes; a man of deep science and infinite modesty—if he can be detach'd from the others I dare say you'll wish to countenance him in Barbary, where he seems inclinable to go in pursuit of his object: the other gentlemen behave with great propriety, but I don't hold out the journey to them, as neither you nor I are very fond of supernumeraries: however if they do go, a caution shall be given them by some private hand, not to expect being included in your suite.

A Newspaper of 27th March; no Ministry fix'd. I have receiv'd no letter. Vessels of all kinds coming daily to us.

Dear Curtis

Yours ever truly

G. A. Eliott.

Gibraltar

Feb 26th 1784

Dear friend

I am indeed most extremely thankfull for your letter of 28th Jan I hope to God by this time publick affairs look now more promising than on the 24th altho' letters of the 29th Jan are by no means flattering: little as I like or understand any politicks, what comes from you is very acceptable as they are not ting'd with partiality: one point in the controversy mention'd in your letter gives me great pain; this answer going by post I will not repeat it, but you guess: 'tis cruel you understand they were writing to me upon a certain interesting point, *not a bit*, it is hardly to be expected no help— I am glad the salute is decided, but I have no account; 'tis well my steps are not disapproved but received as they were really *doubts.*

If the Country was quiet I should wish myself in England and for no reason more than to have the happiness of visiting you—My respects, if you see the moment, to Lord Howe thats a man I should like to be well with especially as a private man. My situation here is not one whit more agreable than it was: Head money is in the properest channel between you and Mr. Fuller.

Adieu post going out

Ever yours

G. A. Eliott.

Gibraltar

July 1st 1785

My dear friend

The *Marquis de Seignelay* under weigh, pray tell me what could I say in answer to your two kindest of all letters repeating how much I love and honour you is unnecessary: recollect I never have a pen fit to scrawl and good Mr Rawleigh won't allow me a sheet of tolerable paper, ecce signum: I am fairly reduced to 12 square inches by an accumulation of papers without order as you well guess after all this how unreasonable to expect I should write letters but try me where business is the question.

I hope the good and great man will never leave the vessel whilst she can swim: you can tell him how to stop the leak with the seamen's jacket: for if he goes all's gone: I really believe your minister will do something: he bears hard upon some of the old *Fogies patience* if we have neighbours fare.

I gain ground in training my Garrison, altho' not an inch in discipline, but *dum spiro spero* I never tire.

How happy you make me by telling me I am abused, then there's some hopes; for truly I began to be jealous of the advantages you so boastingly told me you were distinguishd with. I hope now we are nearer upon a footing.

I like Gibraltar more and more not for its magnificence but I am wedded to the climate: to be sure for the happiness of embracing you and the few, I might submit to [leave] it would not be for long: there is no prospect of this suddenly: if I stick by her till she *rights*, not an inch gain'd yet: to the southward we improve but the town continues a sink of abomination. You want something to do, good Sir, shall we go to war again for your diversion? Pray be satisfied, thatch your cottage, shell your Grotto, weave your bower, then we'll eat syllabub together: I wish the *Ganges* would bring the 58 Regt sure tis common sense in oeconomical days. Lt Col Eliott is with me, wishes to be recommended to your favour.

> Dear friend
> Ever yours
> G. A. Eliott.

[What was said at 'Cockcraft's hutt'? General Eliott's friends were no longer in power, and Captain Curtis left his station at Gibraltar on the flimsiest of excuses, to carry the news of the victory to a hostile Ministry. Perhaps the event in which the public was concerned, was that the official story of 13 September 1782 was to be backed by all the friends the General could enlist, against the possible rumours that, as opposed to the Garrison destroying the floating batteries, they inconsiderately destroyed themselves.]

Bibliography

MANUSCRIPTS

In the Public Record Office

The correspondence of the Governors of Gibraltar and the Secretaries for the Southern Department. CO/91.

Letters from General Eliott to the Commander-in-Chief in the Amherst Papers.

In the British Museum. Department of Manuscripts

Correspondence of Lord Grantham. Add. MSS. 24,165, 24,174–24,176.

Letters concerning secret reports from America in the Auckland Papers. Add. MSS. 34,415.

Letters of Admiral Darby. Add. MSS. 38,681.

Letters, notes, and songs, in French and Spanish, concerning the Camp at San Roque. Egerton MSS. EG 375.

General Boyd's Log Book. Add. MSS. 38,605, 38,606.

Diary of the siege by a Spanish Officer. Add. MSS. 30,041.

Richard Cumberland's Report. Add. MSS. 28,851.

In Gibraltar Garrison Headquarters

Garrison Orders.

In the Chief Secretary's Office, Gibraltar

Correspondence with British Consuls.

Correspondence with Minorca & Islands.

Treasury Letters.

War Office Letters.

Journal of the siege kept for General Eliott.

In the Gibraltar Garrison Library

Autographs of Eminent Personages by John Drinkwater.

MAGAZINES AND NEWSPAPERS

The Gentleman's Magazine.

The Annual Register.

The London Gazette.
The London Chronicle.

CONTEMPORARY PUBLISHED WORKS

History of the Herculean Straits. Col. T. James. London. 1771.

A Journey from Gibraltar to Malaga. Francis Carter. London. 1777.

Historia de Gibraltar. Ignacio Lopez de Ayala. Madrid. 1782.

The Siege of Gibraltar from 12 April to 27 May 1781. Mrs Catherine Upton. London. 1781.

History of the Siege of Gibraltar. Capt. John Drinkwater. London. 1783.

A circumstancial journal of the long and tedious blockade and siege of Gibraltar. Samuel Ancell. Liverpool. 1784.

The History of the Blockade and Siege of Gibraltar. Walter Gordon. Aberdeen. 1784.

Journal of the Siege of Gibraltar. Capt. John Spilsbury. Gibraltar Garrison Library. 1908.

A Lady's Experiences in the Great Siege of Gibraltar. (Mrs Green's Diary.) Edited by Col. R. E. Kenyon. *Royal Engineers Journal.* 1912.

An authentic and accurate Journal of the late Siege of Gibraltar. Anonymous. London. 1785.

A history of the late Siege of Gibraltar by sea and land. Anonymous. Falkirk. 1815.

A new history of the late Grand Siege of Gibraltar. Anonymous. London. 1808.

Mémoire pour servir à l'histoire du siège de Gibraltar par l'Auteur des Batteries Flottantes. (Le Michaud d'Arçon.) Cadiz. 1783.

Histoire du Siège de Gibraltar par un Officier de l'Armée Françoise. (Le Michaud d'Arçon.) Cadiz. 1783.

Conseil de Guerre Privé sur l'Événement de Gibraltar en 1782 pour servir d'exercise sur l'art des sièges. Le Michaud d'Arçon. 1785.

Mémoires Militaires de Louis de Berton des Balbes de Quiers. (Duc de Crillon.) Paris. 1791.

Tableau de l'Espagne Moderne. Bourgoing. 1797.

An historical sketch of Gibraltar with an account of the siege. J. Heriot. London. 1792. (With pencil notes by W. Booth.)

Correspondence of King George III. Edited by Sir John Fortescue. Macmillan. 1928.

Remarks on the rescript of the Court of Madrid and the Manifesto of the Court of Versailles. Memorial to the Court of Versailles by Benjamin Franklin. London. 1779.

The Propriety of Retaining Gibraltar Impartially Considered. (John Sinclair.) London. 1783.

Naval and Military Memoirs of Great Britain, 1727 to the Present Time. Robert Beatson. London. 1790.

Memoirs of the Kings of Spain of the House of Bourbon. William Coxe. London. 1813.
The Last Journals of Horace Walpole. London, John Lane. 1910.

LATER PUBLISHED WORKS ABOUT GIBRALTAR

The History of Gibraltar. Frederic Sayer. Chapman & Hall. 1865.
Gibraltar in British Diplomacy in the Eighteenth Century. Stetson Conn. Yale University Press. 1942.
Gibraltar. C. F. Carrington. Chatham House Publications. 1956.
An Introduction to the Documents Relating to the International Status of Gibraltar. Wilbur C. Abbott. New York, Macmillan. 1934.
The Hussey-Cumberland Mission and American Independence. Samuel Flagg Bemis. Princetown. 1931.
The Gibraltarian. H. W. Howes. London. 1951.
The Jews of Gibraltar under British Rule. A. B. Serfaty.
D'Arçon. Sa Vie et ses Ecrits. M. A. de Roche d'Aiglun. Besançon, Societé d'Emulation de Doubs. Serie 4. Vol. 2. 1866.
Elliot traditions also Family Anecdotes. Lt-Col. the Hon. Fitzwilliam Elliot. Edinburgh. 1922.
Gibraltar under Moor, Spaniard and Briton. Col. R. E. Kenyon. London. 1938.

SOME GENERAL WORKS

The British Navy in Adversity. Capt. W. M. James. Longmans, Green & Co. 1926.
The French Army before Napoleon. Spenser Wilkinson. Oxford. 1915.
The Organisation of the British Army in the American Revolution. E. E. Curtis. Yale. 1926.
History of the British Army. J. W. Fortescue. Macmillan. 1902.
The British Army 1783-1802. J. W. Fortescue. Macmillan. 1905.
The Influence of Sea Power upon History 1660-1783. Capt. A. T. Mahan. Sampson Low, Marston, Searle & Rivington. 1889.
Life of Howe. Sir John Barrow. John Murray. 1838.
The Diplomacy of the American Revolution. Samuel Flagg Bemis. The American Historical Association. 1935.

Index

Captain BRADSHAW SMITH,
of the Navy.

SIR ROGER CURTIS,
Commanding Officer a-float.

EARL HOWE.

The Painting is 25 feet wide, by 22½ feet high, divided into two Compartments; the upper describing the Victory of the Garrison, and in the moment of their triumph, a display of humanity, that highly exalts the British Character; it is composed of three large groups; that on the right contains the Portraits of the principal British and Hanoverian Officers, of the size of life, who are assembled on the Rampart (the Action being over) to view the dreadful scene which ensued from the battering Ships being set on fire. LORD HEATHFIELD, on horseback, in conversation with GENERALS BOYD, DE LA MOTTE and GREEN; pointing to SIR ROGER CURTIS, and a detachment of British Seamen, who, at the hazard of their own lives, are rescuing their vanquished enemies from destruction. Several of the seamen are seen at the stern of one of the battering Ships, striking the Spanish Ensign; whilst others generously relieve a number of the unfortunate Spaniards from a sinking wreck: these form a second group, on the left. The third group occupy the centre, where a number of the enemy are represented in extreme distress, endeavouring to escape from a floating battery that is enveloped in flames. At a distance is a view of the Camp of the Allied Army, and the head quarters of the DUKE DE CRILLON. In the under Compartment is represented the Relief of Gibraltar, by the British Fleet, under the command of EARL HOWE; on the right is seen the ROCK OF GIBRALTAR, and a number of Store-ships entering the Bay, protected by a Detachment of the Fleet, which extends itself through the Picture, to the left.

At a distance is a View of the Bay of GIBRALTAR; and the Combined Fleets of France and Spain appear at anchor.—The Spanish Coast terminates the view. Portraits of EARL HOWE and ADMIRAL BARRINGTON are placed on the sides of this Compartment.